Ismailism and Islam in Modern South Asia

This book explores the evolution of a Shia Ismaili identity and crucial aspects of the historical forces that conditioned the development of the Muslim modern in late colonial South Asia. It reassesses the tortuous legal process that, since the 1860s, recast a Shia Imami identity for the Ismailis culminating with the installation of a line of successive living Imams, the Aga Khan(s), at the apex. It illustrates how, under the Imamate of Aga Khan III, the community virtually reinvented itself in the transregional western Indian Ocean and gradually in the global arena. This process reflects the complexities of heightened internationalist organizational activities that animated several of world's major religions since the late nineteenth century— an age of 'religious internationals', as this book posits. Marshalling a rich corpus of neglected primary sources, the book elaborates on questions such as the Aga's understanding of colonial modernity, his ideas of India, restructured modalities of community governance and the evolution of Imamate-sponsored institutions. It illuminates key strands in scholarship that characterized the development of the Muslim and Shia Ismaili modern, and above all, Muslim universality vis-à-vis denominational particularities that often transcended the confines of the modular nation and state structure. These are questions of crucial contemporary relevance that both inform the functioning of the present Imamate and forge what this book calls an 'Ismaili international'. The book will interest historians, students and scholars in related disciplines working on Islam in modern South Asia and its wider networks.

Soumen Mukherjee, FRAS, is Assistant Professor at the department of History in Presidency University, Kolkata. His research interests lie widely in the fields of socio-religious and intellectual history of modern South Asia.

Ismailism and Islam in Modern South Asia

Community and Identity in the Age of Religious Internationals

Soumen Mukherjee

CAMBRIDGE
UNIVERSITY PRESS

CAMBRIDGE
UNIVERSITY PRESS

University Printing House, Cambridge CB2 8BS, United Kingdom
One Liberty Plaza, 20th Floor, New York, NY 10006, USA
477 Williamstown Road, Port Melbourne, vic 3207, Australia
4843/24, 2nd Floor, Ansari Road, Daryaganj, Delhi – 110002, India
79 Anson Road, #06–04/06, Singapore 079906

Cambridge University Press is part of the University of Cambridge.

It furthers the University's mission by disseminating knowledge in the pursuit of
education, learning and research at the highest international levels of excellence.

www.cambridge.org
Information on this title: www.cambridge.org/9781107154087

© Soumen Mukherjee 2017

First published 2017

Printed in India at Thomson Press (India) Limited

A catalogue record for this publication is available from the British Library.

ISBN 978-1-107-15408-7 Hardback

Contents

Acknowledgements

The better part of the research that has graduated into this book was carried out during my stint as Research Fellow at the Zentrum Moderner Orient, Berlin, and was funded by Germany's Federal Ministry of Education and Research (BMBF). However, some of the questions explored here are traceable in part to my earlier works, albeit in significantly different forms. A teaching secondment at the Freie Universität in Berlin, and my subsequent appointment at the Presidency University in Kolkata substantially helped widening my academic horizons and, in the process, conditioned this evolution to no small extent.

Over the years a number of remarkable individuals—teachers and mentors, colleagues and friends, relatives and above all staff of the several institutions that I had to explore in search of primary sources—have provided support, critical insights, and encouragement. I would hasten to add though that their support of my academic quest need not be necessarily taken to mean their endorsing, or even sharing, the arguments made in this book. Likewise, all limitations and inadvertent errors that may have crept in are my own. I am grateful in particular to Gwilym Beckerlegge, Michel Boivin, Katrin Bromber, Bhaskar Chakrabarty, Subhas Ranjan Chakraborty, Kingshuk Chatterjee, Faisal Devji, Amit Dey, Gita Dharampal-Frick, Harald Fischer-Tiné, Monika Freier, Ulrike Freitag, Margret Frenz, Kashshaf Ghani, Rajarshi Ghose, Bernhard Gißibl, Nile Green, Thomas Gugler, Hans Harder, Justin Jones, Kai Kresse, Prabhat Kumar, Heike Liebau, Shireen Maswood, Sajal Nag, Ali Usman Qasmi, Mridu Rai, Dhruv Raina, Dietrich Reetz, Sajjad Alam Rizvi, Francis Robinson, Dietmar Rothermund, Shukla Sanyal, Torsten Tschacher, Hari Shankar Vasudevan, Theodore P. Wright Jr., and Benjamin Zachariah. In addition to the archivists and librarians of institutions listed under the section of the primary sources in the bibliography of this book, authorities and staff of the libraries of especially the Aga Khan Foundation (Geneva), Institute of Ismaili Studies (London), Ismaili Tariqah and Religious Education Board, India (Mumbai), the South Asia Institute of the University of Heidelberg, the Zentrum Moderner Orient, and the Freie Universität provided significant support. My sincere thanks to all of them. At the Cambridge University Press, I wish to thank the entire editorial team, and especially Qudsiya Ahmed, Suvadip Bhattacharjee, Jayati Das, Sohini Ghosh, Anwesha Rana, Anurupa Sen, the anonymous reviewers who read the chapters, and above all the Syndics and the competent authorities.

My extended family—the Banerjees and Gangulys in India and the Chatterjees in Switzerland—have been extremely supportive. Suranjana, my companion for over a decade, have stood by me through thick and thin. I do not have sufficient words to express my gratitude to her. Even as this book now comes out, I pause for a moment to reflect on a couple of reminiscences from my early childhood: memories of those first steps in the journey of my learning to read and write, and especially of those two individuals who would read with me the occasional nursery rhymes or help me hold a pencil. Neither of them, however, have lived long enough to see this book come out. It is to the memory of these two individuals, my parents, that I dedicate this book.

List of Abbreviations

AKA	Aga Khan Academies
AKAM	Aga Khan Agency for Microfinance
AKDN	Aga Khan Development Network
AKES	Aga Khan Educational Services
AKF	Aga Khan Foundation
AKFED	Aga Khan Fund for Economic Development
AKHCP	Aga Khan Historic Cities Programme
AKHS	Aga Khan Health Services
AKPBS	Aga Khan Planning and Building Services
AKRSP	Aga Khan Rural Support Programme
AKTC	Aga Khan Trust for Culture
CSASUC	Centre of South Asian Studies, University of Cambridge
EAMWS	East African Muslim Welfare Society
FBO	Faith-Based Organization
FOCUS	Focus Humanitarian Assistance
IIS	Institute of Ismaili Studies
IOR	India Office Records
ISA	Ideological State Apparatus
ITREB	Ismaili Tariqah and Religious Education Board
LG	Lloyd George Papers
LON	League of Nations
MD	Malcolm Darling
MEC	Muhammadan Educational Conference
MSA	Maharashtra State Archives
NAI	National Archives of India
NNI	Norwegian Nobel Institute
OUP	Oxford University Press
REC	Religious Education Centres
RNGO	Religious Non-Governmental Organization
STEP	Secondary Teacher Education Programme
UNAG	United Nations Archives at Geneva

Glossary

Ajam	the Persian cultural sphere; a person not born Arabian
Allama	an honorary title for highly regarded scholar of Islamic thought
Anjuman	community assembly
Asabiyya	group solidarity
Bandobasts	rules of conduct instituted by communities such as the Parsis for governance
Bekhudi	selflessness instrumental in creating a community, as conceptualized by Muhammad Iqbal
Bida	deviant innovations
dai al mutlaq (abbreviated as *dai*)	religious leader of the Mustali Ismailis, or the Bohras; hidden Imam's vicegerent
dawat	religious establishment of communities such as the Bohras, religious missions
farman	edict
ginan	religious literature of Ismailis of the Indo-Pakistan subcontinent
hadith	sayings of the Prophet Muhammad
Haẓir Imam	lit. Imam of the time, refers to the spiritual head of the Ismailis
Hiẓmet	in Turkish, Islamic principles and ideas of service of the Gülen Movement
Ijma	consensus of the Muslim community, or of the *ulama*
Ijtihad	independent reasoning in interpreting Islamic sources
Iman	belief
Islah	amendment, improvement
Isnad	means of assessing the *hadith* traditions on the basis of chain of transmitters
Jamaat	assembly; congregation
Jamaatkhana	assembly hall used for religious and social activities of community

Jihad	lit. 'to strive', with significant moral connotations for both internal or spiritual sphere as well as external or physical 'holy war'
Kamaria	*jamaat* accountant
Khudi	self; individual, a key component of Muhammad Iqbal's politico-religious thought
Malahida	heretic
Mehfel	association; assembly; gathering
Millat	community; an Ottoman Turkish system of administration of different ethnic and religious groups
Mujtahid	one who is qualified to perform *ijtihad*
Mukhi	*jamaat* treasurer
Mukti	liberation
Mumin	believer
Mutaa	temporary marriage
Nurcu (or *Nur*)	light
Panchayat	a community organization governance constituted originally of five members
Pirs	saints
Qaum	community; nation
Sharia	Islamic law
Sunna	tradition orienting conduct of life, more specifically referring to Prophetic tradition
Tanzimat	a series of Ottoman administrative and constitutional reforms in the nineteenth century
Tafsir	exegesis, especially Quranic exegesis
Talim	authoritative teaching
Taqlid	acceptance of religious ruling coming from higher religious authorities; blind adherence
Taqyyia	religious dissimulation; doctrine of mental reservation
Tarjuman	interpretation
Tawil	classical interpretive approach in Ismailism; science of elucidating particular meaning of the Quran
Ulama	theologians (sing. *alim*)
Umma	people; community, usually refers to the Muslim community

Note on Transliteration

I have not used any diacritical marks but have, naturally, retained those used in quotations while citing other works. Non-English words are usually italicized (e.g. *jamaat*), while well-known terms are not (e.g. Imam). Such words and expressions have been all glossed in their first usage. In addition, a separate glossary has been also provided for the readers' convenience. Names of places, institutions etc. have been spelt according to their contemporaneous spellings (e.g. Bombay; Simla Deputation; Muhammadan Anglo-Oriental College).

Introduction

Ismailism has survived because it has always been fluid. Rigidity is contrary to our whole way of life and outlook. There have really been no cut-and-dried rules, even the set of rules known as Holy Laws are directions as to method and procedure and not detailed orders about results to be obtained. In some countries—India and Africa for example—the Ismailis have a council system, under which their local councillors are charged with all internal administrative responsibility, and report to me as to [sic] their doings. In Syria, Central Asia, and Iran, leadership… is vested in either hereditary or recommended leaders and chiefs, who are the Imam's representatives and who look after the administration of the various Jamats or congregations.

From all parts of the Ismaili world with which regular contact is politically possible a constant flow of communications and reports comes to me. Attending to these, answering them, giving my solutions of [sic] specific problems presented to me, discharging my duties as hereditary Imam of this far-scattered religious community and association—such is my working life, and so it has been since I was a boy.[1]

Sultan Muhammad Shah Aga Khan III, 1954

This book explores the history of development of a Shia Ismaili identity in colonial South Asia. What follows in the pages below, in this introductory chapter, is an outline of the key arguments that I develop in the course of five subsequent chapters and the analytical tools and conceptual categories I employ to explore the history of Ismailism that the above longish quote from the memoirs of the community's forty-eighth Imam encapsulates. However, I would like to outline my choice of diction at the very outset. My occasional use of the expression 'sect' with reference to the Shia Muslims should not be seen in the light of any core-periphery or the Church-deviance paradigm. Also, this expression is invoked quite regularly, if also somewhat loosely in its usages, by Aga Khan III himself, and certainly eschewed of its pejorative slant.[2] On a related note, I use 'denomination' to refer to the Ismailis as a short-hand and by divesting the term of its Christian traits. Before we proceed any further, a word or two about working definitions of the Ismailis and Ismailism in line with contemporary understanding, and the way we in the present book understand them, will be in order. The underlying idea to sketch a concise overview of the contemporary notions and only thereafter proceeding on to engage with the key aspects of the historical process is an endeavour to invite readers to participate in a dialogic exercise with contemporary categories in the light of their historical and/or recorded past(s). This, in the present context, in effect means an engagement with the changing nature of certain epistemological concerns that had been pivotal in larger identitarian questions in South Asia since, at least, about the middle of the nineteenth century.

The conventional contemporary understanding of the Ismailis thus is as a minority among the Shia Muslims divided broadly into those still believing in a line of living Imam (the Imami Ismailis), and those who hold that the Imam is hidden and is represented by the Imam's vicegerent, *dai al mutlaq* (the Mustali Ismailis, or the Bohras in South Asia, East Africa etc. further split up into several sub-groups). I am concerned in this study with the former group, i.e., the Imami Ismailis, also called the Nizaris (referred to as the Khojas in South Asia and East Africa where there had been sizeable migrations of Ismailis for the better part of early modern and modern history). Unless otherwise qualified, throughout the present work, 'Khoja', 'Khoja Ismaili', 'Khoja Imami Ismaili' – with the latter in particular hinting at the followers of the Hazir Imam (Imam of the time), the Aga Khans – are all used to indicate the Nizari Ismailis of South Asian origin, while the terminology 'Ismaili' or 'Nizari Ismaili' refers more generally to those followers of the Hazir Imam hailing from other parts of the world, such as Central Asia.[3] The community is led by the Aga Khans, presently Shah Karim Aga Khan IV (1936; Imam since 1957), residing in Europe but frequently travelling across the world reaching out to his followers. His immediate predecessor as Imam – the forty-eighth in line who is also quoted above – was his grandfather Sultan Muhammad Shah Aga Khan III (1877–1957), who first shifted his residence from India to Europe while also setting a pattern of frequent travels to connect to his Ismaili followers across the globe. The very establishment of the Aga Khans as the leaders of the Ismailis was orchestrated through a prolonged legal process since the times of Aga Khan I (1800–81) in the latter part of nineteenth century Bombay that marked a dynamics of religio-legal forces and not least wider discourses of public good.[4] This language of public good was ensconced in a vision of modernity that, not unlike developments in other metropolitan centres in the colonial world, characterized the cosmopolitan nodal port-city of Bombay. It came to be invoked by the city's vanguard Khoja reformers who went on to pillory Aga Khan I for subverting their modernist projects while impelling in the process the Aga Khan's establishment to respond in accordance with this grammar of modernity.

In more general terms, Sudipta Kaviraj points to the divaricating notions of modernity so that in South Asia the idea, somewhat differently from its counterpart in the western political thought, emerged more than anything else as a matter of rational truth contra untruth or error.[5] While Kaviraj has in mind the 'structure of nationalist discourse', as announced in the title of his essay, one can hardly afford to overlook the larger socio-cultural meanings, and even anticipations, of the expression and the uses to which they were put in the sites of various forms of identitarian polemics. As we shall see, this is what our self-styled Bombay Khoja reformers in question precisely illustrate, by their invocation of idioms of 'reformation' and 'liberty', a rationally propelled progress, vis-à-vis medieval barbarism embedded in the occult, and indeed, in the form of the response they provoked from the Aga Khan's camp in the process. The ground that the South Asian variant of modernity, then, still shares in common with the western version is a crucial idea of newness of the future, whereby the modern future becomes intelligible only with reference to a rupture from its present and past, marking no simple replication with some variations of past or present events but anticipating something unprecedented. Crucial to this reconceptualization of the relation between the past, present and the future within the discursive rubric of 'modernity' is an emphasis on the knowledge of historical 'processes' as opposed to 'events'. Kaviraj here takes a cue from Reinhart Koselleck. Koselleck's narrative of an epistemic shift from the early modern (*Früher Neuzeit*) to the modern (*Moderne*), located in the so-called *Sattelzeit* (a transitional phase straddling roughly the mid-eighteenth and mid-nineteenth centuries when the new grammar of modernity was worked out), foregrounds the changing contours of temporal consciousness.[6] My efforts to understand this history of the Ismailis, then, is also informed by the idea of a larger framework, one characterized by historical *processes*, often contested, and balancing religio-cultural particularities with perceived universal values and ethics. The processes also involved both internalization as well as celebration of human intellect and activism at the level of the individual, and institutional articulations through the creation of new spaces of communication at the level of the collective. While the project of reading the rational as crucial component of the religio-cultural complex of Islam in modern Ismaili history has to be seen in part as a response to overwhelming appeal of the enlightenment-propelled notion of rationality, its association in particular with the Shia Ismaili strand of Islam needs to be problematized with reference to the denomination's engagement with ideas of both universality and specificities mediated by its Imamate since especially the times of Aga Khan III.

Much of this question about universal values and ethics also informed religious change and introspections in Islamic and Muslim societies, and indeed such developments in other religious communities, in late colonial South Asia. In as much as we locate the history of modern Ismailism since the latter part of the nineteenth century at the intersection of this quest for universality – which in itself was no uncontested terrain – and defence of denominational specificities, we shall also endeavour to understand some relatively less-explored aspects of socio-political change in Islam in modern South Asia. Of particular importance in this context will be the crucial role that Aga Khan III played in South Asia's Muslim politics, with increasingly transregional-global aspirations. In other words, the dynamics of these forces, since especially the Imamate of Aga Khan III, defined the contours of Ismaili history in the modern times and their relation with the larger Islamic world in general. While the religio-legal experimentation in Bombay during the times of Aga Khan I provides a general backdrop to the history of the community in modern times (see chapters 1 and 2 below), we shall see in the subsequent chapters that much of the complexities that characterize the globally-spread community along religio-political and socio-intellectual planes becomes intelligible in the context of the Imamate of Aga Khan III, and the crucial shifts and breaks it brought about.

The postnational, the denationalized and the cosmopolitan

The early phase of Ismaili identity formation since the latter part of the nineteenth century drew upon the dynamics of a range of forces at socio-religious, legal, and political planes in the immediate context of colonial Bombay. However, the process also bore significant transregional and, increasingly, global ramifications in the subsequent times. It involved the development of a distinctive Shia Ismaili identity – with South Asia's Khojas at the vanguard under the messianic and charismatic leadership of the Aga Khans (especially Aga Khan III and since the late 1950s, Aga Khan IV) – drawing upon wider pan-Islamic aspirations and postnational sensibilities. My idea of the postnational, I should point out, is informed by a line of scholarship that underscores the importance in the development of the 'self' in the colonial context of the urge to transcend the barriers of the national, questioning in the process the totalizing and homogenizing idea of nationalism. Such quest for the self, as has been pointed out, does not necessarily signal 'the disintegration of any sense of collective polity', but rather indicates resistance to 'the oppressive potential of collective nationalist identities'.[7]

Our invocation of the notion of the postnational, then, must not be seen as an autarkic enterprise positing a discursive formation cordoned off from the numerous ramifications that the ideas of nation and state imply or entail.[8] While the Ismaili Imamate's idea to both transcend and render redundant the boundaries set by the western model nation ensconced in the idea of territory becomes better intelligible within the conceptual rubric of the postnational, such engagements scarcely mean an outright denial of the very ideas of nation and state. Rather, they characterize an endeavour to critically engage with – and depending on the historical specificities, defy – the kindred conceptual cluster of the nation, state, and territoriality. While I am trying to suggest at one level that the question of defiance must not be seen as a denial to engage with ideas of the nation, or the state, or territorial boundedness, at another level the notion of the postnational then emerges as a far more leavening category than a hollow transcendental aspiration. In this, I am in effect echoing a critical inflection that recent scholarship on the idea of the postnational has persuasively argued. I have in mind a line of intervention that seeks to iterate the relevance of location in the face of global flows, fluidity, and translatability at a conceptual stratosphere of the 'global civil society'. As has been pointed out, 'the term *location* does not imply *indigeneity* or *authenticity*', but rather 'the *materiality* of spatial and temporal coordinates that inevitably suffuse *all* theorising' (emphases in original).[9] It is this intellection around the idea of the postnational, situated at the universality/particularity intersection that we strive to understand in this book.

The present study demonstrates that the form in which the ideas of the individual and the community, with all their corollaries, existed in Aga Khan III's discursive realm, elicits a pressing need to go beyond the contemporaneous modular notion of nation-state. We then also see how such critical engagements spurred creative possibilities, thanks to his enduring attempts at reworking, and selectively appropriating at times, such ideas. Aga Khan III's engagement with this conceptual constellation thus entailed, in effect, their virtual reconceptualization leading to significant implications for both his deterritorialized and depoliticized global Ismaili community as well as his discourse of a Muslim ecumenism. This is where the notion of 'denationalized', as a cognate conceptual framework to understand changes in ideas of self, citizenship and rights becomes apparent, especially in the context of more recent developments under the Imamate of Aga Khan IV. The notion of the denationalized occasions engagement with these categories within the confines of the nation even as the very idea of the nation also changes in the process, a development that becomes visible than ever before in its contemporary manifestations of the Ismaili Imamate's institutions. To be sure, the postnational and the denationalized so conceptualized are not entirely mutually exclusive either.[10] Aga Khan III's critical engagements with these conceptual categories, then, are among his most enduring legacies.

Within this larger framework we see that the Ismaili experience involved, furthermore, the activation of a cluster of socio-political idioms feeding into a religiously inflected political culture that had important implications for political ecumenism among South Asia's Muslims. The vocabulary of the political, however, was tempered with qualifications along two axes: first, Aga Khan III's invocation of the rhetoric of pan-Islamism brought with it an emphatic depoliticization of the notion marking a shift towards the spiritual and/or cultural lineaments; second, even as the language of political ecumenism was foregrounded in the context of early twentieth century South Asia, it never really meant an erosion of the Ismaili denominational particularities, which emanate first and foremost from the pivotal and apex location of the Imamate in the community. The complexity of the Ismaili case reminds one of two crucial aspects of the question of ecumenism among South Asia's Muslims that have been underscored especially in recent years. There are, thus, on the one hand scepticisms in scholarship about any linear and monolithic view of ecumenism of Muslim societies in colonial South Asia, which in effect render any argument of a harmonized pan-Islamism somewhat difficult to sustain.[11] On the other hand, scholars have also brought to attention a depoliticized model of Muslim society shored up with appeals to Shia sensibilities and, interestingly, propelled by several key Sunni Muslim thinkers in colonial India.[12] This book reiterates this notion of ecumenism with significant qualifications. It shows, in other words, that in Aga Khan III's thought about Muslim political ecumenism in the context of the subcontinent, his notions of denominational distinctiveness, as well as spiritual pan-Islamism were not incommensurable categories. They formed the very bases of his thesis of plurality in Islam.[13]

As well, the Ismaili community since especially the times of Aga Khan III also witnessed a pronounced emphasis on a range of normative and ethical questions, particularly on the idioms of social service, even as the latter, by late twentieth century, came to be couched in the state-of-art language of 'sustainable development'. The emergence of a universalizing aspirational language of sustainable development underpinned with avowed Ismaili religious ethics – with its own denominational particularities – becomes intelligible against the larger backdrop of a certain 'liberal Islam'.[14] The process, in other words, has to be seen as one developing over a *longue durée* with particular reference to the role of the Ismaili Imamate, and its tryst with the critical components that recent scholarship tends to situate within the analytical rubric of 'liberal Islam'. I emphasize here the need to see the universalizing idioms of progress and development not only in conjunction with an underpinning idea of an avowed Ismaili ethical system, but also the dynamic dialogic process that connected the universals to the specifics and the modalities that translated such projects. It is this dynamics, I suggest, that gives the Ismailis' tryst with modernity its salient character: one that invoked key aspects of colonial modernity, i.e., questions of identity, community development, social service, and progress and yet strips them of the coercive nature that the colonial venture entailed.[15] In doing so, it virtually re-inscribed the history of the Ismailis within a larger discourse of Islamic pluralism, critiquing especially the constraints that the western model of territorial nationalism imposed. Indeed, in their more recent articulations in the form of non-state actors under the aegis of the Imamate, the Ismaili institutions celebrate in no ambiguous terms the plural ethos of Islam and the need at the same time for the Imamate's mediation. This wedding of larger universalizing features to the ethical idioms entrenched in a distinctive religio-cultural, or even sectarian, matrix with its characteristic historical feature(s) is a reminder, in more general terms, of the idea that modern history could be better appreciated 'as an interplay of multiple and competing universalisms',[16] or a 'diversity of universals' as noted at the turn of the twenty-first century.[17]

This is the larger framework within which I endeavour to situate the history of the Ismailis in the modern times, pointing at the same time to the more recent implications with reference to the lineaments of the 'liberal' in 'liberal Islam'. But allow me to pause here and elaborate on some further aspects of the notion of, and arguments for, a nuanced Ismaili universalism on which this book is premised, especially the more practical aspects of the modalities of bringing the universal and the specificities in dialogue that I am alluding to. The nuances of the Ismaili universalism, as foregrounded by the Imamate, can be located at a number of planes. Aga Khan III's understanding of a religion drawing at once upon reason, belief, and ethics was part of a sweeping historical process. The emphasis on a correlated nature of reason, belief, and ethics defined his understanding of a certain universality that, he argued, characterized both Islam and Ismailism. Also, his emphasis on fluidity of Ismailism facilitated, for one, the remoulding of inherited traditions and structures with crucial implications. The same language of pliability, moreover, enabled religious inspiration enter a dialogic exercise with cultural and civilizational discourses, eliciting at once re-appraisal of ideas of accommodation, assimilation, and community membership. The notion of universality, then, both subsumed and drew strength from a plurality of forces, different interpretive possibilities, intellectual traditions, and a re-invigorated quest to rehabilitate the individual in any interpretive exercise. This idea of plurality in turn also enabled an accommodation, and even a repositioning, of the Ismaili denomination within the wider Islamic world with its own set of beliefs and practices, most notably the belief in a living Imam. The universal thus conceptualized was far from any closed 'given'; rather it underscores the need to take note of the plurality of historical possibilities, and to the unfinished nature of the Ismaili enterprise in contemporary times.

The notion of 'universalism with a difference', located in the family of vernacular and rooted cosmopolitanism, albeit 'diverging in subtle points of emphasis', addresses some of these issues.[18] Posing a riposte to the Eurocentric idea of cosmopolitanism as a legacy of Enlightenment metanarrative – labelled as 'colorless cosmopolitanism' operating typically at the level philosophical abstraction – this model looks for an antidote in the shape of 'colorful cosmopolitanism' that not only takes note of the 'inherited traditions' of the non-West but also underscores 'the dynamic process of creating and recreating traditions as well as flows between cultures and the fluidity of cultural boundaries'.[19] As indicated, our engagement in the following pages with the protean nature of the Ismaili universalism, with all its nuances and cosmopolitan allusions, is premised, first and foremost, on an axiom of certain pliability: viz. of its inherited traditions, institutions and structures, as expatiated on by Aga Khan III in the epigraph provided at the head of the present chapter. In our efforts to understand the history of the Ismailis and their universalizing aspirations in modern times with particular reference to the Imamate, rather than moving along any abstract stratospheric plane we emphasize their historical rootedness and contingent nature.[20] In the upshot, I hope, we are able to unpack their universalizing project as 'forms of power in their own right, which rest on their own politics of truth and enable forms of inclusion and exclusion'.[21] We do so moreover with reference to the complexities that have characterized the community since the latter part of the nineteenth century from a historical perspective.

Religious internationals and cosmopolitanism: The religious, the secular and Ismaili subjectivity

The emergence of a distinctive Shia Ismaili identity is a history that originated in Bombay with the Aga Khan Case of 1866. Also known as the Great Khoja Case, it signalled in certain respects a critical rupture with the Perso-centrism that Aga Khan I had until then symbolized. Located at the intersection of religio-legal experimentation and political and administrative imperatives of the colonial establishment, it brought to the forefront a new set of indices to determine community membership, and re-defined in the process the very bases of religious/spiritual authority of the community embodied in the Aga Khans. Supplanted gradually by colonial epistemic props, this Perso-centrism found itself in an alternative space, viz., in a subtle celebration of the Persian traditions with all its cultural paraphernalia that later flavoured part of Aga Khan III's cultural proclivities even as he welcomed modernist experiments, especially in social and political spheres, along western lines.[22] In the process, community institutions such as the *jamaat* (assembly/ congregation) too were restructured and remoulded. The process, it seems, was not insular. In particular, certain parallels in institutional formations can be gauged from the *panchayat* (a traditional form of community governance) and *anjuman* (community assemblies) systems of the Parsis, and the shifts they witnessed over the nineteenth century, due in large part to changing perceptions of religious authority amid colonial religio-judicial experimentations.[23] Under especially Aga Khan III the *jamaat* underwent significant changes in conjunction, as well as in consonance, with a new-found constitutionalism. The recurrent invocation of idioms of voluntarism and community development since the Imamate of Aga Khan III marks a throwback to the vocabulary of public good that emerged in the course of the 1866 law case. Thus, the Aga Khan Case marks a crucial moment of realization, albeit not uncontested as we shall see, for the Ismaili community, viz., the growing importance of the Imam of the time, i.e., the Aga Khan, in not only the realm of the sacred and spiritual but also in the domain of the temporal. The idiom of public good, then, came to provide an intricate balance between the universal and the specific. A crucial point of reference for the posterity, the 1866 law case anticipated a language of ethical community that under Aga Khan III would later graduate into a coherent discourse, cutting across boundaries of ethnicity and nationality, while remaining responsive to the transregional-global locations of the Ismailis.

The universal message of public good voiced through the Ismaili vocabularies of morality and ethics, mediated by the pivotally located Imamate through community protocols and *farmans* (edicts) that came into force from the early 1900s, served a two-pronged purpose. It came to provide the bases for both criteria of community membership as well as a complex equipoise of rights and responsibilities. It meant on the one hand a reconfiguration of the boundaries of the community in terms of the language of socio-religious ethics. On the other hand, the centrality of the Imamate in this socio-religious fabric provided a specific Ismaili imprint, even as recasting the Imamate in increasingly secularized nomenclature. A dynamics of these forces conditioned the development of a distinctive Ismaili ethics as alluded to above, i.e., one that gravitated around an Imamate, drawing upon an understanding of Islam celebrating plurality, human intellect and interpretive possibilities while also wedding them to the universalizing language of human progress, improvement and, more recently, 'sustainable development'. I should note, in passing for now and will elaborate on its larger ramifications later in the course of the book, that the idea of secularism that underlies the present study is one that sees its distinctiveness in the fact that it 'presupposes new concepts of "religion", "ethics" and politics and new imperatives associated with them'.[24] In the process, we argue, the dynamics between the secular vis-à-vis the religious result in the projection of new meanings of each of these categories.

In the course of what follows below we shall also see how the protean Ismaili universalism manifested itself through a language of cultural and civilizational mission extolling the role of the Indians, and more specifically Ismaili Muslims, in large parts of Africa.[25] Lest readers translate this as a thinly garbed language of a somewhat crude internal colonialism underpinned with a nationalistic fervour, I should add, that crucial to Aga Khan III was also a stress on cultural assimilation, occasionally *voluntary* religious conversion and,[26] as already indicated, efforts to both critique and rework existing models of nation and state. Part of the Aga Khan's endeavour to relate South Asia and Africa through a transoceanic grid has to be seen in the light of a line of thought that emphasized the transcolonial interactions since especially the late nineteenth century. Scholars have thus suggested a re-examination of India's locus in this re-conceptualized imperial web, one in which India appears to have acquired a central and pivotal role, from which 'peoples, ideas, goods, and institutions ... radiated outward', spurring in the process new ideas of being Indian, and indeed imperial citizen.[27] While part of this larger politico-intellectual circle, we shall see in the following pages, the Aga Khan however also foreshadowed significant innovations in his engagement with ideas of citizenship. Moreover, his very reconceptualization of India as an epitome of Asiatic cultural/civilizational forces – categories he largely used interchangeably – and located at the heart of an imagined entity that he called the 'South Asiatic Federation', marked a crucial commentary on the very idea of India. In the upshot, Aga Khan III was in effect evoking a language of defiance, if not denial, of the very existence of an array of cognate notions in the nation-state family: of territoriality, territorial nationalism, and ethnicity, hallmarks of modernity and typically sacrosanct to the hegemonic European line of political thought.

In this defiance of indices of the nation and territoriality, I do not read evasive efforts to repose the colonized self in the 'inner' domain as opposed to the 'outer'. Rather, I see in the Aga Khan's conceptualization of a cultural and civilizational project of Islam accompanied with a selective emulation of western-inspired modernity, an ambitious endeavour to envision certain spiritual pan-Islamism. I see in this venture efforts towards intellection of an alternative language of religio-cultural community with its own variations as well as cultural and civilizational claims beyond the confines of the nation.[28] And yet, interestingly, in spite of the promise of the postnational, several trappings of the state – rules and regulations, constitution, flag, and anthem – were, and still are, also sought to be imbibed by the Imam's establishment that lends them to a sublime semiotic exercise at the hands of the Imamate. This is part and parcel of a process whereby the Ismaili Imamate had been striving since the times of Aga Khan III to reformulate its vocabularies of community governance. This, then, is a process marked by oppositional forces. On the one hand, the Ismailis see themselves as part of historical developments brought about by the forces of globality, cosmopolitanism and decolonization in larger parts of Asia and Africa, although not necessarily with the same results or homogenized religio-cultural metanarratives. On the other hand, it also stoked efforts to rise above the logic of capital and idioms of territoriality and territorial nationalism, recasting in the process new languages of community membership based on a protean understanding of Ismailism.

In my endeavour to shed light on the cosmopolitan vision that the Imamate especially since the times of Aga Khan III sought to promote, I also seek to problematize the production of the Ismaili subject. As hinted at in the foregoing pages, the very idea of the Ismaili subjectivity as professed by the Imamate has to be situated at the intersection of the larger historical forces spiralling originally from colonial Bombay. As also mentioned, they had momentous implications for the community's identitarian quest since the mid-nineteenth century entailing crucial institutional articulations. My concern to problematize the Ismaili individual vis-à-vis at one level, the Ismaili collective and, at another, the institutional articulations, echoes to some extent scholarly efforts to locate the meanings of individual's actions in transcendent projects and/or temporal structures. As Talal Asad argues:

> The medieval Christian monk who learns to make the abbot's will into his own learns thereby to desire God's purposes. In an important

sense, the meaning of his actions is what it is by virtue of their being part of transcendent temporal structures ... Even among nonbelievers, few would claim that the human agent is sovereign, although post-Enlightenment moral theory insists that she ought to be autonomous.[29]

Asad is equally concerned about the translatability of cultural projects, adding a note on the heterogeneity in nature as well as in versions of power spawned by translations of projects from one site to another.[30] In my effort to understand Ismaili subjectivity, I try to see the didactic modalities of its Imamate as the strategies of 'fashioning'. Such strategies relate to the creation of a distinctive Ismaili personality to shaping her/his attitude towards the community and the world to inculcating a particular code of conduct. At the same time, the translatability of the Imamate-mediated centralized project at multiple locations brings us to the question of inculturation.[31] I am, thus, concerned here to understand the critical balance that defines the Ismaili Imamate's view of the Ismaili subject. We intend to interrogate here how a messianic religious authority, reinventing itself within colonial epistemological framework and with its own institutions and set of protocols – akin, interestingly, to several of the state's mechanisms – produces an idea of a religious community with its trademark particularities and yet, at an essentially deterritorialized plane, addresses an array of larger universalist questions. Evidently, this also hinged upon domestication of certain colonial epistemological categories that were ensconced in prolonged religio-judicial exercise. Indeed, this history, with all its variations, was part of more general process of taxonomization of the colonized communities that often resulted, in turn, in heightened politico-intellectual activities of self-fashioning on the part of several of those communities as well.

The earliest experiments of the Imamate-led Ismaili community governance emerged out of Aga Khan III's venture to redefine community boundaries in response to the dogged secessionist developments among the Khojas in the western Indian Ocean world in the early twentieth century. Thus, the first of the rules and regulations of the community emerged in the 1900s, in parts of littoral eastern Africa and western India, connecting for the first time the community spread in those parts of the world through a language of governance and constitutionalism.[32] This system of protocols, sensitized as it was to the specificities of the regions, was at the same time regulated by the Imamate through its complex mechanism. It contributed to no less extent to the galvanizing of a new language of community development in the western Indian Ocean rim, a transregional arena with remarkable cosmopolitan character.[33] This was the cradle of what I call the 'Ismaili international' of more recent times. In invoking the expression 'Ismaili international', I am borrowing and customizing a recent intervention that posits a conceptual framework of 'religious international' which, it is argued, emerged and proliferated in the nineteenth and the twentieth centuries. Its gradual development led to 'reforging of religious identities in transatlantic or imperial encounters, and the emergence of new forms of sectarian politics, philanthropy and the press', at the very heart of which is certain '*mobilization* and *religiously inflected voluntarism*' (italics in original).[34] As we shall see, these are also forces that defined the Ismaili experience under the leadership of its Imams, and especially since the times of Aga Khan III.

The idea of cosmopolitanism that informs the present work, then, invites us to explore the 'internal developmental processes within the social world' – instead of looking at 'globalization as the primary mechanism' – leading to certain 'critical' and 'post-universalistic' understanding of cosmopolitanism.[35] This is in no way to ignore the implications that global processes and globalization entail,[36] nor the universalizing aspirations of specific historical processes. Rather, when we invoke notions of globalization, we do so bearing in mind its role as a larger overarching background, not as a sweeping wave with any underpinning teleological argument of homogenizing cultural venture.[37] My use of the expression 'Ismaili international' is, in fact, an effort to underscore the critical balance between the different pathways of Ismaili inculturation across the world on the one hand and the community's avowed religio-cultural core held together by the Imamate on the other. The different pathways of inculturation, furthermore, also entail crucial introspections within the conceptual rubric of cosmopolitanism. They range from the emphases on the dynamic nature of internal processes in line with Gerard Delanty, as noted above, to what I see, with certain qualifications, as essentially anticipations from the times of Aga Khan III of an ideal Ismaili as champion of an idea of 'cosmopolitan citizenship', as theorized by Andrew Linklater. Linklater draws upon the Kantian idea of the moral bases of cosmopolitanism while extending it further by reminding 'citizens of the unfinished moral business of the sovereign state and to draw their attention to the higher ethical aspirations which have yet to be embedded in political life' creating, in the process, 'universal frameworks of communication'.[38] While this represents a relatively recent social scientists' critical evaluation of the nation and the sovereign state consummating in the founding of universal frameworks for communication, I strive in this book to look for its historical antecedents beyond the narrow confines of academic practice, focusing attention instead on the religio-cultural and intellectual sites beyond the remits of the state in the non-West. Indeed, one wonders if there are also not anticipations of such critiques since the early twentieth century in Aga Khan III's social thoughts, articulated moreover through a range of institutions that evolved under him.

It has been argued that the model of citizenship propped up by the colonial dispensation was essentially limited by the criteria of property qualifications, religious orientations, caste, and kinship patterns, a project that was even in such burgeoning urban hubs as Bombay sustained more often than not by the communitarian structures of major mercantile groups, promoting respective group interests, and only an incomplete notion of civic consciousness.[39] However, I suggest that while this may have well been the dominant narrative, the Imamate that evolved under Aga Khan III presents a crucial counter-narrative in certain respect. Thus, while the Imamate's institutions – ranging from a restructured *jamaat* through a system of protocols, to a protean language of religio-cultural sensibilities evolved through a dynamic relation between the universal and the specifics – were central to the redefinition of an Ismaili community both in transregional and global arenas, they became in the course of time no less crucial in foregrounding a language of a holistic participatory and sustainable development, and indeed an inclusive citizenship, beyond the constricted boundaries of a nation-state. The process thus also spurred since the Imamate of Aga Khan III the development of both spheres as well as idioms of a complex communication.

In my emphasis on the universalizing aspirations that a particular religious denomination under its spiritual leadership has been striving to come to terms with, for about a century now, I am in effect trying to engage key aspects of the two lines of cosmopolitanism in dialogue. This becomes intelligible with reference to both Aga Khan III's religious leadership among the Ismailis, and his political leadership among South Asia's Muslims, without necessarily and exclusively dwelling on Kantian philosophical abstractions. His languages of community development and voluntary social service transcending the boundaries of the nation-state sensitized remarkably to its universalizing prospects would provide one with a case in point. In effect, therefore, I am suggesting here a *longue durée* history of an ideational lineage, with all its nuances, of the postnational and universalizing possibilities of a cosmopolitan citizenship. Ours then is an exercise – with the particular reference to the history of a religious denomination – in tracing the genealogy of postnational subjectivity. We see here how Aga Khan III's efforts in this direction emanated from the crucible of the internal developments of his Ismaili denomination since the late nineteenth century, discernible first among the Khojas in the western Indian Ocean world, and gradually in wider global circles. At another level, the universalizing prospects have subsequently come to mean incorporation within the religiously underpinned discourse of progress and development of large sections of non-Ismaili beneficiaries. A study of the overlapping discourses of Ismaili subjectivity, fashioning and, indeed, cosmopolitan citizenship would also elicit reflections, in particular, on the life and times of Aga Khan III.

Religious authority and the question of articulation

In my effort to understand the process of an Ismaili identity formation emanating from colonial Bombay and leading to an Ismaili subjectivity in relatively recent times, I am, to reiterate then, concerned with a set of questions that were integral to the community's changing contours even as it marked a passage from the transregional to the global arena.

This was a process that was connected to the evolution of what I have above referred to as the Ismaili international. This global space for an essentially religious denomination spread across the world was not an outcome of any linear historical process, and nor do I intend to give any triumphalist teleological narrative of a homogeneous Ismaili experience. A further complexity stems from the critically important position that the community's forty-eighth Imam Aga Khan III held as a leading Muslim nationalist in the political sphere in late colonial South Asia, even as working out his own ideas of pan-Islamism and Asian solidarity. For Aga Khan III, spiritual pan-Islamism and the rhetoric of Asian solidarity, albeit eliciting ideas of depoliticization, were part of a larger ideational repertoire of internationalism. To be able to navigate with these vocabularies at such platforms as the assemblies of the League of Nations, which was after all premised on an understanding of internationalism involving multilateral intergovernmental initiatives, is then indicative of the creative possibilities within the framework of internationalism, or for that matter the variations of the very idea. This also brings to the forefront the question of balancing a specific denominational vision with a language of political ecumenism, underscoring simultaneously the commensurability in Aga Khan III's thought of spiritual pan-Islamism and pan-Asian aspirations. Aga Khan III's engagement along these planes hinged on, foremost, the inflections he brought about to reconceptualize categories that had already had some currency and, in the process, creating his own brand of conceptual repertoire. For one, even the idea of Ismaili specificities, streamlined and regulated by the Imamate through its own mechanisms and recast in new idioms of community membership, are critical reminders of the complexities of the historical context in late colonial South Asia and East Africa from which it emerged. It also illustrates how inherited traditions and institutions were, under the auspices of the Imamate, systematically reworked. We shall also see how an enduring academic engagement in the course of time carved out an epistemological entity called 'Ismaili Studies' raising a range of questions, part of which were clairvoyantly anticipated by Aga Khan I's Defence Counsel in the wake of the 1866 Aga Khan Case. The most important legacy of these questions had been of both methodological as well as ethical nature, which not only conditioned the contours of an academic sub-field that started taking shape under Aga Khan III, but also facilitated the Imamate's envisioning of an Ismaili, and indeed Islamic, conscience.

We have suggested above that Aga Khan III's denial of the project of what he called 'political pan-Islamism' could be read as an effort to surmount the strictures of territoriality, and indeed the very idea of 'nation' with all its paraphernalia, that a western model of territorial nationalism imposes. In this, he echoed some of the most crucial concerns that other contemporaneous South Asian Muslim thinkers of the time expressed, perhaps most notably, albeit not exclusively, Sir Muhammad Iqbal (1877–1938). The critique of the modern western model of nation-state and its totalizing venture formed part of a much wider intellectual exercise, one that was felt and articulated in the metropole as well. Thus Lord Acton, the Regius Professor in Modern History in Cambridge, around the time when *Allama* (an honorary title for highly regarded scholar of Islamic thought) Iqbal was a student at Trinity College, was one of the most vehement critics of the hegemonic nation-state discourse. For no insignificant reason, therefore, one recent historical account sees plausible connections in their thought.[40] Likewise the valorization of the federal/confederal model, which underpins Aga Khan III's project of Indian reconstruction in his 1918 book *India in Transition: A Study in Political Evolution*, too can be seen as a part of this larger critique of centralization that homogenizing mono-cultural nation-states entail.[41] As well, the idea of pan-Islamism too has to be problematized. Syed Ameer Ali (1849–1928), leading Shia Muslim politician and an exegete of Shia Muslim traditions among his other *avatars*, had serious reservations about that expression. In a polemical exchange with the Orientalist D. S. Margoliouth (1858–1940), Ameer Ali pointed out that 'pan-Islamism' was but a figment of western brain, a tool to reduce all legitimate grievances of the Muslims – suffering at the hands of unfettered colonial greed – under a pejorative portmanteau construct.[42]

Recent scholarly works have, moreover, pointed to the tortuous history of the very idea of pan-Islamism since the middle of the nineteenth century. The notion of a 'Muslim world' underlying a pan-Islamism with Ottoman Turkey at the apex and involving resolute anticolonial and anti-imperialist voices stretching from West to South Asia, thus, has been seen as one among several other forms of internationalisms emerging in the late nineteenth century.[43] Evolving out of dialogues since the 1880s among Muslim reformers and essentially anticolonial figures – thinkers, politicians, activists – from among the colonized Asian societies, pan-Islamism acquired three enduring features: a discourse of an Islamic civilization contesting hegemonic European pejorative constructs; a discourse of anti-Westernism; and an anticolonial internationalism embracing eventually non-Muslim colonized societies in Asia and Africa.[44] What is at stake here is the way the universalist aspirations revolving around visions of an Islamic solidarity came to be seen in dialogue with national, regional, and even local predicaments. In this vein, it has been illustrated how commentaries, and the resultant intellectual exchanges, on the Caliphate by the towering Muslim thinker-activist Muhammad Rashid Rida (1865–1935) and the Indian National Congress leader Maulana Abul Kalam Azad (1888–1958) developed both commonalities and divergences: commonality in terms of the pivotal position they both accorded to the Caliphate; divergences, since, their ideas of the Muslim world were still conditioned by the specificities of their nationalist experience, a pronounced Arabism for Rida as opposed to Azad's insistence on disaggregating religion, territoriality and race in line with the Indian National Congress' visions.[45] Against this larger backdrop, Aga Khan

III's quest for a spiritual pan-Islamism cutting across ethnic and national lines balanced with a language of political ecumenism in South Asia represented yet another variation of the idea. Aga Khan III's thesis, then, was as much part of global flows in ideas as it was ensconced in the particularities of the South Asian historical context: his religious and political location as well as the transregional nature of the Muslim community of which he was the spiritual leader.

There are, then, substantial reasons that we focus in this book on the life and career of Aga Khan III. And this is where, among other questions which it addresses, the present book will mark a point of departure from existing scholarship. To make my point clearer, I should mention in particular a recent intervention that seeks to explore 'how individuals and localities become more closely affiliated with a transnational, non-territorial organization than with the territorial nation-state of which they are citizens or administrative units'.[46] The preponderant thrust in such works as this, though, is towards understanding from an ethnographic – and only secondarily historical – perspective the Ismaili institutions. Doubtless, the Ismaili institutions formed an important site where some of the most crucial aspects of the community's identitarian venture were worked out. My unease with an almost exclusive focus on institutions, however, is not because of any lack of sophistication in these studies, but is due to other reasons. This is because of the emphasis in such accounts on institutional formations often at the expense of exploring the mental worlds or the ideational complexities of individuals who are crucial to historical processes that condition the institutional structures. This, however, is not to be so naïve as to say that individuals necessarily dictate, or succeed in dictating, in all respects the trajectories of institutions. Indeed, there is an immense indexical value of the life and career of Aga Khan III that provides us with a window into the larger implications of the socio-political, religio-cultural, and not least economic forces of the times. For all the singular nature of the life of Aga Khan III in the Ismaili spiritual *topos*, his career illuminates nevertheless a complex process of Ismaili identity formation, marking a passage from the transregional space of the western Indian Ocean seaboard to a wider global arena. This is also a history of the Imamate's vision of what it meant to be an Ismaili. With especially the Indian-origin Khoja Ismailis at the vanguard,[47] however, Ismailism under Aga Khans III and IV had also undergone its own process of inculturation, signifying a history of different political trajectories and cultural pathways that the Ismailis experience in large parts of the world. The quotation from Aga Khan III that stands as epigraph in this introductory chapter is a reminder of some of these complexities.

With this larger project in mind, I try here not only to understand his intellectual profile, but also his authorial role and intent. By authorial role and intent I imply authorship of both historical processes through which he led the Ismailis and South Asia's Muslim aspirations in a crucial phase of their history, as well as its articulation through the significant corpus of literature he produced.[48] While I have already outlined above some aspects of individual authorship in relation to historical processes, an account of the conceptual bases of authorial voice, or for that matter silences or elisions that inform my study will be in order. The two foremost textual interventions of Aga Khan III come in the form of his 1918 work entitled *India in Transition: A Study in Political Evolution* and his 1954 memoirs entitled *The Memoirs of Aga Khan: World Enough and Time*, with a Foreword by W. Somerset Maugham (1874–1965). While the latter is clearly a memoir, as announced in its title, in the former case, exploring the authorial 'I' and the individual's voice in relation to the wider historical forces and processes is especially facilitated by the narration in an articulate first-person. In *India in Transition* the underlying project is to envision the future of a country standing at crossroads, after the World War I and on the eve of the 1919 constitutional reforms.[49] *The Memoirs*, by contrast, conjures an image of a life that had come full circle, having witnessed momentous changes, the 'duty', as Aga Khan III notes,

> to give an account in some detail of my experience over this long, momentous epoch, and to record my personal acquaintance—often, indeed, my real and deep friendship—with some of those who have had their share in bringing about its vast political, social, and economic changes.[50]

But the very opening few sentences in the Prologue, in particular, are also telling: they point to the urgency of an onus on the Aga Khan to undo all the myths and legends that surround his persona.[51] The cumulative outcome of such myths and legends perhaps comes most forcefully from one of Aga Khan III's staunchest political opponents, Jawaharlal Nehru (1889-1964). Nehru wondered at the alleged contradictions that the Aga Khan personified, playing 'such varied roles, combining the thirteenth century with the twentieth, Mecca and Newmarket, this world and the next, spirituality and racing, politics and pleasure'.[52]

Yet, in all fairness, the attempt to correct spurious legends and respond to visceral critiques should not be seen as the dominant trend of the memoirs of the Aga Khan. If anything, the memoirs should be read first and foremost as key to understanding the mental world, as much as the persona, of the Aga. This effort to retrieve the authorial 'I' is aware of the charges often brought against the life histories as a form of expression: as an instrument of bourgeois cultural history or of the autonomous individual associated with the cultural project of late capitalism.[53] The present study, however, proceeds from the idea that life histories, after all, are both part of the historical matrices from which they emerge as well as critical commentaries on them in turn. Aga Khan III's example illustrates how the numerous anecdotes of the youth projected themselves into the Imam's life and thought, even as a youth from Bombay who became Imam of the Ismailis at the tender age of eight grew up under the tutelage of a team of private tutors in the family's palaces in Bombay and Poona. Allow me to elaborate on this. I have in mind in particular the Aga Khan's valorization of the plural ethos of Islam that formed the hallmark of his socio-religious thought. A clue to some aspects of his ideational disposition, for instance, his lifelong 'prejudice against professional men of religion' can be traced back to his childhood as he contrasted in his memoirs the parochial Shiite outlook of his teacher of Arabic, Persian and Islamic traditions with the three much-praised European tutors that the Jesuits in Bombay and Poona chose for instructing him in 'western matters'.[54] Consider, furthermore, the maturing youth immersed in learning Arabic, Persian, English, French, a good mix of the sciences, 'Mill's system of logic', in a family with a penchant for everything aesthetic, in literature and spirituality.[55] Consider also the way the near-octogenarian Imam engages with his childhood recollections through the chapter: the precociously insatiable hunger for reading more and an occasional impish thrill in attempting to steal, along with his cousin, books in a Bombay bookshop and the shame in getting caught, juxtaposed with the rigorous daily schedule that his religious position required, superimposed, finally, on imageries of a much profound stream of mysticism of Rumi and Hafiz that memories of his mother evoked and remained with him for the rest of his life.[56] In the light of his personal account of admiration for physical culture in general and his own emulation of the model sportsman juggling with cycling to boxing to Eugen Sandow's (Friedrich Wilhelm Müller, 1867–1925) exercise,[57] it is not difficult to trace a part of his larger discourse of health and muscle power for 'reconstruction' of society and the nation developed in greater detail in his *India in Transition*. These are handful random examples. The outcome, though, is not an image of a distant and sombre religious head, but of someone who derived pleasure in everything human, someone who could stitch together with his characteristic élan vignettes of his own experience on the turf, to more serious discussions about his role at the Round Table Conferences, at the League of Nations, and not least his concept of Islam and his own role as Imam of a particular branch of the Muslim community that underwent a sea change under his more than half-a-century long Imamate.[58]

Outline of chapters

Before we move on to outline the chapters that follow, a brief pause devoted to narrating what it does not offer will be perhaps in order. While this book posits the idea of possible myriad pathways of what I venture to call Ismaili inculturation across different parts of the globe, it is clearly not an effort to dissect them on a comparative scale. Indeed, one can barely accommodate a detailed narrative of this multisited inculturation within the remits of the present book. Likewise, it is not an objective of the book to engage with questions such as the phenomenon of missionary activism, often associated with the conceptual category of inculturation. Nor is this book an exhaustive account of *all* aspects of the history of the Ismailis in modern times, such as histories focusing on gendered experience(s) and women's issues in modern Ismaili discourse or, for instance, accounts of the community emanating from vernacular Gujarati literature from the western Indian Ocean world. This is not because such questions are not important or were of no concern to the Imamate, but because once again of the difficulty in accommodating all of such questions within the existing scheme of the book, and do justice to them.[59] This, then, is not to be oblivious or dismissive about possibility of such histories, but merely to suggest one possible way of writing the history of the Ismailis in modern times while also recognizing other possibilities. This book pays a particular premium on the life and times of the community's forty-eighth Imam Aga Khan III. Under his Imamate, from the late nineteenth to about middle of the twentieth century, i.e. a stretch covering the two World Wars and a rapidly decolonizing world, the community virtually reinvented itself as, what I have alluded to above, an Ismaili international. In view of the immense indexical value that Aga Khan III's career bore, I try to retrieve the questions asked, and answers arrived at, in the literature produced by the Imamate, and more specifically by Aga Khan III himself, whose works are almost invariably, in their originals, in the English language. I also juxtapose the impressive body of literature, produced in particular under the Imamates of Aga Khan I (the living Imam during the 1866 Aga Khan Case) and Aga Khan III in different literary forms, with those gleaned from a wide variety of archives and repositories, some of which have been hardly ever used in the existing scholarship. One of the most unfortunate implications of not having consulted such literature manifests itself through the blinkered twentieth century scholarship still tethered to re-invented Orientalist idioms. I do not see any plausible historical merit in such positions, but find it imperative to point to the rather disturbingly persisting nature of at once the absurd and seductive character of Orientalist tropes in some academic circles, and their overall neglect of the critical intellectual exercises that redefined the very bases of an Ismaili community since the late nineteenth century.[60]

In Chapter 1 I provide the background to the momentous changes since the mid-nineteenth century that conditioned modern Ismaili history. I trace the contours of the legal process that spiralled from colonial Bombay and came to (re)define the category of the 'Khoja' within the framework set by what historians have called the 'Anglo-Muhammadan judiciary'. While I agree with the established view that the Imamate was repositioned centrally within the Khoja Ismaili community in the colonial times, I argue however, by drawing upon a corpus of neglected archival sources, that this centrality was by no means irrevocably settled in the wake of the Aga Khan Case (1866), as conventional knowledge would have us believe. I look at the social profile of both the self-proclaimed reformists, who opposed Aga Khan I, as well as that of the Aga Khan's supporters. Moreover, I explore the vocabularies that were invoked in the legal polemics, and the tortuous judicial experiments in the latter half of the nineteenth century in which the colonial establishment also vacillated in its position. In doing so, I show how antithetical voices emerged contesting hegemonic languages of religious standardizations.

Chapter 2 fills in a major gap in scholarship on the Ismailis. In the first place, it shows how in the wake of the Aga Khan Case the category of the 'Ismaili' was invoked and came to be used interchangeably with the 'Khoja'. Second, by making extensive use of hitherto neglected primary sources, I explore the larger moral argument that was invoked to defend and rehabilitate the Shia, and more particularly Ismaili Shia, position within the framework of Islam, while also bringing to the forefront questions of racial and cultural sensibilities. Third, I draw upon such primary sources to show how they were in effect, if somewhat unwittingly, anticipating a range of methodological concerns that subsequently resurfaced and defined the project of 'Ismaili Studies'. In tracing the production, consumption and subsequent institutionalization of scholarship on the Ismailis through re-invigorated efforts of the Imamate since the times of Aga Khan III, I point to the continuities and breaks in the intellectual process, and contextualize them against the backdrop of larger discourse(s) of 'world religions'. It is against this background that Aga Khan III successfully dovetailed his role as the Ismaili Imam with that of a leading political personality. As argued in the following pages, Aga Khan III did so, furthermore, by championing wider Muslim causes in South Asia in the early part of his career, and gradually and ever so increasingly reaching out to a range of internationalist concerns.

Chapter 3 examines Aga Khan III's thoughts on, and aspirations about, India in the light of the constitutional experiments of the early twentieth century. Aga Khan III's *India in Transition: A Study in Political Evolution* (1918) was, first and foremost, an exposition of his thoughts on India's reconstruction and development, with ambitious theses on models of social service and governance. Yet the text also breaks new ground by foregrounding cultural concerns outside the remits of the western notions of nations and statism that he later went on to articulate in international platforms such as the League of Nations, of which India was also a founding member. In the upshot, the reader encounters a critical balance between an array of internationalist aspirations and hopes about, and even more concretely his blueprint of, a country 'in transition'. A key component of the cultural internationalism was Aga Khan III's discourse of spiritual pan-Islamism championing a remarkable degree of cultural plurality. The argument of plurality with a postnational promise was an important one, given that it subsequently came to condition a global Ismaili identity, which we revisit in greater detail in chapter 5.

Chapter 4 explores the complex nature of the public career of Aga Khan III ranging from his role as the Ismaili community's Imam of the time, even as the community was being continually reconfigured, to an important political leader among South Asia's Muslims. In this chapter, I problematize and interrogate the entanglement of a range of dynamic historical forces, and the possibilities they entailed: of denominational particularities within Islam in the context of modern South Asia against the background of contending religious nationalist politics; the issues gravitating around political ecumenism; charismatic spiritual authority drawing upon a re-activation of a language of messianism; overlapping discourses of spiritual pan-Islamism and postnationalist sensibilities; and not least, the historical roots of the ethical and institutional forms of the contemporary global ecumene that the Ismailis signify. While rooted in the historical context of late colonial South Asia this complex entanglement, then, also had significant internationalist ramifications that become further intelligible in terms of the postnational imagination that the global Ismaili formations have, especially in more recent times, come to evoke.

Taking cue from the earlier discussions in chapter 5 we illustrate how, mediated by the messianic authority of the Imam of the time at the apex, an Ismaili identity gradually coalesced around languages of Ismaili denominational specificities and spiritual pan-Islamism in a deterritorialized world. The centrality of the Imamate, in particular, is an important issue that had transregional and increasingly global significance. But no less salient are the idioms of 'Ismaili ethics', and religious normativity with universalizing aspirations and a cosmopolitan appeal. Also crucially important in this Ismaili experience, as we highlight in our study, is the sphere of praxis within which we see generations of Ismaili children being tutored in the language of Ismaili normativity and ethics, sensitizing them to the idioms of active community membership. Drawing upon conceptual reflections on 'habitus' and 'potentiality', I draw upon literature coming from within the Ismaili community while also alerting my readers to the organizational and/or structural aspects of the process. This survey from the times of Aga Khan III to the present Imamate of Aga Khan IV underscores at one level the variegated nature of both the Ismaili community-specific structures as well as Ismaili inculturation across the world that gives the Ismaili international its very versatility. At another level, it also brings to the forefront the mutually potentiating nature of the inclusive holistic developmental *imaginaire* of the contemporary Ismaili institutions (e.g. the Aga Khan Development Network and its affiliated bodies), and not least the role of religious inspiration that underpins such institutions. This chapter traces this process from the early twentieth century, when the earliest of the experiments in this direction were conducted in South Asia and East Africa under the aegis of Aga Khan III.

In the section on 'Concluding Reflections' we shall not only summarize and wind up the discussions, but also shed light on some more recent and contemporary aspects of the subject, both in conceptual and empirical terms. The study, thus, raises an array of issues straddling the fields of intellectual and religious history, and provokes further questions in the fields of history of South Asia and South Asian religions. It does so by situating the core questions raised in the book in the context of larger socio-religious and intellectual processes at transregional and global arenas.

Endnotes

1   His Highness the Aga Khan III, *The Memoirs of the Aga Khan: World Enough and Time*, 185 (London: Cassell & Co. Ltd., 1954).

2   For instance Aga Khan III, *The Memoirs of the Aga Khan*, 4, talks about his inherited position as 'the Imam of the Ismaili branch of the Shia sect of Muslims'. Few pages down the line, the Aga Khan refers to the 'Ismaili sect of the Shia Muslims' (Ibid., 7).

3   Throughout the book, I prefer the expression 'Ismaili' and 'Ismailism' to 'neo-Ismaili' and 'neo-Ismailism', respectively. This choice has to be seen in the light of my effort to retrieve the nomenclature in currency in the self-depicting literature rather than recycling expressions that have come to the forefront in relatively recent scholarship. Thus, in a recent work Nile Green, *Bombay Islam: The Religious Economy of the West Indian Ocean, 1840-1915*, 156 (New York: Cambridge University Press, 2011)observes that while 'Ismāʿīlism is regarded as a stable religious formation passed down through an ancient pedigree of familial imams ... the prominence and characteristics of the Āga Khāns' "family firm" were very much a product of the religious economy of nineteenth century Bombay'. Thus, Aga Khan I (1800–81) and his sons, in this view, emerge as the 'intellectual and logistical promoters' of neo-Ismailism in an urban religious space marked by stiff competition (Ibid., 162). More generally see, ibid., chapter 5, entitled, 'The Making of Neo-Ismāʿīlism'.

4   Amrita Shodhan, *A Question of Community: Religious Groups and Colonial Law*, 3, 82–116 (Calcutta: Samya, 2001) shows that the legal disputes were cast in languages of 'public issues'. Having raised the banner of rebellion against the Qajar Shah of Iran, Aga Khan I arrived in Bombay in the 1840s. It is only in the subsequent period that the language of public good became a crucial index in the polemics between the pro- and anti-Aga Khan factions, even as the Aga Khan sought to engraft his version of Shia Ismailism on the Khojas of India. Shodhan illustrates, furthermore, how this tortuous legal exercise also came to replace the idioms of caste with that of sectarian identity. For an overview of the developments in the nineteenth century Bombay, also see J. Masselos, 'The Khojas of Bombay: The Defining of Formal Membership Criteria During the Nineteenth Century' in *Caste and Social Stratification among the Muslims*, edited by Imtiaz Ahmad, 1–19, especially 8–15 (New Delhi: Manohar, 1973).

5   Sudipta Kaviraj, 'On the Structure of Nationalist Discourse', in id., *The Imaginary Institution of India*, 85–126, especially 122 ff (New Delhi/ Ranikhet: Permanent Black, 2012 [2010]).

6   See Reinhart Koselleck, *Futures Past: On the Semantics of Historical Time*, translated and introduced by Keith Tribe (New York: Columbia University Press, 2004).

7   See Javed Majeed, *Autobiography, Travel and Postnational Identity: Gandhi, Nehru and Iqbal*, 4 (Basingstoke and New York: Palgrave Macmillan, 2007).

8   The idea of the transnational, by comparison, had had a longer history if also becoming

relatively indeterminate in the course of time, thanks to its appropriations in different politico-cultural contexts. The early twentieth century use of the expression 'transnational' in America by the likes of Randolph Bourne (1886–1918) thus defined itself in terms of a heterogeneity of cultures in opposition to the contemporaneous hegemonic European model of predominantly monocultural nation, thus exhorting to not only go beyond the national characters but undermining them as well, and anticipating later discourses of the multicultural model. However, later inflections, especially in Cold War academic scenario, arguably did little to challenge the idea of nation and its constraints, and still later usages of the ideas of the 'transnational' and 'transnationalism' as an ideological paradigm had significant ramifications in the fields of sociology, anthropology, and cultural studies with focus among other things on issues of migration. Thus the cluster of transnational/ transnationalism arguably came to be associated especially with understanding the making of the contemporary multicultural world rather than exploring the past, or historical experiences. For a concise and scholarly treatment of the genealogy of the idea and the diverse implications for different academic disciplines, see the lexical entry, Pierre-Yves Saunier, 'Transnational' in *The Palgrave Dictionary of Transnational History*, edited by Akira Iriye and Pierre-Yves Saunier, 1047–55 (Basingstoke and New York: Palgrave Macmillan, 2009).

9   Nivedita Menon, 'Thinking through the Postnation', *Economic and Political Weekly*, XLIV, 10 (2009) (Special issue 'The Postnational Condition'): 70–77, at 70.

10 The idea of this postnational/ denationalized dyad, conditioning discourses of citizenship has been underlined in recent times by Saskia Sassen, *Territory, Authority, Rights: From Medieval to Global Assemblages* (Princeton: Princeton University Press, 2006). We shall have the opportunity to revisit this dyad with particular reference to the idea of community membership that informs the Ismaili Imamate's project under Aga Khans III and IV in particular.

11 For a critique along this vein see, for instance, Justin Jones, *Sh'ia Islam in Colonial India: Religion, Community and Sectarianism*, especially chapter 4 titled, 'Aligarh, *Jihad* and Pan-Islam: The Politicization of the Indian *Sh'ia*' (Cambridge and New York: Cambridge University Press, 2012).

12 Faisal Devji, 'The Language of Muslim Universality', *Diogenes*, 57, 2 (2010): 36–49.

13 I am invoking the expression 'plurality' to conjure the idea of diversity, while 'pluralism' has a more cogent ideological structure. See, e.g. T. N. Madan, 'Introduction- India's Religions: Plurality and Pluralism' in *India's Religions: Perspectives from Sociology and History*, edited by Idem, 1–35, especially 26 ff (New Delhi: Oxford University Press, 2015 [2004]).

14 This point comes to the forefront in particular in Faisal Devji, 'Preface' to Marc van Grondelle, *The Ismailis in the Colonial Era: Modernity, Empire and Islam*, ix–xvi (New York: Columbia University Press, 2009).

15 This, taking a cue from Christopher A. Bayly, *Recovering Liberties: Indian Thought in the Age of Liberalism and Empire* (Cambridge and New Delhi: Cambridge University Press, 2012), I see as part of a much wider political and intellectual process that shaped mental worlds of generations of Indian intellectuals in colonial India. Ever since the Imamate of Aga Khan III this domestication hinged on a critical balance between the oppositional forces of universals and specifics. See chapter 3 of the present book for further discussions.

16 Sugata Bose, 'Different Universalisms, Colorful Cosmopolitanisms: The Global Imagination

of the Colonized', in *Cosmopolitan Thought Zones: South Asia and the Global Circulation of Ideas*, edited by Sugata Bose and Kris Manjapra, 97–111, at 97 (Basingstoke and New York: Palgrave Macmillan, 2010).

17   Sheldon Pollock, Homi K. Bhabha, Carol A. Breckenridge, and Dipesh Chakrabarty, 'Introduction: Cosmopolitanisms', *Public Culture*, 12, 3 (2000): 577–89, at 583: 'No true universalism can be constructed without recognizing that there is a diversity of universals...' While sympathizing in the main with the histories of universalisms and cosmopolitanisms in the non-West, I will, however, stop short of claiming that such universals are often not 'universals at all, but rather interpretations devised for particular historical and conceptual situations... more in the nature of arguments for the universal' (Ibid., 583). One understands that this scepticism stems from a disenchantment with 'the capitalized "virtues" of Rationality, Universality, and Progress...' that makes cosmopolitanism of 'our times' different from triumphalist languages of 'cosmopolitical coexistence' (Ibid., 581, 582). However, my agenda is precisely to understand the discursive nature of such argumentations as well as their praxis vis-à-vis perceived notions of universality.

18   Bose, 'Different Universalisms, Colorful Cosmopolitanisms', 98. Cf. 'Vernacular cosmopolitanism' of Homi K. Bhabha, *The Location of Culture* (New York: Routledge, 2004 [1994]), and 'rooted cosmopolitanism' of K. Anthony Appiah, *Cosmopolitanism: Ethics in a World of Strangers* (New York: W.W. Norton, 2006).

19   Bose, 'Different Universalisms, Colorful Cosmopolitanisms', 98.

20   Most of these questions have hitherto remained by and large the preserve of anthropologists, with their focus in particular on the modern ramifications. For a sophisticated ethnographic treatment of Ismaili globality in largely contemporary times in northern Pakistan bordering on Central Asia, see Jonah Steinberg, *Isma'ili Modern: Globalization and Identity in a Muslim Community* (Chapel Hill: University of North Carolina Press, 2011). In his conceptualization of a global community through conduits that promote imagined identities transcending different forms of disparateness, Steinberg resonates ideas voiced in the classic, Benedict Anderson, *Imagined Communities: Reflections on the Origin and Spread of Nationalism* (London and New York: Verso, 1983). Contesting overused discourses of 'globalizing modernity', and with an exclusive geographical focus on Chitral in northern Pakistan, Magnus Marsden, 'Muslim Cosmopolitans? Transnational Life in Northern Pakistan', *The Journal of Asian Studies*, 67, 1 (2008): 213–47 also underlines the relevance of 'premodern forms of Muslim cosmopolitanism'.

21   John M. Willis, 'Azad's Mecca: On the Limits of Indian Ocean Cosmopolitanism', *Comparative Studies of South Asia, Africa and the Middle East*, 34, 3 (2014): 574–81, at 576. Cf. the concern in recent scholarship, as one commentator points out, to go beyond philosophical abstractions and, instead, to see 'universals... grounded in particularities of the history in which they are imbricated' and to interpret them in the light of 'vested interests and consumerist needs of specific constituencies.' See Rustom Bharucha, *Another Asia: Rabindranath Tagore and Okakura Tenshin*, 115 (New Delhi: Oxford University Press, 2014 [2006]).

22   More generally, the extolling of the cultural superiority of the Persian-speaking world (Ajam) vis-à-vis the military and political superiority of the Arabs has been seen as part of a much larger historical phenomenon that defined the early history of Islam. See Muzaffar Alam, *The Languages of Political Islam in India, c. 1200-1800*, 7 (New Delhi/ Ranikhet: Permanent

Black, 2014 [2004]). The Aga's conceptualization of Islam, we shall see, was characterized by an effort to cut across lines of ethnicity, nationality, and sectarian variations, not by denying them outright, but valorizing instead their plurality.

23 Steinberg, *Isma'ili Modern*, 212 (n. 9). For a concise overview of the Parsi case see, e.g., John R. Hinnells, 'Changing Perceptions of Authority among Parsis in British India' in *Parsis in India and the Diaspora*, edited by John R. Hinnells and Alan Williams, 100–18 (London and New York: Routledge, 2008). Kenneth Jones, *Socio-Religious Reform Movements in British India*, 146 (Cambridge and New Delhi: Cambridge University Press/ Orient Longman, 1989) points to the institution of *bandobasts* (rules of conduct) instituted by the Parsi *panchyat* (community organization originally constituted by five members) in 1818 for promoting cohesion in the community.

24 Talal Asad, *Formations of the Secular: Christianity, Islam, Modernity*, 1–2 (Stanford: Stanford University Press, 2003). Cf. Charles Taylor, *A Secular Age* (Cambridge, MA: Harvard University Press, 2007). Scholars such as Taylor have tended to posit a thesis in which the 'secular' becomes meaningful not necessarily at the expense of 'religion' but rather in terms of breaks with the past whereby religion reinvents and articulates itself in new forms.

25 In his recent work Jonah Steinberg, *Isma'ili Modern*, 46 ff. has foregrounded the relevance of the Ismaili diasporic experience in the western Indian Ocean world in the evolution of the community's institutional formations. Cf., for instance, my 'Universalising Aspirations: Community and Social Service in the Isma'ili Imagination in Twentieth Century South Asia and East Africa', *Journal of the Royal Asiatic Society*, Series 3, 24, 3 (2014): 435–53, especially at 439, 443–44.

26 Scholars have noted (and as we still discuss later in the book, especially in chapter 5) the changing contours of the Ismaili community in parts of Africa. Cf. 'the utmost satisfaction' Aga Khan III expressed at his becoming instrumental, in contrast to his father and grandfather, in 'the conversion to Islam of some 30,000 to 40,000 caste Hindus' who, thanks to their conversion, he thought would have better future in Pakistan. Aga Khan III, *The Memoirs of the Aga Khan*, 4, 5. Also see Chapter 4 below for discussions of his views on conversion in relation to uplift of 'depressed classes' in India.

27 Thomas A Metcalf, *Imperial Connections: India in the Indian Ocean Arena, 1860-1920*, 1, 3 (New Delhi/ Ranikhet: Permanent Black, 2007).

28 A still influential theory of nationalism in the colonies posits a 'material domain' (in which the colonized was little more than silent spectator) vis-à-vis the 'spiritual domain' (in which the colonized could meaningfully imagine their communities). See Partha Chatterjee, *The Nation and its Fragments: Colonial and Postcolonial Histories*, 6–11 (Princeton, New Jersey: Princeton University Press, 1993). For critique of this model with reference to other South Asian thinkers, see this chapter, especially n. 40. One might be further tempted to add that this endeavour to go beyond western categories, e.g. the frameworks of nationalism and/ or territoriality, had significant variants in other parts of Asia, especially East Asia where older spiritual and religious ideals, incorporated in new ideas of civilization, emerged as fount of moral authority. For further discussions along this line with particular reference to East Asia, see for instance, Prasenjit Duara, 'The Discourse of Civilization and Pan-Asianism', *Journal of World History*, 12, 1 (2001): 99–130.

29 Talal Asad, *Genealogies of Religion: Discipline and Reasons of Power in Christianity and Islam*, 13 (Baltimore and London: The Johns Hopkins University Press, 1993). The production of

such subjectivity can entice one to see it as analogous to the complex process of interpellation, to invoke loosely the Althusserian terminology. Yet, certain major qualifications are in order for the present purpose. While referring to the Althusserian commitment to locate the individual in a larger discursive web critiquing the Enlightenment claims of individual autonomy one has to be, nevertheless, careful not to invoke notions of repression central to Althusser's model of ideological state apparatuses (ISAs). It is equally important to be cautious not to dismiss the celebration of human intellect and interpretive possibilities, which are argued to be central to the Ismaili Imamate's project, by stretching the Althusserian idea of erosion of individual autonomy too far. Cf. Louis Althusser, *Essays on Ideology* (London: Verso, 1984, English edition).

30 Asad, *Genealogies of Religion*, especially 11–13. Asad here acknowledges some debt to Stephen Greenblatt's classic work on self-fashioning in the sixteenth century. Asad draws the readers' attention to especially chapter 6 of Greenblatt's *Renaissance Self-Fashioning: From More to Shakespeare* (Chicago: University of Chicago Press, 1980), a chapter in which Greenblatt elaborated on his idea of improvization as typical of the Western world, an ability that enabled the Europeans, since the classical and medieval times but more vigorously from the Renaissance onwards, to 'insinuate themselves into preexisting political, religious, even psychic structures of the natives', and turn them to their advantage. See Greenblatt's *Renaissance Self-Fashioning*, 227.

31 The idea of inculturation refers to the process(es) whereby Christian societies adapt their liturgical formations to diverse non-Christian socio-cultural contexts across the globe. I am invoking the concept here divesting it of its Christian particularities. The crux here is in understanding the diverse pathways of cultural adaptations even as one is also reminded of the enduring importance of a certain religious core nevertheless. For an overview of the Christian framework, see Jaco S. Dreyer, 'Theological Normativity: Ideology or Utopia?: Reflections on the Possible Contribution of Empirical Research' in *Normativity and Empirical Research in Theology*, edited by Johannes A. van der Ven and Michael Sherer-Rath, 3–16, 5 ff (Leiden: Brill, 2004).

32 But even predating this constitutionalism, the commands issued by Aga Khan III in 1899 in the course of his visit to Zanzibar had brought to sharp relief the shifting nature of community boundaries: thus in contrast to the Sunnis and the Ithna Ashari Shia, the Aga Khani Khojas were subjected to stringent endogamous marriage rules, which in fact meant a re-instatement of traditional caste endogamy among the Aga Khani Khojas. This prohibition of interracial marriages, naturally, had bearings on demographic compositions and matters relating to property inheritance. See the recent intervention by Iqbal Akhtar, 'Negotiating the Racial Boundaries of Khōjā Caste Membership in Late Nineteenth-Century Colonial Zanzibar (1878-1899)', *Journal of African Religions*, 2, 3 (2014): 297–316. Indeed this is also in contrast to later history of the Aga Khani Khojas; see chapter 5, and especially n. 4, for insights on the nineteenth century developments and n. 45 for discussions on twentieth century histories of an assimilative Ismailism. The late nineteenth century moment of exclusivism, then, has to be seen in the particular context of heightened anxieties spawned by secessionist movements of the time.

33 The present book is not a history of the Indian Ocean. Nevertheless, outlining briefly the key strands of scholarship in this field will be in order since we are here concerned with the history of a religious community that had its tryst with colonial modernity precisely in the

littorals of its western rim. Drawing upon the Braudelian framework, K. N. Chaudhuri, in *Trade and Civilisation in the Indian Ocean: An Economic History from the Rise of Islam to 1750* (Cambridge: Cambridge University Press, 1985) and *Asia Before Europe: Economy and Civilisation of the Indian Ocean from the Rise of Islam to 1750* (Cambridge: Cambridge University Press, 1990) sees the Indian Ocean as a space for human transactions, both temporal and spatial. In doing so he sees the Indian Ocean as a matrix within which to engage with comparative studies of civilisations. Kenneth McPherson, *The Indian Ocean: A History of the People and the Sea*, 3 (Delhi: Oxford University Press, 1993), points to the Indian Ocean as a world that had its very distinctive and heterogeneous forms of 'cultural diffusion and interaction'. More recently, the idea of the Indian Ocean as 'a space on the move' has come to the forefront, underscoring thereby long-term historical processes. See Brigitte Reinwald and Jan-Georg Deutsch (eds.), *Space on the Move: Transformations of the Indian Ocean Seascape in the Nineteenth and Twentieth Century* (Berlin: Klaus Schwarz, 2002). Sugata Bose, *A Hundred Horizons: The Indian Ocean in the Age of Global Empire*, 6 (Cambridge MA. and London: Harvard University Press, 2006), argues that rather than a rigid 'system' the Indian Ocean should be seen as a diffuse 'interregional arena', as a space of human interactions with immense 'depth of economic and cultural meaning'.

34 See Abigail Green and Vincent Viaene, 'Introduction: Rethinking Religion and Globalization' in *Religious Internationals in the Modern World: Globalization and Faith Communities Since 1750*, edited by Abigail Green and Vincent Viaene, 1–19, at 1, 2 (Basingstoke and New York: Palgrave Macmillan, 2012). The transregional-global history of the Ismailis under the Aga Khans that we endeavour to understand in the present study is also a history of internationalist aspirations, imaginations, and indeed, to borrow the words from a recent intervention, ideas and hopes about future that were thought to be realizable through the vehicles of '*non-state or supra-state actors*' (emphasis in original). See Ali Raza, Franziska Roy and Benjamin Zachariah, 'Preface' to *The Internationalist Moment: South Asia, Worlds, and World Views, 1917-39*, edited by Ali Raza, Franziska Roy and Benjamin Zachariah, at viii (New Delhi: Sage, 2015). Cf. 'The Introduction: The Internationalism of the Moment— South Asia and the Contours of the Interwar World' for a conceptual agenda of the project. See ibid., xi ff. While the amorphousness of categories and labels have also been aptly pointed out, (Ibid., xii), I should perhaps add that our present study is neither restricted to the interwar years, nor specifically to any organized political movement, although the interwar phase as well as wider socio-political forces had had their share of influence on the mental world of Aga Khan III, our key protagonist.

35 Gerard Delanty, 'The Cosmopolitan Imagination: Critical Cosmopolitanism and Social Theory', *The British Journal of Sociology*, 57, 1 (2006): 25–47, at 25.

36 Taking a cue from French scholarship on early modern Mediterranean and Indian Ocean worlds, Christopher A. Bayly and Leila Fawaz, 'Introduction: The Connected World of Empires' in *Modernity and Culture: From the Mediterranean to the Indian Ocean*, edited by L. Fawaz and C.A. Bayly, 1–27, at 7 (New York: Columbia University Press, 2002) thus contrast the conspicuous absence in the early modern period of Indian merchants, in spite of regular circulation of Indian commodities, in the port-cities of West Asia and North Africa with the spread of more direct Indian mercantile activities in the nineteenth century in the wake of British commercial expansion. Chhaya Goswami, *The Call of the Sea: Kachchhi Traders in Muscat and Zanzibar, c. 1800–1880* (Hyderabad and New Delhi: Orient Black Swan, 2011) traces the history of merchant networks, of especially the Kutchi

traders, connecting western parts of India with parts of East Africa and Oman in a key phase in colonial history.

37 Here I draw upon the scepticism expressed by Frederick Cooper, 'What is the Concept of Globalization Good for? An African Historian's Perspective', *African Affairs*, 100, 399 (2001): 189–213. Cooper questions the overdrawn homogenizations implicit in globalization theories that tend to conceal the unevenness of different processes and linkages between different territories.

38 Andrew Linklater, 'Cosmopolitan Citizenship', *Citizenship Studies*, 2, 1 (1998): 23–41, at 24. Cf. Sassen's postnational/denationalized dyad, elaborated on in the course of this book.

39 Sandip Hazareesingh, *The Colonial City and the Challenge of Modernity: Urban Hegemonies and Civic Consciousness in Bombay, 1900–1925*, 168 (Hyderabad: Orient Longman, 2007).

40 See Iqbal Singh Sevea, *The Political Philosophy of Muhammad Iqbal: Islam and Nationalism in Late Colonial India*, 131 (Cambridge and New Delhi: Cambridge University Press, 2013 [2012]). The thesis of the creation of an alternative Islamic polity thus also critiques the bases of Partha Chatterjee's two-fold theory of nationalism in the colonies that posit the 'material domain' vis-à-vis the 'spiritual'. See above, n. 28. Cf. Sevea, *The Political Philosophy of Muhammad Iqbal*, 133.

41 Sevea, *The Political Philosophy of Muhammad Iqbal*, 207 sees this as a key prop of several Muslim thinkers who tried to come to grips with alternative political structures for the India they envisaged.

42 Ibid., 205–06

43 This is the underwriting idea in Cemil Aydin, *The Politics of Anti-Westernism in Asia: Visions of World Order in Pan-Islamic and Pan-Asian Thought* (New York: Columbia University Press, 2007).

44 Idem, 'Globalizing the Intellectual History of the Idea of the "Muslim World"' in *Global Intellectual History*, edited by Samuel Moyn and Andrew Sartori, 159–86, especially 168–72 (New York: Columbia University Press, 2013).

45 John Willis, 'Debating the Caliphate: Islam and the Nation in the Work of Rashid Rida and Abul Kalam Azad', *The International History Review*, 32, 4 (2010): 711–32.

46 Steinberg, *Isma'ili Modern*, 19.

47 Interestingly, Steinberg, *Isma'ili Modern*, 57 suggests an enduring predominance of Indian-origin (and most often Kachchhi Gujarati) Khojas in Aga Khan IV's inner council of advisers.

48 The copious writings of Aga Khan III addressing both an Ismaili and non-Ismaili audience, in conjunction with key mechanisms of the Imamate, present a contrastive picture of formalization of charismatic authority. We have here an active mediation on the part of the Aga and his Imamate, rather than a passive scriptural tradition developed exclusively by hagiographers, as other nineteenth and twentieth century South Asian examples sometimes seem to suggest, for instance the case of the Bengali mystic saint Ramakrishna Paramahamsa (1836–86), or competing strands of the Maijbhandari Sufi tradition illustrate. See, e.g., Hans Harder, *Sufism and Saint Veneration in Contemporary Bangladesh: The Maijbhandaris of Chittagong*, 27 (London and New York: Routledge, 2011).

49 See the Foreword to His Highness the Aga Khan, *India in Transition: A Study in Political Evolution*, vii–x (London: Philip Lee Warner, 1918).

50 Aga Khan III, *The Memoirs*, 3.

51 Ibid., 1.

52 J. L. Nehru, 'His Highness the Aga Khan', *Selected Works of Jawaharlal Nehru, Vol. Six*, 470–74, see 473–74 (New Delhi: Orient Longman, 1974). The tract was originally written when Nehru was interned in the Almora District Jail and was published in *Modern Review*, November 1935, 505–07.

53 For life histories as bourgeois cultural project see J. Comaroff and J. Comaroff, *Ethnography and the Historical Imagination*, 26 (Boulder: Westview Press, 1992); cf. Ivor Goodson, 'The Story So Far', in *Life History and Narrative*, edited by J. A. Hatch and R. Wiesniewski 89–98 (Washington DC: Falmer Press, 1995). My own position is informed by a line of scholarship that situates life histories at the intersection of different forces in society, along lines of 'gender, modernity, colonialism and nationalism, religion, social change, family and kinship, and interrelationship between self and society'. See David Arnold and Stuart Blackburn, 'Introduction: Life Histories in India' in *Telling Lives in India: Biography, Autobiography, and Life History*, edited by idem, 1–28, at 6 (Bloomington and Indianapolis: Indiana University Press, 2004).

54 Aga Khan III, *The Memoirs*, 15–19, at 17. The strong association with the Jesuits is coupled with an idea of a benign Empire that the Aga Khan thought had not, till that point of time, been eclipsed by the intolerant imperialism of subsequent times. See, e.g., ibid., 24.

55 Ibid., Chapter 1 'Childhood and Youth'; also, at especially 30.

56 Ibid., 11–13, 18–19, 20.

57 Ibid., 13.

58 Ibid., Chapters IX, X, XI and VIII, respectively.

59 For a succinct outline of especially Aga Khan III's views on the women question see Zayn R. Kassam, 'Gender Policies of Aga Khan III and Aga Khan IV', in *A Modern History of the Ismailis: Continuity and Change in a Muslim Community*, edited by Farhad Daftary, 247–64 (London and New York: I.B. Tauris, 2011 [2010]).

60 I have in mind here works such as the Bernard Lewis, *The Assassins: A Radical Sect in Islam* (New York: Basic Books, 2003 [1967]). First published in 1967, Lewis eventually discovered in 2002 that especially in respect to the practice of self-annihilation in the wake of or following a mission, the Ismaili Assassins of Alamut of eleventh-thirteenth centuries have their modern day avatars. While he points out that rather than the Christian West, the victims of the Assassins had historically been preponderantly the political elites within the Muslim world, there is also a disturbing effort to compare and contrast the 'medieval Assassins' with the present-day suicide bombers. See the Preface to the 2003 edition referred to above. See ibid., 134 ff. for his views on 'Ismaili terror' in its early history. In Chapter 2 of my book I limit my critical discussions of the debates in colonial Bombay, resulting from the dynamics of contesting Orientalist scholarship, and the larger implications they subsequently came to bear. I do so remaining sensitized to the larger historical context and with particular reference to the idioms of the community's identity formation.

1

The Khoja Ismailis and Legal Polemics
Religion and Customs in Nineteenth Century Bombay

I am a Shia— no a Suni; I was twice married in the Suni form, that
is why I know.[1]

Mohamed Dama, 1866

The preponderant thrust of the academic scholarship on the theme of production
of colonial knowledge and epistemological practices related to South Asia's diverse
socio-religious groups and communities tends to highlight the overarching concern
to see such communities in terms of clear-cut neat boundaries.[2] This had also, in turn,
conditioned the mental world of sections of the colonized to varying degrees. The
above quotation, for instance, marks an interesting oscillation between the rival claims
of Shia and Sunni consciousness, a question which becomes intelligible particularly
in the light of the shifting colonial epistemological concerns since especially the
latter part of the nineteenth century. In all likelihood, one would imagine, Mohamed
Dama's vacillation was greeted with a roar of laughter. Lest the readers find this
to be somewhat facetious, it should be clarified that it was, however, no staged
performance, but a moment that captured the key question at stake in a crucial law
case in the rooms of the Bombay High Court. The court had assembled to decide
the exact sectarian status of the Khojas and the position of the Aga Khan within
that community.[3] Recognized as one of the key founding figures of the Sunni Khoja
jamaat in Bombay, the witness Mohamed Dama was impelled to think – probably for
the first time in his life in front of an audience – about his identity along a specific
sectarian line as laid down and required by the colonial judicial apparatus. Justice
Arnould later adjudicated that the Khojas are Shia Muslims with Aga Khan I – who
had in the 1840s arrived in British India after fleeing from Qajar Persia – at the apex
as their spiritual guide, the Imam.[4]

Interestingly, however, at the levels of individual consciousness and religious
sensibilities, and above all in specific matters of private law (intestate inheritance, in
particular), antithetical trends defying wider processes of standardizations persisted
among the Bombay Khojas even after this landmark judgement. Examples such as the

one recounted above make one wonder that in spite of all the commendable empirical and sophisticated discursive analyses of the colonial epistemic framework, if there is also not a danger of glossing over the occasional antithetical voice coming from within sections of the communities for which the very categories were designed. Our example of the Khojas in colonial South Asia then is on the one hand a study in the antinomies of the colonial project of religio-judicial standardization, intelligible in part within the frame of liminality, while on the other, an effort to understand the development of contending sectarian worldviews in an intensely competitive and active religious cosmos. The latter, in part, can be attributed to the indigenous expectations and efforts to come to terms with the evolving regimented colonial classificatory episteme even as retaining some of the liminal traits.[5] Our understanding of liminal traits takes cue from interventions that urge the need to look beyond the monoliths of the 'Hindu' and the 'Muslim', but with no underlying naive idea of religio-cultural syncretism.[6] 'Liminality' thus emerges as a specific phenomenon where religious identity (in the modern sense) appears ambiguous, and therefore should be carefully distinguished from other interactions that belong rather to the sphere of 'composite culture'.[7] While a detailed survey of scholarship on the colonial episteme will be redundant, suffice it to say that it will be ahistorical to claim that the Bombay Khojas' experience was like no other. For one, scholars have ended up comparing the Khoja case with similar contemporaneous identitarian projects within the framework of colonial religio-judicial experiments, while others have pointed to the poverty of Euro-centric categories in understanding the South Asian specificities.[8] Also, not all such socio-religious groups responded to the new interventions in the same way, although the Imami Khoja position under the successive Aga Khans eventually made a virtue of articulate sectarian, and even politically-inflected ecumenical argument even as clinging on to an avowed denominationalism that only underlined their interstitial nature in popular religious sensibilities and religiosities. The forces that went into the process of identity formation of such groups as the Khojas, then, were often dissonant, and accounted for much of its complexity. The dissonance – in the particular case of the Khojas – was further compounded by the fact that it emanated not only from the contending ideas of the Hindu or the Muslim, but even from emerging competing sectarian and denominational (Shia versus Sunni, and then subsequently Ithna Ashari Shia vis-à-vis Imami Shia) consciousness drawing upon contending strands of Orientalist scholarship.

Our concern here, though, is not so much to debunk the historical relevance of the discourse of streamlining socio-religious categories that generations of scholars have brought out since the later decades of the twentieth century. Rather, ours is an attempt to underscore the irrelevance, or even danger, of any overemphasis on such projects that often tend to gloss over the internal nuances and antinomies of grand narratives. This, therefore, is also an effort to point to the pertinence to explore such antinomies, viz., that contrary to established knowledge, there still were contesting voices, as late as down to the early decades of the twentieth century that made the process of standardization of a Khoja identity much more complex than one would tend to think. Indeed, as the case of the Bombay Khojas shows, even the very process of creating clear-cut socio-religious categories was far from a linear march towards one defined goal. For one, the discordant forces from within the colonial establishment reflected the indecisiveness that characterized colonial policymaking about the Bombay Khojas from the 1870s for some four decades. This indecisiveness undermines any argument of a teleological progression. More specifically, it also shows that the support given to the Aga Khan by the colonial judicial system in 1866 by recognizing him as the religious head of the Khojas, declared as Shia, was by no means a final definitive moment in the community's history. Developments from the 1870s onwards suggest certain preoccupation among some sections of the colonial administration to circumscribe both the Aga Khan's and the *jamaat's* authority. These crosscurrents were also reflected in the general irresoluteness of colonial judicial policy with regard to the Khojas until at least 1909 when in the wake of another law case the equation changed in favour of the Aga Khan to an extent like never before.

In this effort to see the 1866 Aga Khan Case as an episode in a much longer narrative, one with its own internal nuances and crosscurrents, I try not to restrict this study to one specific moment in history that characterizes several other works in this field.[9] By exploring the critical crosscurrents of the post-1866 period and the numerous vacillations within the administrative circles, I try to recover the other possible narratives that are otherwise lost on the existing scholarship in the field. While this is an endeavour to critique triumphalist accounts that accord to the 1866 moment certain definitiveness, in no way do I seek to undermine the historical relevance of the Aga Khan Case. The importance of the 1866 case has to be seen, first of all, in the light of the rhetoric of burgeoning civic awareness, and of public good, as scholars have shown. Second, the other salutary implication lay in the successful reclamation of an Ismaili past by Aga Khan I's establishment, most notably by the main Defence Counsel E. I. Howard. What has often been glossed over is the fact that the crux of Howard's defence speech lay in his rehabilitating the Shia Ismaili credentials, in his relating the Khojas to the Ismailis of the past by laying claims to a different set of universals than the predominant Sunni order. However, this project too was no less Islamic, but one with a distinctive Ismaili Shia imprint with the Imam of the time at the apex upholding the values of modernity and using the Fatimid Caliphate as the model. These are issues that we take up in greater detail in chapter 2. In order for us to appreciate the implications of the social and judicial experiments, however, in the present chapter we start by charting out the broad contours of the colonial epistemic paradigm. We then go on to explore the lineaments of religious orientations that underlay the consciousness of the contending Khoja groups involved in this process. In the remaining parts of the chapter, we juxtapose the discrete tendencies with the wider process of standardization and finally examine the social profile of the different groups involved.

The broad contours of the colonial episteme

A comparison of the census operations in South Asia with that in Britain offers interesting insights. Kenneth Jones thus points out how rarely 'religion' figured in the census operations in Britain as compared to its central importance as a basic criterion to understand and categorize population in India.[10] This marked tendency towards standardization – albeit not without critiques and crosscurrents, as I argue below – was fed by colonial ethnography as well as the census operations, a subject much traversed by academics for several decades now. By the first all-India census operations of 1871–72 some idea of a Shia identity of the Ismailis – categorized as 'Shia Imami Ismailies' – had already emerged, thanks largely to the 1866 Aga Khan Case.[11] The 1881 Census recorded that the Shia in the Bombay Presidency were represented by the merchant classes of principally the 'Boráhs' and the 'Khojahs' who also happened to be 'strongest in the capital city [Bombay]' for commercial reasons.[12] A tortuous discursive exercise, occasionally drawing upon supposed indigenous semantic and/or cultural traditions,[13] was then subsequently adopted to reconstruct a history of the Khojas, to measure its distance from one religious tradition or another and the degree of its 'orthodoxy' (or the lack of it) in religious behaviour. Interestingly, regional variations played a significant role in the process. There had been, thus, Khojas in other parts of the subcontinent, such as the Punjab.[14] Yet, not all groups known by the same semantic denominator (i.e., 'Khoja') were part of the long-drawn process of formation of an Ismaili identity that started in Bombay with especially the developments of the 1860s. Thus, the process of reconfiguration of community identity along new conceptual planes necessitated and/or inspired by the colonial epistemic practices that I am expatiating on here concerned first and foremost the Bombay Khojas, and thereafter the Khojas on the eastern littorals of Africa.

A brief excursus to delineate the multiple socio-cultural meanings of the very term 'Khoja', however, will be in order, if only to gesture at efforts on the part of colonial scholarship to understand regional variations with reference to socio-cultural particularities, which were often hierarchical. H. A. Rose's *A Glossary of the Tribes and Castes of the Punjab and North-West Frontier Province*, employing as it did the multiple connotative possibilities of nomenclatures as the lens of analyses, might help us illustrate the point. Rose's understanding of the Khoja takes him first to the *Arabian Nights*, where the term is said to mean a man of wealth and respectability. As distinct from this comes its three-tier classification, at a regional level, in the context of the Punjab: a eunuch, a scavenger converted to Islam and a Muhammadan trader, contrasted in Rose's narrative with his counterpart in Bombay, who is said to be different from the Punjab Khoja, though sharing in common a 'dissent from orthodox Muhammadanism'. Most importantly, Rose is no less concerned with tracing the pre-conversion caste affiliations of the Khojas in the Punjab with the sub-texts of wealth distribution and social standing writ large. In north-west Punjab and the northern districts of the North West Frontier Province, for instance, the 'Parácha', was a wealthy Hindu trader converted to Islam, and was up in the hierarchy displacing the Khoja to a category of miscellaneous Muslim traders, chiefly hawkers and peddlers, or petty traders. By contrast, in the eastern districts and in the Derajat, the Khojas were noted for their commercial importance.[15] Rose's account was based on the Punjab Census Report (1883) by Sir Denzil Ibbetson, and was later supplemented by findings of the census operations of 1892 by E. D. MacLagan. Ibbetson's was a sophisticated approach to understand indigenous groups, one that preferred a dynamic role of 'status' shifting according to the general turns in socio-political developments, and no static worldview predicated on unchanging discourses of 'caste' and superior/inferior 'race'.[16] This question of flux in status and social standing, depending on the variegated patterns of regional specificities even within a single province, formed the intellectual backdrop to Rose's ethnographic accounts.

While it is not the focus of this chapter to dwell on the colonial ethnographic accounts based on empirical studies from the Punjab, this passing survey still provides a window into our underlying concern to highlight the key lineaments of the colonial ethnographic practices, their heterogeneous (if also dissonant) intellectual lineages, and above all the significance of regional and/or local specificities. Moreover, by contrast, the conceptualization of the rival Bombay Khoja groups along religious/sectarian lines was an outcome of experiments that, rather than invoking the question of 'dissent from orthodox Muhammadanism', phrased the polemics in terms of adherence to either the Shia or the Sunni sect of Islam. While the argument of 'dissent' became a standard charge that the self-styled reformist Sunni Khojas brought against the Aga Khan's group, the Aga Khan's arguing for a Shia identity, consequently, was based first and foremost on a strong defence of the Shia faith as no less Islamic than the Sunni. The idiom of 'dissent' in the context of Bombay, then, was a strategic tool at the hands of the Aga Khan's Sunni opponents in the law court. The polemics that developed and the modalities of articulation that were resorted to in the process were entrenched in the maritime mercantile culture that defined the very character of the port-city. Propelled exclusively by sections of the Bombay Khojas this process of community formation predicated upon emulation of colonial ethical and normative categories, operating above all within an essentially colonial judicial space. In other words, and taking a cue from some recent interventions on the 'public uses and appropriations' of classificatory mechanisms such as the census operations, we need to highlight both the importance of the process(es) of reception as well as widen the remits of our understanding of such administrative exercises; it is important in particular that we examine the eventual uses to which such administrative ventures were subjected in the larger identitarian projects, by precisely those who were the subjects of the studies.[17] Within a broader colonial episteme, the experience of the Bombay Khojas rooted in the historical practicalities of the port-city, as we see, did not find echoes among the Punjab Khojas. Indeed, Rose's Khojas and Parachas were not part of the grand narrative of Khoja Ismaili community formation that swept western parts of South Asia as well as East Africa – regions connected along an axis that only strengthened with the passage of time in the late colonial period. Nor did E. I. Howard, the Defence Counsel of Aga Khan I in the 1866 law case, had much to say about the Punjab Khojas, except for his passing comment, drawing upon an earlier edition of *Dabistan*, on the Ismaili population in 'Hindustan', nearly 30,000, settled in Multan, Lahore, Delhi and Gujrat (Punjab).[18] What it does illustrate, however, is the diverse range of connotations and alternative narrative possibilities – depending on social, cultural and regional variations – of given socio-religious categories and/or social groups. Except for the commonalities the Punjab Khojas shared with their counterparts in western India in terms of their the pursuit of commercial activities as occupation, it is doubtful if there was much in common between the hinterlands in the Punjab and the maritime cosmopolitanism that late colonial Bombay embodied.[19] This is also the point we shall have to leave H. A. Rose and his Punjab Khojas behind for an exploration in greater detail of the socio-religious world of the rival Khoja groups of colonial Bombay.

Unravelling religious attitudes

The polemics of contesting Islamic sectarian consciousness that the rival groups of the Bombay Khojas developed (and/or appropriated) was worked out primarily in the colonial judicial sphere, thanks to the social location and orientation of their authors in these competing camps. Revolving first and foremost around issues of property and inheritance, the polemics gradually activated the ever-widening socially relevant rhetoric of public good and welfare. The development of the competing sectarian positions and the discourse of public good went hand in hand taking shape within the colonial judicial apparatus at a time when legal approaches and methodologies themselves were being reconstituted, reshaped and experimented with all over in British India as well as elsewhere in the Empire. We shall shortly have the opportunity to return to the question of these experiments and their implications. But before we do, it might be useful to pause for a brief while and try to understand a general conceptual question: if adherence to a religion or denomination, in the first place, follows any specific functionalist pattern. While it will be unwieldy to rehearse here in great detail the complex debate around the issue of religious choice, we can still underline the fact that the idea of 'rationality' has undergone crucial inflections in social theory and religious studies especially in recent times with the effect that the idea is now increasingly seen both in epistemic as well as a normative (the Weberian *wert rationalität*) terms.[20] This appeal to the culturally ensconced normative and ethical bases of rationality vis-à-vis a narrowly interpreted instrumentality rooted in economistic terms is a reminder to the creative relationship between the rational and the ethical. Recent scholarly works on religious experience and/or preference thus further iterate the aporia of approaching questions of normativity as 'reason's other', a rather facile assumption of mutual exclusiveness that conditions academic – especially religious studies – and public discourse no less than it informs projects of theologians.[21] We shall have the opportunity to revisit the larger question of normativity elsewhere in the book, and see how an emphasis on the mutually constitutive nature of the normative and the rational underwrote Aga Khan III's – and indeed, in more recent times the Ismaili Imamate's – social and religious projects. Our particular concern here in this chapter, though, is to strive to understand the different facets of this rational/normative dyad, and their manifestations, in religio-legal developments that the Bombay Khojas witnessed in the latter half of the nineteenth century.

Indeed, the narrative we are striving to glean from the literature at our disposal – some of it hitherto hardly explored – is one of dynamics, at once with significant internal shifts in expressions of normativity, morality and an Enlightenment-inspired reason. Cumulatively, they gesture at far reaching repercussions for the posterity. Our study of resistance to religious authority among the Bombay Khojas points to the transformative aspect of the justificatory rhetoric of religious attitudes: from the crude vocabularies of pecuniary interests characterizing Khoja resistance in the 1820s,[22] into one proclaiming to champion the interests of civilization and public issues in the 1860s leading, furthermore, to reinvent the very ideational bases of the religious authority in the subsequent period. Indeed, the rhetoric of 'public good' and the polemics gravitating around it had come to define much of the urban socio-political cultures in colonial South Asia for the better part of the nineteenth and twentieth centuries.[23] However, the present study of the Bombay Khojas is a pointer to the potential range of possibilities that the idioms of 'public good' promises, especially when wedded to religious and/or sectarian identitarian issues predicating upon reformist vocabularies.

It can be argued that the choice of the reformists in the 1860s for Sunnism meant, above all, conceptualizing a religious *topos* sans the Aga Khan, even as their anti-Aga Khan rhetoric was couched in a set of languages emanating from the Enlightenment: of community interests, public good and liberty. At one level, this increasing thrust towards vocabularies under the umbrella of public issues becomes intelligible in part against the backdrop of an intensely competitive religious landscape in colonial Bombay where contesting Islamicities had to defend their ground not only against the Christian missionary activities but also against each other, clinging on to contending claims to Islamic as well as sectarian identities.[24] At another level, even if one tends to see the resistance to the Aga Khan in somewhat functionalist terms entrenched in instrumental rationality, one is nevertheless left clueless as to why the reformists' justificatory rhetoric of public good still had to hinge itself on adherence to a contesting religious belief, Sunnism, in the particular context of the 1860s. This is where the relevance of unpacking the conceptual component of rationality / normativity surfaces. It drives home the need to explore rationality beyond its immediate functionalist paradigm and emphasize instead the norms and ideals in deontological normative rationality. Moreover, we shall see how established ideas and beliefs, such as those of charismatic authority and messianism, were both invoked and reworked in the course of the nineteenth century, and especially in the subsequent decades under Aga Khan III, to redefine the bases of the Ismaili community with the Bombay Khojas in the vanguard. This too is indicative of the importance of beliefs deriving from warrants and norms that epistemic rationality gestures at. This in turn enjoins one to historicize development of such conceptual categories like 'reformism' against the backdrop of temporal and culturally specific contexts. The very articulation of the question of religious commitment, as well as resistance, to an order through the vocabularies of 'public issues' and 'civilization' by the mid-nineteenth century culminating in the 1866 law case, then, reflected very distinctive and contesting deontological understandings of norms, values and duties. The employment of such idioms by the self-styled reformists – later to become the Plaintiffs in the 1866 law case – not only rendered an altogether different dimension to the anti-Aga Khan movement in the 1860s, but actually came to foster an idea of competitive reformism in both the camps in the decades to come. This competitive nature, moreover, also had to do in part with the dynamic religious economy that Nile Green sees characteristic of maritime Bombay.

Antinomies of socio-religious standardizations: Customs and religious traditions

A study of the dynamics between customs and religious traditions through the lens of the legal experience of the different branches of the Bombay Khojas provides a classic case to understand the complexities of socio-religious perceptions and sensibilities, and their implications, in an age characterized by an overarching thrust towards socio-religious classifications and streamlining. Even though the bulk of the Khojas elsewhere in the subcontinent – say, those in the Punjab – remained largely unaffected by this, there were significant reverberations on the other side of the western Indian Ocean, thanks to the steady migration of Gujarati-speaking merchant communities to East Africa over centuries. In Zanzibar, for instance, in the subsequent decades the British colonial administration had to weigh and measure the possibilities of replicating much of the judicial lessons it had learnt in Bombay. It can be suggested, then, that the 1866 law case signified, in a qualified way, a crucial moment in a historical passage; one when religious commitment seen in terms of articulations of belief in general had started to evolve into a more regimented ideological understanding, drawing upon new textual and legal ventures characteristic of the times.[25] The emergence of the Khoja identity out of the crucible of the 1866 law case has been seen, furthermore, within the episteme of 'community', a nomenclature used to encapsulate the idea of the social and religious collective, as opposed to the political, that developed systematically in the nineteenth century colonial judicial context. The Khoja and Memon Case of 1847 – a case in which customs were somewhat upheld by the colonial judiciary, as elaborated below – and the Aga Khan Case of 1866 are thus seen marking a shift from a conceptualization of the Khojas as a socio-religious polity governed by its own customary laws (hence in principle beyond the state's concerns) to a clear-cut 'sect', a community subject to neatly demarcated legal tradition (religiously underpinned and upheld by the state).[26]

A close study of the Khoja case, to bring back one of our central arguments into the ongoing analysis, shows a chink in the armour of any triumphalist grand narrative of standardized socio-religious classification propelled by the colonial establishment. For one, the colonial project itself was not without its crosscurrents, even after the landmark 1866 law case. Besides, for communities such as the Khojas, the question of interstitial practices with which many of them had been accustomed for generations, regardless of their pro- or anti-Aga Khan position that articulated themselves only since the 1820s, was not simply a matter reduced to the private domain of religious practices either. They entailed, furthermore, a degree of liminality till at least 1937 in key areas of legal episteme and practice when the Shariat Act finally redefined the locus of customs. These crosscurrents and complexities remained in force in spite of their contesting claims of sectarian identity that had come to the forefront in 1866. For the colonial establishment at the apex it meant, in addition to carving out an Islamic identity of the Khojas and redefining customs and institutions – religious or otherwise – in terms of legality, also establishing set patterns and hierarchy of legal traditions.

The process of hierarchic schematization was in turn connected to contemporaneous intellectual and socio-political endeavours, entrenched in their own administrative pragmatism. A varied range of forces – customs, practices and religious normativities, and their interplay orchestrated by the colonial dispensation in their courts of law since the 1840s in particular – had been crucial in defining religious identities for the Khojas in the Bombay Presidency. The increasing number of law cases over property rights, with bearing on the understanding of the socio-religious location of the Khojas from about the mid-nineteenth century onwards mirrors the complex dynamics of these forces. The Khoja and Memon Case of 1847 adjudicated by Sir Erskine Perry captured one of the earliest moments of this tension, one in which customs were accorded some degree of supersession, under certain circumstances, over religious scriptural traditions. It was pointed out:

> If a custom, as to succession, is found to prevail amongst a sect of Mahomedans, and be valid in other respects, the Court will give effect to it, although it differs from the rule of succession laid down in the Koran.[27]

This preference for customs came to be reassessed substantially in the subsequent decades gradually leading to its replacement by certain 'Islamic law'.[28] By the time the Aga Khan Case of 1866 had ended, let us recall, the Khojas had been labelled as Shia (as opposed to the Sunni claims of the self-proclaimed reformists) with the Aga Khan as their spiritual head.[29] It can be argued that subsequent claims of rival identity even among the Shia Khojas – Ithna Ashariya (the Twelvers) as opposed to the Aga Khan's version of Imami Shiism (the Seveners) – was a logical extension of the classificatory schematization process that the 1866 case set in force. This culminated in articulations of a Sevener Shia (as opposed to the Twelver Ithna Ashariya) identity of the Khoja Ismailis by the turn of the century. This schism too started around a property case in which it was decided that the spiritual head of the Khoja Imami Ismailis is Aga Khan and all offerings made to the Aga Khan were labelled as his absolute property not subject to any trust. The law case had its origin in a lawsuit filed by one Haji Bibi, widowed daughter of Jungi Shah (an uncle of Sultan Muhammad Shah Aga Khan III). Haji Bibi claimed a share in the estate left by the Aga Khan I on the ground that offerings made to the Aga Khan were not for his sole consumption, but for the whole of the Aga Khan's family. This began as a familial fall-out over property but before long assumed the shape of a much more nuanced internal polemics within the Shia group over the extent of the Aga Khan's rights to offerings and over the very sectarian nature of the Khoja community. The judgement had two significant and definitive aspects: in the first place, it was decided that offerings made to the Aga Khan were only for *his* personal use, thereby sealing off much of the debate about his exact position and giving him a veritable free-hand over property matters; second, Justice Russell adjudicated that the Khojas were, and had always been, Shia Imami Ismailis.[30]

The four decades or so that separated the Aga Khan Case of 1866 and the Haji Bibi Case of 1909, however, had been far from being smooth. One sees in this phase no indubitable sign of any linear development within the colonial episteme to install the Aga Khan in a manner that it ended up doing by the turn of the century. The ultimate importance of the 1866 Aga Khan Case emanates partly from the invocation of a new rhetoric of public good, which set a new vocabulary of socio-religious debates and legitimation shared alike by the contesting groups. The implications of this development informed a discourse of accountability, a deontological predicament, surfacing continually from the 1870s onwards in public debates and in the long run occasioning active response from the Aga Khan's establishment. The importance of the 1866 case lies also in the fact that it epitomizes that decisive moment when the Khojas came to be defined not only in terms of birth or intermarriage, but also by the need to adhere to a specific creed or a carefully configured sectarian belief. As one historian has pointed out, this marked a passage from 'the informal and implicit basis of membership that had hitherto existed... [to] formal and rigid criteria which had the effect of excluding some members and appreciably altering the actual structure of internal power'.[31]

However, as noted, the decades that followed witnessed a complex process of drawing and redrawing the boundaries of this community along religious sectarian lines. It was a process, to reiterate one of our core arguments, one in which the antithetical and/or liminal socio-religious customs and traits still continued to co-exist with discourses of religio-legal standardization based on scriptural and textual methods. And it continued to do so until the early decades of the twentieth century. There is, therefore, a need that we look beyond the confines of discourses of religio-legal regimentation at the stratospheric level. This will also help us appreciate, not fully perhaps, but nonetheless quite substantially, the relevance of antithetical voices, and of plurality in socio-religious practices amid arguments of an overarching impact of streamlined religious laws.[32] The question of customs meant, moreover, that markers of identity were not only sought to be negotiated in terms of sectarian specificities, but also with reference to customary legal traits often closer to Hindu laws rather than Muslim laws. The complexities continued to develop over questions of claims to, and management of, properties. Thus barely a decade after the 1866 case, the Hirbae versus Gorbae Case of 1875 brought to the forefront the importance of Hindu laws as the ultimate resort: 'in the absence of satisfactory proof of a custom, differing from the Hindu law, the Courts of this [Bombay] Presidency apply to the Khojás the Hindu law of inheritance and succession'.[33] Furthermore:

> ... the great majority of the community consider that, according to the *customs* of their caste, the mother ought to have management of the property in preference to a childless widow, and that that custom has (so far as there is any evidence before the Court) been invariably adopted by the *Jamáts* of *Bombay* and *Zanzibar, and also in all cases of private arbitration.*[34]

(Emphasis mine)

The question whether the Bombay Khojas should be placed under the Hindu Wills Act (XXI of 1870) in the end became a critical predicament for the colonial establishment for a major part of the late nineteenth century. Sir Richard Temple's government formed a judicial commission to determine views of the majority of the Khoja community on the matter, living both within and outside Bombay city. The commission originally had four members and its president was Justice Maxwell Melvill. The four members represented the contending groups within the Khoja community, viz., Aga Ali Shah, Ahmedbhoy Hubeebbhoy, Jairazbhai Peerbhoy and Rahimtula Sayani. Later two more members, viz., N. Spencer and Dhurumsey Poonjabhoy, were admitted at the suggestion of the Aga Khan. Four of these members represented the Shia division of the Khojas, while one (Ahmedbhoy Hubeebbhoy) came from the Sunni branch.[35] The Aga Khan's camp objected to the very formation of such a commission and in doing so reflected the Aga Khan's general lukewarm attitude towards the idea of opening up deliberations on questions of inheritance, especially with regard to intestate succession, to other stakeholders. He saw in this an effort on the part of the government to circumscribe his and his *jamaat's* control over a key area of inheritance. Only after quite persuasion by the Bombay government did the Aga Khan agree to have his son Aga Ali Shah on the commission.[36] The Aga Khan's stand on the issue of intestate succession was to place himself immediately after the first cousin. This stemmed from his underlying concern to ensure the authority of the Khoja *jamaat* in matters of adjudication as opposed to giving a freehand to the English judicial system.

To read the history of customary traditions under colonial rule as linear history of marginalization would be, then, to do immense disservice to understand a complex historical process. The reconstruction of, and preference for, textual sources and a scriptural tradition over customary sources became the predominant force gradually feeding into certain Muslim (and by the extension of the logic, contending Hindu) identitarian politics from the late nineteenth century onwards. The process, though, was incomplete, in the sense that not all antithetical forces and customary traits were ever eroded in totality. The codification and application of such customs were in effect bowdlerized to facilitate the 'political and economic imperatives of colonial rule' creating in the process a certain 'Anglo-Muhammadan judiciary' which, with its preference for textual sources to customary traditions and aimed at reconstructing a scriptural tradition, gradually became the crucible of a new form of Muslim identitarian politics.[37] The result was a gradual shift in conceptualization of legal pluralism that characterized the colonial legal order, viz., a shift from a 'relatively fluid legal pluralism' to a more 'hierarchical model of legal pluralism' erected by the colonial state,[38] but drawing substantially from the interventions of the indigenous litigants. Translated into the present case, it meant a marginalization, and selective absorption, of Khoja customary traditions to feed into broader colonial imperatives, and not their total annihilation. This tension came to relief in the wake of the colonial efforts to set succession rules specific to the Khojas first within South Asia and then elsewhere where there had been significant Khoja expatriates. Thus the 'Khoja Succession Act, 1884' was argued to be applicable for *the whole of India* and, furthermore, the Indian law applicable 'to all moveables left by a deceased Khojá in British India' could, in the course of time, be applied in the consular jurisdictions in the Persian Gulf, Zanzibar and places outside British India where a considerable number of Khojas lived.[39]

However, the critique of the *jamaat*-centric Khoja legal apparatus by sections of the colonial administration came not on the bases of blatant claims of textual or scriptural sanctity vis-à-vis customs. It was argued above all on moral grounds that certain sections of the colonial administrative circles thought were at risk due to the overwhelming presence of *jamaats* virtually under the Aga Khan's almost exclusive control. C. P. Ilbert's definition of the law of testamentary and intestate succession of the Khojas is a case in point. Ilbert took a cue from Joseph Arnould's definition of the *jamaat* as 'an assembly in council of all the adult male members of the Khojá community of that place'. The difference with Arnould, though, was that, Ilbert meant to precisely subvert its moral claims. A range of factors were thus brought up by Ilbert to restrict the remits of the *jamaat's* and, by extension, the Aga Khan's authority; the exclusivist nature of *jamaat* composition; the relation it could possibly bear with any deceased Khoja and its ramifications; the lack of clarity of *jamaat* customs in matters of intestate property succession, which was argued would render the *jamaat* a veritable tool at the hands of the Imam, i.e., the Aga Khan, in matters of such succession.[40] In arguing the way he did, Ilbert was only echoing earlier concerns to constitute a well-represented commission, rather than leaving all questions of inheritance at the hands of the *jamaat* or a select few.[41] The idiom of public good that emerged in the wake of the 1866 law case thus had a crucial afterlife in that it came to be invoked, in the subsequent decades, by the colonial establishment to hedge around the authority of the Aga Khan that they had themselves publicly upheld in 1866. This language, furthermore, set the boundaries of a common ground where the different strands of the Khoja Ismailis with rival denominational claims engaged with each other and sought to validate their own respective positions. Thus, virtually turning the table on the government and underlining the implicit sanctity of the Khoja customs, the Aga Khan's group pointed out in the course of the deliberations regarding the Khoja Succession Bill that the *jamaat* found it 'neither natural nor proper' that 'the suggestions of *a few wealthy or influential Khojás* who hold views hostile to those of the *majority of the community*' were left to prevail (emphases mine).[42] At the same time, it shows that the moral argument about customs – even if at odds with processes of legal standardizations – could still be invoked in support of wider claims to justice. Articulated in the specific context of late nineteenth century South Asia through idioms of public good, this moral argument was to become an overarching ideational concern in the Khoja Ismaili, as well as the Imamate's, history in the subsequent times.

A question of commonalities: Social base, vocabularies and modalities

Understandably, for all the efforts at arriving at streamlined sectarian identities by both the colonial government as well as the rival Khoja groups, the inherent dynamics and distinctiveness that characterized the variegated socio-religious life and the judicial experience of these groups were hardly ever stifled overnight. The growing anxiety of the rival groups to identify with specific forms of religious denomination within the rubric of Islam becomes intelligible partly in terms of the characteristic feature of the times: first, the dynamic religious economy that Bombay represented, and second, the increasing socio-religious categorization that from especially the later part of the nineteenth century gradually gained new socio-cultural shade. Interestingly, though, claims to rival sectarian identities did not mean a hermetic compartmentalization of the different Khoja factions both in terms of their social profile as well in terms of the rhetoric they invoked. The picture, therefore, is far more complex, one in which the reformists (Plaintiffs) and the Aga Khan's establishment (Defendants) were both intimately connected to the colonial economy of knowledge production as well as capital flows that sustained them. Both these parties – the reformist Plaintiffs and the Aga Khan's Defence – were holding their polemics in Anglo-Indian law court seeking the colonial establishment's support in their quest for their community's selfhood with divaricating modes of self-fashioning garbed, once again, in a legal phraseology that emerged out of that colonial framework.

Moreover, the social bases of these competing factions (mostly merchant) were often not radically removed from each other. In other words, the juxtaposition of a compact elite merchant-reformist group vis-à-vis an uneducated pro-Aga Khan coterie provides a blinkered picture of the social profile of the public debate that culminated with the 1866 law case.[43] In fact, even in far-off East Africa, it has been shown, that the *mukhis* (treasurer) and *kamarias* (accountant), important officials in the Khoja *jamaats*, came from similar wealthy – if not from the exceptionally big and famous league of the so-called 'upper establishment' – merchant strata.[44] They were the counterparts of those who purportedly constituted the mainstay of reformist-elite echelon in Bombay. No less important is the question of switching positions. Thus, Dhurumsey Poonjabhoy – the fiery reformer (Sunni Khoja) of the 1850s and early 1860s – gradually ranged himself with his former opponents, the Aga Khan's faction.[45] By the 1880s, he had emerged as one of the representatives of the Shia Khoja *jamaat*.[46] This move had its anticipations in the 1860s itself. The *Bombay Times and Standard* of

14 May 1861 recorded that the Aga Khan came up with his overtures of friendship by investing Dhurumsey Poonjabhoy with a shawl of honour, agreeing to the foundation of a mosque that Poonjabhoy and company were contemplating to erect and 'formally withdrew any interdict that may have been issued in his name against the institution of Khoja schools'; at the same time, however, it was warned that should the Aga Khan oppose the purpose of education, all the trust of the reconciliation would break down that might well require, once again repeating the old demand, his deportation from Bombay.[47] However, for the reformists the reconciliation was 'a masterpiece of duplicity on the part of Aga Khan' as such conciliatory gestures were seen as mere prelude to his policy of aggrandisement by way of introducing Shiite ceremonies and practices in place of those of Sunni ones.[48] Interestingly, though, retrospective official accounts of the Sunni Khoja *jamaat* in Bombay continued to include Seth Dhurumsey Poonjabhoy as one of their key benefactors who, along with his three sons, made the Khoja Sunni *jamaat* what it was.[49] Such instances of switching positions are compounded by further examples of rival sectarian commitments even within the same family. The family of the Poonjas, once again, provides a case in point. Thus even though Dhurumsey Poonjabhoy went back to the Aga Khan's Imami Shia folds along with his three sons, one of his grandsons (Habibhai Dharamsey, born to Dhurumsey Poonja's third son Fazalbhai Dharamsey) had been member of the Sunni Khoja *jamaat* in the twentieth century.[50]

While bearing in mind the complex nature of the shared social base of the two camps, it is also important to remember the growing relevance of deontological issues of normativity, progress and improvement that went on to inform each of these variants of religiously inflected self-definition that the contending groups aspired to emulate. In other words, the understanding of competing religious/sectarian positions came to be predicated ever so forcefully upon discourses of social reforms and progress – an entanglement that has been a blind-spot for several scholars. In one such study – otherwise a useful intervention – the reformers' move towards modernization is thus reduced to a process involving '*paradoxically* a move towards orthodox Sunni Islam' (emphasis mine) vis-à-vis the position of the Aga Khan, who is argued to be, 'in his own way a reformer ... determined to bring the Khojas back into the path of orthodox Shiaism' of the Persian variety.[51] Thus, the Aga Khan's claims to *his* version of reformism are underscored, even as implicit in the construction is an assumption of modernization at odds with the Sunni world order, rendering in effect any association of Sunni Islam with 'modernization' 'paradoxical'.

In an age when we are striving to appreciate the implications of deprivatization of religion and religious sensibilities, and locate religion in public discourses about a gamut of issues characterizing civic life, it is important that we rise above constricted models of binarism such as this. Indeed, the next chapter seeks to reconstruct the contours of the Aga Khan's defence in the 1866 law case with particular reference to the issues of morality and community interests. In doing so we strive to understand not only the role of the colonial judicial context in the shaping of socio-religious identities, but also the nature of polemics that developed out of such endeavours connecting as they did the questions of redefined socio-religious identities to community norms, public good and morality. A particular aspect we take up in the next chapter is the epistemic implications of this dynamic process.

Conclusion

The history of identity formation of the Khojas, closely tied up with religio-legal experiments in colonial Bombay, was marked by a preference for religious laws over customary laws. However, this chapter argued that the notion of a resolute linear process in this programme of standardization of religious identities is quite overdrawn. In the nineteenth century a section of the Bombay Khojas, self-styled reformers identifying themselves as Sunni Muslims, challenged the authority of the Aga Khan (I), and his claims of a Shiite Khoja identity. In the 1866 Aga Khan Case that followed, the Khojas were declared by the Bombay High Court to be Shia with the Aga Khan as the apex authority, splitting the community into Shia and Sunni denominations. In the subsequent decades further schisms occurred in South Asia and East Africa within the Shia group of the Khojas, claiming contending identities of the Twelver (or Ithna Asahariya) Shia and Sevener (Imami) Shia, the latter following the Aga Khan. Such contestations mostly revolved around inheritance and property matters, culminating in the 1909 judgement in the wake of the Haji Bibi Case that declared the Khojas to be Imami Shia with the Aga Khan as the head of the community. Yet, for greater part of the late colonial period customary rules were often adhered to by different sections of the Khojas, defying in the process any ultimate form of standardization. At the same time, the position of the colonial establishment on the location of the Aga Khan in the socio-religious framework that they sought to shore up, i.e., the Imami Shia Khoja head along with the *jamaat*, remained anything but firm in spite of the 1866 judgement in favour of the Aga Khan. Only in 1909 did the colonial government finally take a more resolute stance. In other words, then, the history of the legal experience(s) of the different branches of the Bombay Khojas and their quest for sectarian identities for the better part of the late nineteenth century, is one of irresolute moments and possibilities. This history of vacillations reflects the larger predicament that the colonial government witnessed in its efforts at arbitration and restructuration of socio-religious categories in large parts its Empire.

The renewed interest in upholding the Aga Khan's position within his community by the turn of the century – and indeed the re-invigorated state support that the 1909 judgement lent – needs to be appraised against the backdrop of the politico-historical context of the period. The following chapters in this book connect the internal religio-legal polemics studied in the present chapter with the broader political and socio-religious forces sweeping South Asia and to some extent the Muslim world in general. A particular issue in that study would be on the nature of translocal/transregional networks, their socio-religious and internationalist aspirations, imaginations and imageries. But before we proceed in that direction, it will be pertinent to unpack the immediate epistemic legacy that the Aga Khan's Defence Counsel left behind. Indeed, except for treatments in the form of passing references, E. I. Howard's long speech in the 1866 law case has not really received the kind of scholarly attention it deserves. In the following chapter we strive to recover the moral argument that Howard developed in his defence of the Shia and the Ismaili. In the process to reconstruct an Ismaili history, Howard foregrounded what eventually proved to be a crucial methodological position. In the following chapter we shall endeavour to appreciate his intervention in the broader context of Orientalist scholarship while assessing, furthermore, the implications of the conceptual reorientation. This conceptual reorientation meant, in short, significant methodological innovations that had to wait for few more decades to enter the realm of consistent and organized academic practice, buttressed by an enduring process of institutionalization sponsored by the Imamate. A crucial ideational legacy of the Howardian moment, then, lies in its conceptual possibilities.

Endnotes

1   Evidence of Mohamed Dama (later to become one of the founders of the Sunni Khoja *jamaat*, or congregation) in the Aga Khan Case of 1866; reported in E. I. Howard, *The Shia School of Islam and its Branches, Especially that of the Imamee-Ismailies. Being a Speech delivered by Edward Irving Howard, Esq., Barrister-at-Law, in the Bombay High Court in 1866*, 67 (Bombay: Oriental Press, 1866).

2   See Neeladri Bhattacharya, 'Notes Towards a Conception of the Colonial Public' in *Civil Society, Public Sphere and Citizenship: Dialogues and Perceptions*, edited by Rajeev Bhargava and Helmut Reifeld, 130–56 (New Delhi: Sage, 2005). Bhattacharya provides a useful overview with a much refreshing programmatic statement to explore the relevance of Habermasian formulations in colonial Indian context, and not least, the implications the socio-legal experiments bore while transforming the colonized individuals into legal subjects (Ibid., 135).

3   E. I. Howard, Aga Khan I's main Defence Counsel, was not particularly comfortable with the categories 'caste' and 'tribe' but conceded nevertheless the use of the former in common parlance See Howard, *The Shia School of Islam and its Branches*, 5. The use of the expression of sect with reference to the Shia in general, and the Ismailis in particular, however, should also be pointed out. For respective references to each of them see for instance, ibid., 15, 59.

4   *Advocate General* v. *Muhammad Husen Huseni*, (1866), 12 Bombay High Court Reporter (Bom. H.C.R.) 323. See for the judgement, A. A. A. Fyzee, *Cases in the Muhammadan*

Law of India and Pakistan, 504–49 (Oxford: Clarendon Press, 1965). There are a number of accounts of the political history of Aga Khan I's relationship with the British. For the most recent scholarly treatment with reference to the socio-religious aspects as well as the pre-1866 tussles between the Aga Khan and the Bombay Khoja leaders, see Teena Purohit, *The Aga Khan Case: Religion and Identity in Colonial India*, chapter 1 (Cambridge, MA. and London: Harvard University Press, 2012).

5   One of the earliest classic interventions in this vein to capture the idea of reception of colonial tropes by the colonized comes from Bernard S. Cohn, 'The Census, Social Structure and Objectification in South Asia', in Bernard S. Cohn, *An Anthropologist among Historians and Other Essays*, 224–54 (New Delhi: Oxford University Press, 2006 [1987]). Thus, in what was a much deeper and complex series of developments, 'not only have colonial peoples begun to think of themselves in different terms, not only are they changing the content of their culture, but the way that they think about their culture has changed as well' (Ibid., 228).

6   An early sketch of this idea of liminality with reference to the Ismailis in South Asia is developed in Dominique-Sila Khan and Zawahir Moir, 'Coexistence and Communalism: The Shrine of Pirana in Gujarat', *South Asia: Journal of South Asian Studies*, XXII, Special Issue, (1999): 133–54. The argument is based on the analysis of the multiple entangled narratives on the life of Imam Shah and his tradition. In the upshot we get a highly complex picture of the Imam Shahis, one that cannot be readily accommodated within any other category like the Hindus, Muslims, or even any Sufi tradition.

7   Subsequent investigations by Dominique-Sila Khan have brought to light the 'threshold' nature of groups such as South Asia's Nizaris. Khan's idea of the 'threshold' or the 'liminal' is informed by a historical understanding of an array of forces that characterized Nizari Ismaili history in medieval South Asia, viz., certain universalistic claims, combined with dissimulation and also particular conversion strategies by Ismaili preacher-saints (*pirs*). Khan's narrative of the historical trajectory of the Ismailis in medieval South Asia, furthermore, emphasises the actors' agency. See Dominique-Sila Khan, *Crossing the Threshold: Understanding Religious Identities in South Asia*, 4–7 and 44–50 (London: I.B. Tauris, 2004).

8   Shodhan, *A Question of Community* and Purohit, *The Aga Khan Case*, thus, compare the Khoja case with formation of Vallabhacharya Vaishnava and Hindu Swami Narayana sectarian identities respectively. Harjot Oberoi, *The Construction of Religious Boundaries: Culture, Identity and Diversity in the Sikh Tradition* (New Delhi: Oxford University Press, 1994) illustrates with a study of the Sikh case how the impact of the colonial epistemic categories on the mental world of those who they sought to describe was a complex process, and one seriously facile too, because such Euro-centric norms scarcely did justice to the diverse South Asian practicalities.

9   For instance, the recent scholarship of Shodhan, *A Question of Community* and Purohit, *The Aga Khan Case* restrict themselves to studying the various aspects of the 1866 law case paying scant attention to subsequent developments.

10   Kenneth Jones, 'Religious Identity and the Indian Census' in *The Census in British India: New Perspectives*, edited by N. Gerald Barrier, 73–101 at 78 (Delhi: Manohar, 1981). Jones, much like Bernard Cohn, was one of the earliest scholars to show how the employment of religion as an important component in the construction of the imperial knowledge of the colonized Indian 'races' gave the census reports a much more active agency than has usually

been recognized. Recent works, such as Peter Gottschalk, *Religion, Science, and Empire: Classifying Hinduism and Islam in British India* (New York: Oxford University Press, 2013) see in this classificatory mechanism propelled by the criterion of religion a deep-rooted Christian impulse that developed a close relationship with the evolving 'scientific disciplines', and indeed scientism.

11 *Census of the Bombay Presidency: General Reports and Tables of the Population, Houses, & c., 1872, Part II*, 76–77 (Bombay: Government Central Press, 1875). One is told that the island of Bombay had Khoja inhabitants as early as 1806–07, although the census of the 'Bombay Mahomedans' for 1807–08, given in Volume 1 of *(The) Transactions of the Bombay Literary Society*, or appended to Sir J. Mackintosh's *Preliminary Discourse* does not count the Khojas as Muslims. Captain James Macmurdo, Resident at Anjar, however categorized the Khojas in 1818 as Muslims, a 'Mohammadan cultivator' to be precise; cited in Howard, *The Shia School of Islam and its Branches*, 74–75.

12 J. A. Baines, *The Imperial Census of 1881: Operations & Results in the Presidency of Bombay, Including Sind, Vol. I*, 48–49 (Bombay: Government Central Press, 1882).

13 This often involved selective yet systematic employment of putative indigenous speech ('entextualization' of the 'colonized speech') in colonial disciplinary discourse. For elaborations along this line, see e.g., Gloria Goodwin Raheja, 'Caste, Colonialism, and the Speech of the Colonized: Entextualization and Disciplinary Control in India', *American Ethnologist*, 23, 3 (1996): 494–513.

14 See J. N. Hollister, *The Sh'ia of India* (London: Luzac & Co. Ltd., 1953), 340 ff. for accounts of Fatimid presence in Multan and the adjoining areas in early medieval Punjab. As we shall see, one of the most crucial repercussions of Howard's 1866 intervention was his relating the Khojas of the subcontinent with the Fatimids of the past.

15 H. A. Rose, *A Glossary of the Tribes and Castes of the Punjab and North-West Frontier Province*, 536–38 (Chandigarh: The Language Department of the Punjab, 1990 [1883]).

16 Susan Bayly, 'Caste and "Race" in the Colonial Ethnography of India' in *The Concept of Race in South Asia*, edited by Peter Robb, 165– 218 and esp. 204–16 (New Delhi: Oxford University Press, 1995).

17 Kathrin Levitan, *A Cultural History of the British Census: Envisioning the Multitude in the Nineteenth Century*, 5 (Basingstoke and New York: Palgrave Macmillan, 2011).

18 Howard, *The Shia School of Islam and its Branches*, 59.

19 Howard notes their commercial activities in the northern parts of the subcontinent (See Ibid., 59, Cf. Rose, as noted above). However, the scale of commerce seems to have varied to a great extent. For account of trade of the Khojas of Gujarat and Sialkot, Punjab recorded in 'System practised by the Khojas of fostering trade by sales on credit', see Home Department, Public Branch, Proceeding 188B (May 1879), National Archives of India (NAI). For discussions on trading patterns of the peripatetic Punjab Khojas, see Neeladri Bhattacharya, 'Predicaments of Mobility: Peddlers and Itinerants in Nineteenth Century Northwestern India' in *Society and Circulation: Mobile People and Itinerant Cultures in South Asia*, edited by Claude Markovits, Jacques Pouchepadass, Sanjay Subrahmanyam, 163–214 and esp. 171 ff. (Ranikhet/ New Delhi: Permanent Black, 2003).

20 The narrow economistic/instrumentalist version persists with some variations, among others, in R. Stark and R. Finke, *Acts of Faith: Explaining the Human Side of Religion* (Berkeley: University of California Press, 2000). For overview of its critique in recent times

see especially Colin Jerolmack and Douglas Porpora, 'Religion, Rationality, and Experience: A Response to the New Rational Choice Theory of Religion', *Sociological Theory*, 22, 1 (2004): 140–60.

21 For a critique see, Thomas A. Lewis, 'On the role of normativity in religious studies' in *The Cambridge Companion to Religious Studies*, edited by Robert A. Orsi, 168–85 (Cambridge: Cambridge University Press, 2011).

22 While there might well be much more than sheer 'economic' angle to attitudes to religion and/or dissent, the paucity of sources clearly articulating the dissenting position of the 1820s coming directly from that period (unlike the literature that articulated the 'reformist' programme in the 1860s) leaves studies of the 1820s' dissent somewhat incomplete at the present. If anything, Aga Khan I's main Defence Counsel E. I. Howard, *The Shia School of Islam and its Branches*, 60, pointed out that it was not until 1851 that the Plaintiffs actually came to affirm their Sunni identity. See Christine Dobbin, *Urban Leadership in Western India: Politics and Communities in Bombay City, 1840-1885*, 113–21 (London: Oxford University Press, 1972) for a succinct narrative of resistance by sections of the Bombay Khojas to the Aga Khan since the 1820s; see also Masselos, 'The Khojas of Bombay', 8–15.

23 Douglas E. Haynes, *Rhetoric and Ritual in Colonial India: The Shaping of a Public Culture in Surat City, 1852–1928* (Berkeley: University of California Press, 1991) thus shows how the Surat city notables, rooted strongly in local traditions and culture and distinct from the Anglophile elite or the burgeoning bourgeoisie, first picked up idioms of 'public good' inviting furthermore the English-educated elite's response, who, too, saw themselves as the carriers of the 'common good' and 'progress' in their own ways. This signified a much wider trend and was not necessarily part of any religious reformist ventures *per se*.

24 Green, *Bombay Islam*, argues, if somewhat provocatively, for using the lens of 'religious economy' to analyse the plural and competitive nature of the religious terrain in colonial Bombay. Green's is an analytical frame entailing the idea of individual choices in 'religious consumption', drawn from a clientele that had Anglophile reformers with Western education at one end of the spectrum and the labourers of the dockyard at the other, with various intermediate categories filling up the gulf in the middle. A further key aspect of Green's work is his underscoring the connections colonial Bombay's religious landscape bore with the western Indian Ocean arena, to which we shall have the opportunity to turn in the subsequent chapters. Our present concern especially in this chapter, though, is the specific question of rhetoric used in this competitive dialogic process among the Bombay Khojas, which was no less crucial in carving out sectarian identities from erstwhile caste groups and polities.

25 Ashis Nandy, 'The Politics of Secularism and the Recovery of Religious Tolerance' in *Secularism and its Critics*, edited by Rajeev Bhargava, 321–44 (Delhi: Oxford University Press, 1998) provides some clue to understanding religion as faith and religion as ideology. The former, according to him, summarizes the view of religion as a plural and non-monolithic tradition, as a way of life, if one were to invoke a cliché. The latter refers to it as certain subnational, national or crossnational identifier used by populations in matters of political and or socio-economic interests. The latter, moreover, has the tendency to develop into patterns of pure religions, drawing upon textual authority (Ibid., 322). The question of the subnational, national or crossnational dimension does not directly relate to our present study of contending Khoja identities in the immediate context of the 1860s, although the

nature of ideational moorings with increasing emphases on textual and legal traditions – themselves evolving as well – has to be problematized.

26 Shodhan, *A Question of Community*, 18, 35 ff., 58–111. Crucial to Shodhan's argument is the influence of Ferdinand Tönnies's conceptualization of *Gemeinschaft*. Shodhan, however, diverges from Tönnies in not accepting its evolutionary aspect. She concludes thereby that individuals naturally belong to a community and that its 'public mobilization' becomes inevitable under certain political conditions. Ibid., 19–23. Ferdinand Tönnies's conceptualization of *Gemeinschaft* (community) and *Gesellschaft* (society) – albeit not unchallenged – has still remained a classic intervention in understanding evolution of communities. Thus the former can be taken to mean relations based on bonds of empathy and kinship and the sentiment of belonging to a group; the emphasis is thus on organically grown rules, i.e. mores, customs or 'folk ways'. As opposed to this, but to which *Gemeinschaft* evolves in course of time, is *Gesellschaft*, representing civic life, relations based on contracts and notions of self-interest, embodied in constitution and administered through law. See Ferdinand Tönnies, *Community and Association*, translated by Charles P. Loomis (London: Routledge and Kegan Paul, 1955).

27 *Hirbae* v. *Sonbae,* or the *Khojas and Memons' Case* (1847), 'Cases Illustrative of Oriental Life and the Application of English Law to India, Decided in H.M. Supreme Court at Bombay by Sir Erskine Perry, 110', reprinted in *The Indian Decisions, (Old Series), Vol. IV,* 707 ff. (Bombay and Madras: T.A. Venkaswamy Row and T.S. Krishnaswamy Row, 1912).

28 This preference for customs (and later religious laws) was, however, subject to repugnancy test. According to the principles of repugnancy test, religious and customary laws were allowed to prevail provided they were not repugnant to the British statutes and interpretations of justice and morality. Much of these experiments in colonial South Asia and Africa resulted in critical conflicts even within the different wings of the British colonial administration. See e.g., Abdulkadir Hashim, 'Shaping of the Sharia courts: British policies of transforming the kadhi courts in colonial Zanzibar', *Social Dynamics: A Journal of African Studies,* 38, 3 (2012): 381–97 for insights on developments in Zanzibar, the stepping stone to East Africa.

29 *Advocate General* v. *Muhammad Husen Huseni,* (1866), 12 Bombay High Court Reporter (Bom. H.C.R.) p. 323. Also see Fyzee, *Cases in the Muhammadan Law,* 504–49.

30 *Haji Bibi* v. *H.H. Sir Sultan Mahomed Shah, the Aga Khan,* (1909) 11 Bombay Law Reporter (Bom. L.R.), 409.

31 Masselos, 'The Khojas of Bombay', see 8–10; especially 2.

32 This plurality of socio-religious and legal practices characterized even families close to the Aga Khan's establishment. A classic case in point is Sir Tharia Topan's family from Zanzibar. Two of his sons, Musa and Gafar thus ended up dividing their properties according to Sunni laws: Gafar for a Sunni mosque, and Musa for a Sunni religious seminary (*madrasah*). See Abdul Sheriff, 'The Records of the "Wakf Commission" as a Source of Social and Religious History of Zanzibar' in *Islam in East Africa: New Sources,* edited by Biancamaria Scarcia Amoretti, 27–45, especially 41 (Rome: Herder, 2001). Moreover, in places other than Bombay – in Calcutta, for instance – *jamaats* were shared by all the three branches of the Khojas, and only as late as in 1927 did the Sunni Khojas actually separate themselves constituting in the process the Khoja Sunnat Jamat of Calcutta. See, *The Sunni Khojas: An Account of the Khoja Sunnat Jamat Bombay,* 12 (Bombay: Khoja Sunnat Jamat, 1969).

33 *Hirbae* v. *Gorbae*, (1875) 12 Bom. H.C.R., 294.

34 Ibid., 317.

35 'Bill for regulating succession and inheritance among (Khojas) of Bombay', Home Department, Judicial Branch, March 1880, Proceedings 123- 134 (A), NAI. See also, India Office Records (IOR), Public and Judicial Department Records, The Khoja Succession Bill, 1884, L/PJ/6/131, File 1428. Curiously, however, *The Sunni Khojas*, 33, published by the Khoja Sunnat Jamat of Bombay lists Rahimtula Sayani as one of the leading Sunni Khoja members, probably indicating a switch – by no means uncommon, as a section in this chapter suggests – at some point of time.

36 G. Gonne (Secretary to Government) to His Highness the Aga Khan, 18 December 1878; 'Bill for Regulating Succession and Inheritance among (Khojas) of Bombay', Home Department, Judicial Branch, March 1880, Proceedings 123–34 (A), NAI.

37 Michael R. Anderson, 'Islamic Law and the Colonial Encounter in British India' in *Institutions and Ideologies: A SOAS Reader*, edited by David Arnold and Peter Robb, 165–85, at 177 (Richmond: Curzon Press, 1993).

38 See Lauren Benton, 'Colonial Law and Cultural Difference: Jurisdictional Politics and the Formation of the Colonial State', *Comparative Studies in Society and History*, 41, 3 (1999): 563–88.

39 IOR, Public and Judicial Department Records, 'The Khoja Succession Bill, 1884', L/PJ/6/131, File 1428. The case of Zanzibar is especially interesting as there was no territorial law of succession as such, leaving the door open for the application of personal laws.

40 Ibid; cf. *Advocate General* v. *Muhammad Husen Huseni*, (1866), 12 Bom. H.C.R. p. 323. For Justice Arnould's Judgment, also see Fyzee, *Cases in the Muhammadan Law*, 504–49.

41 G. Gonne to His Highness the Aga Khan, 18 December 1878; see 'Bill for regulating succession and inheritance among (Khojas) of Bombay', Home Department, Judicial Branch, March 1880, Proceedings 123–34 (A), NAI.

42 Letter of Ladukhbhai Haji Mukhi and Mahomedhbhai Choth to the Undersecretary to Government, Bombay, dated 7 October 1885. See IOR, Public and Judicial Department Records, 'Papers Relating to the Khoja Succession Bill', 1885, L/PJ/6/165, File 2185. Ladukhbhai Haji and Mahomedhbhai Choth were respectively the *jamaat* treasurer (*mukhi*) and *jamaat* accountant (*kamaria*) of what was called the 'Jamát of the Shia Ismaili Khojás of Bombay'.

43 Indeed, the Aga Khan's Defence Counsel went on to add that 'the so-called ignorant party', i.e., partisans of the Aga Khan used to send their children to the very same English school which the Aga's opponents used to run. See Howard, *The Shia School of Islam and its Branches*, 6.

44 Hatim M. Amiji, 'Some Notes on Religious Dissent in Nineteenth-Century East Africa', *African Historical Studies*, 4, 3 (1971): 603–16, see especially, 608.

45 See Masselos, 'The Khojas of Bombay', 15. Cf. Rahimtula Sayani's changing position, as noted above in n. 35.

46 See Letter of Ladukhbhai Haji Mukhi and Mahomedhbhai Choth to the Undersecretary to Government, Bombay, dated 7 October, 1885. See IOR, Public and Judicial Department Records, 'Papers Relating to the Khoja Succession Bill', 1885, L/PJ/6/165, File 2185.

47   Anonymous, 'A Voice from India. Being an Appeal to the British Legislature, by Khojahs of Bombay, against the Usurped and Oppressive Domination of Hussain Hussanee, Commonly Called and Known as Aga Khan, by a Native of Bombay, 1864' in Karim Goolamali, *An Appeal to Mr. Ali Solomon Khan, son of H.H. the Aga Khan (Containing "A Voice from India; "Northcote Memorial" etc.)*, 20–21 (Karachi: Khoja Reformers' Society, 1986 Ed. [1932]). Goolamali's is a compilation of select reformist tracts from the 1860s down to the twentieth century. Further details of the collection are discussed in the next chapter.

48   Ibid., 21–22

49   *The Sunni Khojas*, 34–37.

50   Ibid., 36, Cf. the different denominational orientations in Sir Tharia Topan's family, as noted in n. 32 above.

51   Masselos, 'The Khojas of Bombay', 17.

2

The Howardian Moment
Morality, Aryanism and Scholarship

> We have no history of the Ismailis by one of themselves... I will no
> longer call them Assassins, but I will speak of them by the name which
> they themselves employed, namely "Ismailies" and "Batenites".[1]
>
> E. I. Howard, 1866

Scholars have shown how the terms 'Ismā'īliyya', 'Bāṭiniyya', 'Ta'limiyya' and
'Nizāriyya', in addition to the pejorative term *'malāḥida'* (heretic) were all used by
the majority of Muslim writers to refer to Ismailis throughout the medieval times.
Furthermore, the term 'assassin' was used by the Orientalist scholars, and before
them mostly by Crusaders and other European observers, to refer to the Ismailis. Its
etymological root goes back to *'hashīshiyya'*, deriving in turn from the drug *'hashīsh'*,
which the Nizari chiefs allegedly used to control their followers.[2] Without dwelling
on the origin of each of these semantic categories it is still possible to highlight the
preponderantly prejudiced slant in early medieval, and later, Orientalist scholarship on
the community we now know as the Ismailis. However, ours is an effort to understand
in particular an intervention that perhaps for the first time addressed some of these
conceptual issues: the critical inflections, the tortuous narrative of marginalization,
and their receptions in popular psyche. Indeed, scholarship on the Ismailis has come a
long way to appreciate the structural and methodological aporia that characterizes the
vast corpus of the Orientalist venture(s) on the subject.[3] The methodological issues
brought up in this new spate of scholarship are also centrally relevant in conditioning
the ideational bases of the organized academic endeavour now labelled as 'Ismaili
Studies'. Under the aegis of the Institute of Ismaili Studies (IIS, established 1977) in
London in particular – an institution that has been seen as reflecting 'the imamate's
interest in Western-style liberal arts education'[4] – 'Ismaili Studies' now represents an
epistemological entity in its own right, carving out as well as facilitating understanding
of at once a Fatimid cultural past as well as a Muslim universality for the global Ismaili
community. However, what is still glossed over or, to be charitable, only inadequately
addressed in narratives tracing this new spate of scholarship, is the pertinence of the

epistemic intervention that characterized the speech of the Defence Counsel of Aga Khan I in the 1866 Aga Khan Case. Edward Irving Howard's intercessory defence speech – despite foregrounding issues such as what the above quotation illustrates – has thus curiously remained, by and large, peripheral to academic treatments of Ismaili Studies. The irony of what I call the Howardian moment, then, lies in its falling victim to a studied amnesia in the grand narratives on Ismaili Studies, or perhaps even reluctance in institutional circles to directly engage with it with reference to the larger intellectual context of the times. Howard, by and large, thus remains an unacknowledged voice.

That said, it should be also pointed out that it is unlikely that Howard was thinking of an academic venture *per se*, a venture so coalesced and organized as to be accorded the status of an epistemological entity that an institutionalized Ismaili Studies was to later become. What we are suggesting here is that the ideational contours of a process to reclaim the glory of an Ismaili past in the form of an organized academic initiative with the support of Imam Aga Khan III from the early decades of the twentieth century onwards had a nineteenth century background in which contending identitarian quests and discourses of public morality were all inextricably tied up. It was at least in part an extension of certain nineteenth century concerns to recover, and even redound to, an Ismaili religious and cultural history that first originated in the matrix of socio-religious experimentation within the colonial judiciary. An examination of Howard's speech delivered in the course of the Aga Khan Case illustrates at length that the ideational lineage, and the methodological foundations, of Ismaili Studies could be possibly read back in part to the identitarian polemics that had engaged rival Khoja groups in colonial Bombay, predating the organized academic endeavours from the twentieth century. In other words, therefore, the idioms of the conceptual re-orientation consolidated in Ismaili Studies first developed in the course of a colonial judicial experiment before it entered the domain of organized academics.

This chapter is an effort to retrace this ideational genealogy. It is divided into five sections. In the first of these sections we chart out the judicial context in which the socio-religious identitarian polemics developed. In the section that follows we explore the lineaments of the judicial process with reference to the reformist polemics coming from the early 1860s.[5] In the next two sections of the chapter we strive to situate Howard's intervention in both a longer ideational trajectory and within a larger intellectual matrix. This is where we also go beyond the immediate context of the 1866 law case, rescuing his speech at the same time from any possible reductionist interpretation as a wily Defence Counsel's contrivance. Howard's defence of the Khojas', and indeed the Aga Khan's, commitment to community interests and morals – against the reformists' charge of anomie – developed in two parts: first, rehabilitating the moral claims of the Shia in general; and second, that of the Khojas in particular, dovetailed with an effort to establish their Shia identity. Our analysis of Howard's discursive formulation, therefore, is also split up into these two parts, while also connecting them to their wider intellectual and ideational ramifications. In the remainder of the chapter, we seek to understand how knowledge about the Ismailis came to be produced, circulated, received, and not least institutionalized, in the decades following the Howardian moment of 1866.

The historical backdrop

The speech of E. I. Howard has to be seen in the light of an array of social concerns and rhetoric – of liberty, civilization and of progress – invoked by the reformists in their argument against the Aga Khan since years before the culmination came in 1866. By 1866 the vocabularies emerged as a rallying point, available not only to the reformists but also to the Aga Khan's faction in their respective endeavours to uphold their contending claims. The reformist anti-Aga Khan polemics from the nineteenth century came to be included in the compilation, *A Voice from India. Being an Appeal to the British Legislature, by Khojahs of Bombay, against the usurped and oppressive domination of Hussain Hussanee, commonly called and known as Aga Khan, by a Native of Bombay, 1864.* The writer was originally a native of Bombay but apparently (or at least claimed to be, probably to buttress his anonymity) living in London at the time of its publication. The essays and letters document the reformist position of the early 1860s published in newspapers like *Bombay Times and Standard* and *The Times of India* roughly between May, 1861 and December 1862 with copious reference to notes from the *Deccan Herald* and *The Poonah Observer*. Still later, well into the twentieth century, this collection was incorporated, along with some other later reformist tracts such as *Northcote Memorial* and *An Open Letter to H.H. Aga Khan* in Karim Goolamali's *An Appeal to Mr. Ali Solomon Khan, son of H.H. the Aga Khan*, published in 1932 by the Khoja Reformers' Society in Karachi. Goolamali opened his collection with a general *Appeal*. But the very inclusion of the nineteenth century reformist tracts underscores their relevance in the reformist circles even as late as the 1930s. In order for us to reconstruct the history of reformist rhetoric going back further than the specific moment of the 1866 law case, we draw upon the collection under the title *A Voice from India* included in Goolamali's compilation.

An appraisal of Howard's speech shows an acute awareness and trenchant critique of the predominantly prejudiced nature of Orientalist scholarship on the Ismailis. Howard's refutation of such Orientalist position, authored by scholars such as Joseph von Hammer-Purgstall (1774–1856) among others, came first and foremost on grounds of sources and methods.[6] Interestingly, one should perhaps note in passing, Hammer-Purgstall's interactions with India probably had more importance in indirect ways. Hailing from a freemason background, he was himself honorary member of learned societies in India such as the Asiatic Society of Bengal, Calcutta and the two branches of the Royal Asiatic Society in Bombay and Madras. However, it was one of his students, Alois Sprenger who later became a key figure in the so-called 'Mohammedan Controversy' presenting a thesis and methodology to study the life of the Prophet that was critiqued by William Muir.[7] We shall shortly explore part of this debate with a view to situate our key actors in the intellectual map we are trying to draw. But before proceeding along this line it will be perhaps worthwhile to note that Howard was not the only critic of Hammer-Purgstall. Even as Howard developed his methodological critique of Hammer-Purgstall's work, on the ground of its heavy reliance upon literature produced largely by detractors of the Ismailis, there had been others – e.g., Sir Bartle Frere – who were critical of Hammer-Purgstall's project, though not necessarily for the same reason as Howard's.[8] Interestingly, while Howard's rejoinder of Hammer-Purgstall was ensconced in the specific context of a law case in colonial India, in the broader domain of Orientalist scholarship in Europe Hammer-Purgstall had, already during his lifetime, come under fire from the burgeoning philological community on account of dilettantism and was, on the professional front, denied key diplomatic appointment in Constantinople.[9]

Howard's intervention involved a systematic sifting of different layers of 'histories' from an overwhelming corpus of exotic chronicles of the 'Assassin legends'. However, as we shall see, in so far as Howard had to rely on works representing state-of-art contemporaneous 'scientific' Islamic Studies – also products of a specific branch of Western scholarship on the Orient – he too was in essence replacing one set of Orientalist scholarship with another. The crux lay in the fact that Howard's choice of a specific line of the Orientalist scholarship was driven by his overarching concern to realize his grand venture of reconstruction of an Ismaili identity. His speech, therefore, also betrays signs of selective absorptions of Orientalist traits, ones that suited his project. A number of key methodological issues involved in the formulation of a Shia Khoja Ismaili identity by the Aga Khan's defence, later to become instrumental in the evolution of a specific genre of Ismaili Studies, therefore did not develop independent of any Orientalist politico-intellectual concern. It was conditioned by one specific version of Western scholarship on Islam – one that was intricately connected to the project of validating the Aga Khan's socio-religious position, reclaiming an 'Aryan', Persian past – to the exclusion of others. In as much as Howard's venture marked a polemical response to the self-styled reformists' position, which too was no less deeply entrenched in contemporaneous Orientalist scholarship, it can be argued that both the rival socio-religious identitarian claims of Khoja-hood, for all their overtones of public good and sectarian sensibilities, were in the first place conceived in the crucible of competing strands of Orientalist formulations. With specific strands of Western scholarship underpinning the contending Khoja factions' quest for selfhood, the rival Khoja groups and their leaders nevertheless displayed a remarkable degree of activism. Thus, as the next chapter elaborates, Aga Khan III's socio-political endeavours – an exercise intelligible against this long-term historical backdrop – became crucially important in the religious nationalist politics of the subsequent period, even as the socio-religious specificities of the Ismailis came to be defended in terms of a wider understanding of plurality in Islam, and an epistemological venture to carve out an Ismaili Studies progressed.

For the self-styled reformist writer of *A Voice from India*, the Aga Khan (I) – thanks to his allegedly disreputable 'Assassin' background – was a source of danger to public safety. It is interesting to note that the torch-bearers of 'reformation-freedom-liberty' (conceptual categories invoked by the self-styled reformists, as shown below) should depend so crucially, and indeed no less ironically, on strands of Orientalist scholarship that gradually came to be discredited over the next decades, a problem that was already identified by Howard. Howard, in his capacity as the Defence Counsel of the Aga Khan in the 1866 case, had to parry precisely these constructs. His endeavour to recover the innocence and glory of the Ismailis in the process ended up invoking an alternative strand of Orientalist tradition. In a qualified sense, therefore, Howard's discourse was a receptacle of a curious mix of specific Orientalist scholarly traits and a range of socially relevant issues that had come to redefine the nature of urban politics in late colonial South Asia. But in order for us to engage in a meaningful exercise to explicate the implications of these contending and yet overlapping discursive frameworks, it will be pertinent to trace the contours of the reformist position with particular reference to their anti-Aga Khan rhetoric. In other words, this is important, not least, because the Khoja selves that were refashioned through these internal debates also bore significant links to larger intellectual ventures of the time, a complex entanglement that both provides a corrective to and leavens any narrow functionalist interpretation of the respective positions of the two camps.

The reformist rhetoric

For the writer of *A Voice from India*, the Aga Khan was an 'outlaw' in Persia, with fictitious connection to the house of the Prophet, and with an 'assumed sanctity', and thus a pretender and hypocrite, an 'imposture upon the credulity of the uneducated class'.[10] In an unmistakable sign of influence of contemporaneous European ideas of social progress and its diverse yet cognate phraseology, in the subsequent pages the Aga Khan is portrayed as an enemy of educational progress and 'spirit of reformation-freedom-liberty',[11] thriving on the support of the British colonial establishment. The projection of his image as an enemy of public good, at the same time, depended crucially on such Orientalist constructs, and Bombay – in spite of being the 'modern' city that it was in this narrative – emerged in that discourse as the focal point of resuscitation of the 'most terrible exhibitions of man's depravity', the 'practices of the middle ages'.[12]

The particular reference here is to the massacres perpetrated allegedly by the Aga Khan's camp, when members of the anti-Aga Khan reformist group were mercilessly slain by the Aga Khan's adherents in the Mahim area of Bombay in late 1850. It appears that the Mahim *jamaatkhana* (Khoja religious assembly hall) building was divided into two parts, between the Aga Khan's party and his opponents. The Aga Khan's camp ostensibly planned to eject the latter, and having failed to do that peacefully, resorted to violence, in which some 19 or 20 men armed with swords killed and wounded seriously some 6 or 7 men of the anti-Aga Khan camp on the last day of Muharram, 13 November 1850.[13] This was later allegedly followed with life threats to Dhurumsey Poonjabhoy, at that point of time a leading figure among the reformers. This came in the form of a letter sent to Poonjabhoy, written in Gujarati, but later translated into English and published in the pages of *The Bombay Times and Standard*, dated 29 April 1861.[14] This is said to have its roots in 'a new source of division', viz., the Aga Khan's enforcement of 'degrading superstitions' to oppose the enlightenment and the cause of education upheld by the 'informed and wealty [sic] part of the caste'.[15] Indeed, education gradually emerged as a site of contention where a whole array of issues ranging from progress-backwardness to community consciousness could be fought out. It gave a language with which to address all these issues and often itself served as an index to the degree of socio-political consciousness and involvement of sections of the colonial population in cities like Bombay.

Unravelling the morphology of this discourse of reformism/progress vis-à-vis barbarism/backwardness requires us to observe closely the nature of their intellectual bases, which predicated in no insignificant way both upon Orientalist scholarly enterprises as well as received ideas of reformism, progress and modernity. The reactivation of the 'history' of the 'assassins' in the reformist circles to locate the above events from mid-nineteenth century Bombay in a long and allegedly tainted history of the Aga Khan's leadership was thus extension of both an established line of the Orientalist project as well as works authored by other Muslim detractors of Ismailism. The Aga Khan thus figured as a 'wandering occult potentate' in possession of 'secret but great power', the lineal descendant of the lords of Alamut, the stronghold of the assassins, alleged in scholarship from early medieval down to early modern periods with notorious militant activities against the Muslim world.[16] The Aga Khan's adherents, in this discourse, were seen as not much different from the 'fanatical adherents', the 'devoted Fidawi' of the past.[17] In as much as Bombay, despite being the hub of British modernism in the western parts of the Indian subcontinent, became the epicentre of these conflicts, the alleged events emerged in reformist argument as no less than signs of revival of old assassin atrocities marking a confrontation of forces of 'ancient barbarism and modern civilisation'.[18] In the process the Aga Khan came to be projected as the 'open enemy of all *improvement and progress in the caste*' (emphasis mine).[19]

It is predominantly this connection of progress/modernity as opposed to 'ancient barbarism' that gave the whole issue a dimension of 'public interest' on the basis of which the anti-Aga Khan party went on to recurrently demand for physical removal of the Aga Khan from Bombay.[20]

At the same time, it is worth reiterating in this context, the invocation of the question of authority – with the reformist critiques of the Aga Khan's alleged high-handedness – was nevertheless entrenched in contesting Muslim sectarian sensibilities. Developments with more immediate bearing on actual ground, ranging from the issue of opposition to the pro-Aga Khan coterie, participation of members of the so-called 'Reform Party' in the Khoja *jamaat*, and sharing the space of worship had thus all crystallized into a legal polemics culminating in the Aga Khan Case with the Reform party claiming Khoja-hood to be in essence Sunni as opposed to the pro-Aga Khan camp's Shiite claims. The effective linkage of the question of Sunni or Shia affiliation of the Khojas with property disputes and *jamaat* rights at one level, and alleged 'hypocrisy' and high-handedness of the Aga Khan at another thus couched a whole range of disputes in idioms of public interest and safety.[21] The linkage of contending sectarian claims with issues of public safety, civilization, liberty and progress also meant that the defence of such contending religious positions had also to be worked out in a matching way that eventually marked no less than a paradigmatic shift. This shift had far-reaching repercussions on the community of the Khojas (and gradually interchangeably, 'Ismaili', as self-referential category) in the subsequent decades. Most importantly, this related to a heightened emphasis on social responsibilities and norms, and finally on the role of the religious authority, feeding into an array of historical problems that we explore in the course of this book. In the immediate context of the 1866 law case, which we examine in the remainder of the present chapter, this amplified engagement with the argument of morality to redefine the bases of religious authority and community identity brought out a number of epistemic questions into sharp relief.

The Defendants' response I: The moral claims of the Shia

E. I. Howard's was perhaps the first articulate public endeavour to rebut the discrediting imageries about the Ismailis (and the Khojas, in Bombay), the roots of which he traced back to a preponderantly skewed Orientalist scholarship as well as a largely Sunni Muslim polemics against the Shia in general and the Ismailis in particular. Interestingly enough, and as we have suggested above and intend to explore in greater detail now, Howard too buttressed his position with certain strands of Orientalist interventions that he saw compatible with, and in fact furthering, his legal enterprise to uphold the Aga Khan's version of Nizari Khoja Ismaili faith in the face of vehement self-styled reformist critiques. It is this process of reconfiguration of the social and moral bases of a religious order, drawing upon a contending Orientalist scholarly position (that of William Muir's *Life of Mahomet*), that makes Howard especially intriguing. (Muir's work, it should be remembered, has to be seen as part of scholarly polemics that went on to discredit much of the claims made by the Austrian Orientalist Joseph von Hammer-Purgstall.)

Howard started off by pointing to what he called a certain '*Suniẓation* of Indian Mohamedans', especially of the Bombay Khojas since 1830: thanks to Sunni intolerance, the Shia were said to have been increasingly compelled to adopt Sunni customs to shield themselves.[22] While the anti-Aga Khan 'Reform party', claiming Sunni identity, disparaged the Aga Khan's camp as perpetrators of all forms of immorality and heresy, Howard on his part went on to argue that the deviant customs alleged to be peculiarly Shia were actually shared by other Muslims as well. In the process he went on to charge the Sunni faction of bitter intolerance and hostility. To quote him: 'The Shiites seem to have been forced, first to disguise their religion by the superior power and intolerance of the Sunis, and to have ended by professing Suniism altogether, though they still retain unmistakable marks of their old Shiaism'.[23] The rebuttal of the charge of heresy, on the part of the Aga Khan's defence, virtually amounted to a repudiation of charges of immorality lodged against the Shia in general. Refutation of such defamatory charges, and in the process restoring the innocence of Shia doctrines and customs, constituted the first step in Howard's argumentation.

This polemics about the moral question revolved primarily around two specific practices; firstly, the custom of temporary marriage (*mutaa*); secondly, the doctrine of mental reservation, whereby an outward conformity to religious norms of dominant religious traditions is supposedly permitted in times of difficulty in Shia theology (*taqyyia*). The latter, in particular, was of crucial importance in Howard's enterprise in so far as it connected questions of governance, deviance and heresy, persecution, and community identity – all intersecting in the wake of the Aga Khan case with an immense degree of complexity. Here too, the crux in Howard's argumentation lay in imputing the same degree of hostility to the Sunnis which the reformist faction claiming Sunni sectarian identity had until then accused the Aga Khan's party to have unleashed. It is precisely here that Muir gave Howard an academic basis to draw upon. While a detailed account of William Muir's intellectual career would be out of place here, a brief commentary on his intellectual profile might help one appreciate the nature of his scholarship and connect it with the broader politico-intellectual milieu and its ramifications in other spheres, most notably, the colonial administrative problems. By early 1880s, Muir had for instance emerged as an ambassador of Christian goodwill (albeit with a tacit belief in Christian superiority), promoting understanding between Muslim and Christian worlds.[24] William Muir's early interventions were not without their share of controversies though. He spent his early years, from circa 1858 to 1864, in writing his much provocative *The Life of Mahomet*. Muir's *magnum opus* came to engage the attention of a whole generation of Muslim thinkers in colonial South Asia. It came to be critically reviewed by thinkers ranging from Sir Sayyid Ahmad Khan (1817–98), the founding father of the Aligarh Movement, to Sir Ameer Ali (1849–1928), the prominent legal practitioner who later went on to rechart the contours of a Shia consciousness, became a close collaborator of Aga Khan III in matters of crucial socio-political significance, e.g., championing the Khilafat cause that ensued in 1919 after World War I, and sought to provide a moral defence of the Ottoman Caliphate. We shall have the chance to revisit, in the following pages, the intellectual circle of which Aga Khan III was part and in the broader context of which he developed his project of spiritual pan-Islamism.

At the present point, however, our aim is to situate Muir in the wider academic web of his times while also explicating the repercussions his intervention had, especially for Howard. Muir's engagement was occasioned by the need to produce a comprehensive biography of the Prophet in Hindustani language at the instance of the great 'Christian apologist' Reverend Carl J. Pfander. Starting off with the assumption that judicious modifications of existing biographies would fit the purpose, Muir went on to discover much to his disappointment that no such work really existed in Europe. Part of the problem, according to him, was the general lack of knowledge of Arabia prior to the emergence of the Prophet, or the Prophet's character, or too much reliance on 'Traditions', the *sunna* (tradition orienting conduct of life, more specifically referring to Prophetic tradition) and the *hadith* (sayings and accounts of the Prophet Muhammad).[25] Muir's was an attempt to write a history of Muhammad the Prophet and of Islam in the early centuries discrediting what he condemned as 'legendary' narratives based on 'multitudes of wild myths'.[26] While the historical reconstruction of the life of Muhammad depended upon the *Quran* to a great extent in his project, the very conceptualization of the *Quran's* importance as a key text was of utmost importance as well. In doing so Muir also entered into a process of identifying different layers of the *Quran*.

Howard welcomed what Muir had claimed to be authentic history and historical traditions, with his methods of arriving at a systematization of verses along chronological lines. In picking up select threads from Muir's *The Life of Mahomet* to buttress his arguments, Howard was thus actually linking up select strands of Orientalist scholarship with the question of their legal application that had a momentous importance for the Bombay Khojas', and indeed increasingly Ismailis', identity defined along religio-legal lines. Not only was the Aga Khan Case (1866) an investigation into the legal nature of the Khojas of British India, it was also an engagement with some general problems of Orientalist scholarship on Islam that drew attention to such basic questions as the arrangement of the verses of the *Quran* and their exegesis. Moving beyond the sphere of academic polemics, the Aga Khan Case presented the site where the legal applicability of such intellectual engagement came to be tested. Howard took up cue from Muir's comments on the question of mental reservation or religious dissimulation (*taqyyia*), the rallying point of a crucial charge of immorality levelled against the Aga Khan's camp by the Sunni Khoja reformers. Muir's commentary on the origin of mental reservation or the so-called 'pious frauds' was readily taken up by Howard and adapted to suit his legal interpretation of a more general acceptance and applicability of the doctrine.[27] Muir had commented:

> The system of pious frauds is not abhorrent from the axioms of Islam ...
> The Prophet himself, by precept as well by example, encouraged the
> notion that to tell an untruth is on some occasions allowable ...[28]

In footnotes Muir added that 'common Moslem belief' allows deception on grounds of saving one's life, bringing about reconciliation or peace, persuading a woman and on occasions like embarking on journeys and expeditions.[29] Without any specific sign of association of the doctrine with Shia sectarianism, *taqyyia* was thus argued to have been sanctioned by the Prophet himself, an argument readily picked up and redeployed by Howard to further his legal polemics. Having pointed out a more general origin of *taqyyia*, now reclaimed through an endorsement by the Prophet himself in the days when he was 'more indulgent, and less exacting' before he became a 'conqueror', Howard went on to track the historical trajectory of the doctrine, starting with the Prophet's life and tracing the developments after the Prophet's death.[30] According to Howard, the actual reason of the doctrine ultimately becoming so integral to the Shia system of thought lies in the constant persecution to which they were subjected throughout its history.[31] Indeed, such mental reservation was owing to the 'social pressure by the dominant Suni sect', to which 'the timid Hindoos which the Khojas are by race' submitted.[32]

The Defendants' response II: Morality and the 'Aryan' Ismailis

Having salvaged the moral claims of the Shia in general, Howard moved on to establish a Shia Imami identity of the Khojas, and increasingly of Ismailis to invoke Howard, while at the same time striving to reinstate the moral claims of the Khojas. Theories of race, culture, civilization, religious normativity – key conceptual components in currency in contemporaneous Orientalist scholarship – all came to be enmeshed in Howard's defence. And yet, to reiterate our position on Howard, his choice of the strands of Orientalist scholarship was in opposition to von Hammer-Purgstall's version of Orientalism, invoked by the self-styled reformists in their tirade against the Aga Khan.

Thus in Howard's discourse, the Shia – in their veneration of Ali – had commendably moved beyond the 'Shemitic spirit' of 'the narrow, cruel, jealous monotheism of the Arab Sunis' and had introduced a 'more human element'; for Howard, the Shia creed moreover conjured up at once the image of 'Christianity as developed from Judaism', with the idea of a 'semi-divine' Ali deriving probably form Christianity, 'Aryan, or Indo-European in spirit' as opposed to the 'Shemitic groundwork of Mahomedanism'.[33]

It will be pertinent to pause here for a while to understand the locus of Howard's argument in the broader intellectual landscape. Scholars have argued that there had been a time in the pre-modern and early modern Europe when Islam, Judaism, and Christianity were all seen as part of a larger monotheistic family, an argument that gradually petered out by the nineteenth century with the emergence of the science of religion wedded to racial and national consciousness.[34] The Orientalists' discovery of a pristine 'Aryan' Buddhism also meant that there could be other alternative roots of universal religions, beyond the confines of Semitic monotheism.[35] For a religion to qualify as a 'world religion', though, it was crucial for it to pass the litmus test of universality, which had historically been almost necessarily associated with monotheism. How exactly then does one assert a Euro-Christian superiority over others? One way to address this conundrum was to devise a hierarchic schema of universalisms, in effect betraying contradiction in terms. Christianity thus came to signify the only 'true universalism of the Sovereign Deity', with Judaism representing an 'older, undeveloped, fossilized, hence limited universalism', and Islam, as 'latter-day breakaway movement, amounting to a renegade universalism'.[36] By the late nineteenth century strident critics of Islam became busy throwing their strictures on the religion reducing it gradually to no more than a national religion of the Arabs so that its reality as a transnational force was explained away through suggestions of its allegedly particularistic nature carved out of pre-existing universal categories.[37] As for Aryan Buddhism, its glories lay in the past, to be excavated by the European philologists in the nineteenth century. The history of the universalistic Buddhism after the times of the historical Buddha, then, had been a history of degeneration even as Buddhism spread among 'non-Aryan' peoples.[38]

Howard's recovery of a Shia Ismailism within the Aryan/Indo-European framework reflected, as well as hinged upon astute appropriation of, significant epistemic shifts in the politics of Orientalist scholarship. While the grand schema of world religions came to be conceptualized in Orientalist scholarship on the bases of the twin pillars of comparative philology and racial discourses, in course of time, specific strands of German Orientalism would, nevertheless, seek to glean out a certain non-Semitic 'Aryan' Islam in the form of Sufism. A key proponent of this latter view was Otto Pfleiderer (1839–1908) who, for all his preoccupation with Semitic Islam still strove to understand what he called a 'Persian Islamism' vis-à-vis 'Arabian Islamism'.[39] Much of the delegitimization of Arabism and Islam in the nineteenth century, associating systematically the 'Semitic' peoples with fanaticism and decadence as opposed to the enlightened Aryans/Indo-Europeans, was also part of shifting contours of the romantic traditions in Europe. This was a complex process, one that happened, ironically, at the hands of a new generation of German romantics and French radicals.[40] While this delegitimization of the Semitic Arabs formed a central component of the Orientalist metanarrative of the nineteenth century, it was nevertheless in sharp contrast to the earlier eighteenth century fad for the romantic nomadism of the Arabs that many Orientalists had borne.[41] Howard's intervention, then, provides a link to this complex epistemic shift in Orientalist scholarship that had significant repercussions in the subsequent times. More generally, he anticipated a line of later scholarship that was sympathetic to Islamic history, striving to retrieve an Islamic religio-cultural past from the clutches of hostile Orientalist traditions. The Hungarian Jewish polemicist-turned-Islamicist Ignaz Goldziher's (1850–1921) approving endeavour from the late nineteenth century onwards to recover a history of Islam with reference to its Arab as well as 'provincial' versions (Arab vis-à-vis Ajam, for instance), to its law and customs and practices, and not least understanding the Prophet Muhammad as 'pathfinder' (*Wegweiser*) rendering a living and malleable Islam was,[42] one might be tempted to add, eerily anticipated by Howard's apologetic venture to retrieve a 'more human element'. Howard's endeavour to re-inscribe a transregional history of Ismailism, connecting South Asia's Khojas with the Persian and Central Asian Ismailis underpinned with an appeal to moral and humane claims, then has to be seen as evoking a number of critical concerns. Critiquing a reductionist view of Islam associated with the dominant Sunni views, and indeed 'Semitic' Arab characteristics, also gave him a leverage to forestall any understanding of Islam as a national religion of the Arabs. Nevertheless, this did not happen through any denial of ethno-centrism or racial consciousness. For Howard, the Shia claims in general, and the Ismaili claims in particular, to universality were embedded in an understanding of Islam transcending Arab-centrism, reclaiming at the same time a glorious cultural past. Coupled with the vocabularies of civic consciousness reclaimed from the reformist repertoire, Howard thus also toyed with key aspects of a universality that in evolving contemporaneous discourse of the science of religions had emerged as a crucial register of 'world religions'.

Whereas von Hammer-Purgstall reduced the 'Ismailiah sect' of the Shia to the much deplored 'assassins' with 'secret state-subverting doctrine', Howard strove to establish a highly laudable Ismaili pedigree by connecting them with no less than three political establishments (the Fatimid Caliphs, the Druzes of Syria and the followers of Hasan Sabah), and the importance of the Fatimids in the contemporaneous political and intellectual world.[43] Whereas von Hammer-Purgstall had reduced the crowning achievement of the Fatimid educational enterprise to no more than 'a lodge', Howard came to hail the Fatimids for founding the 'first University' in Cairo setting new

standards of pedagogic experiments.[44] Howard's was a three-fold strategy to deal
with the Assassin-paradigm: having criticised von Hammer-Purgstall's labelling of the
Ismailis 'as ill-omened',[45] he went on to normalize violence as survival mechanism in
hostile environment,[46] to finally the masterstroke of dissociating the theological school
of Imamism from the Assassins.[47] The recovery of the moral credibility of the Ismailis
and of the Aga Khan also involved connecting the Aga Khans simultaneously to the
Alid family line,[48] the centrality of veneration of Ali in *Dasavatar* (thus establishing
its Shia identity), while also pointing to its nature as a Khoja conversion text in the
specific context of South Asia.[49] And it is this quest for Khoja texts as opposed to anti-
Ismaili and arguably propagandist tracts – to return to our key concern, summarized
in the opening quotation, in this chapter – that marked an epistemological departure.

Conceptualizing an epistemological entity: Production and institutionalization of knowledge

Between Howard's 1866 intervention and the systematic endeavours at institutionalization
of Ismaili Studies from around the 1940s in Bombay lies a phase when denominational
reconfigurations necessitated a new form of expression of religious sensibilities, and
not least, the beginning of a new modality of governance in the form of streamlined
community protocols.[50] We shall take up the latter in due course, with reference to
Aga Khan III's Imamate. It will be useful at this stage though to see the forms of
self-expression that characterized Khoja Ismaili life in post-1866 Bombay, and to see
which of Howard's ideas did not quite gain traction, at least directly, among the Khoja
Ismailis who he sought to define. For one, post-1866 Ismaili scholarship betrays hardly
any, if at all, overt fixation with the rhetoric of an 'Aryan' spirit that characterized
Howard's project. There are, however, other forms of polemical issues that we see
conditioned subsequent self-depicting literature and scholarship of the community. The
late nineteenth century text *Risala dar haqiqat-i din* by Shihab ud-din Shah Husayni,
the eldest son of Aga Ali Shah (i.e., Aga Khan II), can be seen as an exemplary self-
reflexive intervention of this period. The text has been argued to reflect the competitive
nature of the religious economy that colonial Bombay epitomized. Representing one
of the several religious 'firms' – to invoke Nile Green's metaphors – vying between
themselves to attract clientele, this text strove to carve out a niche for the 'Aga Khan
firm'.[51] Shihab ud-din Shah Husayni died a premature death in either 1884 or 1885,
leaving his infant brother Sultan Muhammad Shah to succeed to the Imamate after the
death of Aga Khan II in 1885. Green's contention is that Shihab ud-din Shah's *Risala
dar haqiqat-i din* drew upon the classic internal/external dichotomy of faith and set a
polemical tone to advance the grounds of religious guidance, and by extension that of
the Ismaili Imamate, by systematic argumentation. Consider this, for instance:

Brother, profession of Islam is the assertion in two formulas of profession (*shahādatayn*). The uttering of these belongings to the outward side of piety, which has nothing to do with the real, genuine *faith*.[52]

Again:

There is a difference between faith (*īmān*), and the mere outward profession (*islām*), as the Prophet emphasised.[53]

And then:

The foundation of (*aṣl*) of faith is love for the Mawlā... Thus love for the Mawlā is everything, being the root of faith. If it is not strong, all the acts of outward piety (*a'māl-i ẓāhirī*) which are like leaves of tree, will fade ...[54]

I am, however, concerned in particular with a different problem, viz., the afterlife of this text which – if we see the developments sustained by institutionalized efforts in the subsequent decades – gained a position at par with other classics. The relevance of Shihab ud-din Shah's tract in the Ismaili intellectual terrain can be thus gauged by its subsequent translation (into English by Wladimir Ivanow and into Gujarati by V. N. Hooda) and inclusion in its list of publications by the Ismaili Society of Bombay alongside classical and medieval Perso-Indic Ismaili literature. The Ismaili Society, established in Bombay in 1946 under the patronage of Sultan Muhammad Shah Aga Khan III, marked a crucial organizational initiative in the process of collection, redaction, and reproduction of Ismaili literature, coming from the Indo-Persian to Syrian and Oxus regions. Typically, and this reminds us of the importance of para-texts, its publications would start with a 'Notice' laying down its aim of promoting critical and independent scholarship on Ismaili subjects while also disclaiming any propagandist goal. As illustrated below, they also represented crucial aspects of a much larger process of canonization. The Russian pioneer Wladimir Ivanow (1886–1970), along-with some of his colleagues from Bombay, was instrumental in the establishment of the Ismaili Society, just as they had been in the foundation of the Islamic Research Association, also in Bombay, in 1933.

This recovery of a range of texts, extremely difficult to access both because of their secretive nature as well as their splintered and dispersed provenance, was made possible by several scholars who could access the vast corpus of sources from Yemen to South, and Central Asia.[55] In fact, the very career of Ivanow illustrates the complexities of this history. Thus, even before he arrived in India in the early 1920s, he had had an experience of extensive travels to remote places deep in inner Asia as well as Persia, and intensive engagement with Nizari literature retrieved by Russian Orientalists such as I. I. Zarubin (1887–1964). It was during his stint at the Asiatic Museum of the Russian

Academy of Sciences, St. Petersburg, that he had opportunities to access a wide array of Arabic and Persian manuscripts, especially those from Central Asia, and came to study for the first time in his life the Ismaili manuscripts from the Upper Oxus region collected by Zarubin. Leaving Russia as the revolution broke out, he settled in Persia for a while, finding employment with the British Government as an interpreter, collecting Persian Ismaili records, eventually becoming a British subject, and thence relocating to India. In India, Sir Asutosh Mookerjee (1864–1924) recommended his name to the Asiatic Society of Bengal in Calcutta for commissioning him to catalogue the Persian manuscripts preserved in the Society's library. Subsequently he was also commissioned to catalogue the Arabic manuscripts kept at the Society. These were also years when he started publishing his own seminal works on the Nizari Ismailis, and eventually went on to lay the foundations of Ismaili Studies based in Bombay. In the late 1950s he left for Persia, where he spent the rest of his life.[56] This brief biographic excursus can hardly do justice to Ivanow's multifaceted personality and scholarly accomplishments in any comprehensive manner, but is perforce instrumental in our understanding of the thriving transregional character of the intellectual milieu from which an institutionalized Ismaili Studies emerged, and within which some of its early pioneers navigated. Ismaili Studies, then, was conceived and sustained by no provincial academic system, but by individuals who defied territorial boundaries both in their intensely peripatetic academic lives as well as in their understanding of an Ismailism cutting across political and territorial borders. In the process, they at once operated along and facilitated the proliferation of complex knowledge networks.

Another significant aspect of this knowledge production had been the active role of a number of Ismailis belonging to branches other than the Nizaris, such as Ivanow's Bohra Ismaili (i.e., Mustali) colleagues from Bombay, like Asaf A. A. Fyzee (1899–1981), Husayn F. al-Hamdani (1901–62), Zahid Ali (1888–1958) *et al*, although a clearly defined 'Ismaili' ecumenical venture took years to galvanize. This organizational initiative owed its success in no less extent to the diversity of the scholarly community – in terms of both denomination and international nature – that not only facilitated access to literature in otherwise inaccessible private repositories, but also expedited the redaction, reproduction and dissemination cycle with much zeal. Such knowledge production, then, both extensively drew upon and was also closely entangled with specific aspects of earlier as well as contemporaneous Orientalist scholarship, but was underwritten with specific Ismaili agendas and was carried forward through the vehicle of a motley of entangled institutional endeavours.[57] Thus in his editorial note in one of the Ismaili Society Series volumes coming after World War II, Ivanow expressed his gratitude to his Egyptian colleague Kamil Hussein, who had arranged for that volume to be published in Egypt, thus enabling the Ismaili Society to bypass the hindrances of strikes and riots that had seriously come to affect post-War Bombay life.[58] In India, the

Shia scholar-jurist Syed Ameer Ali, who had become a close associate of Aga Khan III from the late 1900s and especially in the wake of the Khilafat Movement, pointed to the lack of sympathetic and authentic sources for the history of the Fatimids.[59]

However, it should be added that even Sir Ameer Ali was not much removed from the prejudiced mythical leitmotifs and stereotypes associated with the Ismailis when he sought to trace the genealogy of secret societies of the Crusaders and subsequent times to the Ismailis.[60] Most interestingly though, what compounds this general ambiguity pointing further to the fluid nature of the production, consumption and appropriation of knowledge in general and of such contentious identitarian issues as the Ismailis' in particular, is the significant discrepancy on matters as important as treatment of religious authority in the different editions of Sir Ameer Ali's *magnum opus*. Reflecting a particular form of Ithna Ashari Shia predicament, an earlier edition from 1902, published under a somewhat different title, thus bore a certain disapproving tone:

> At the present moment an alleged or real descendant of Hassan (*Aala-Zikrihi-as-Salâm*) rules the conscience of these Indian Ismailias; and credulity accepts, and superstition trembles at, the fantasies invented by designing brains to control and keep in chain the human mind. But for the presence of this representative of the Grand Master of Alamût, the Ismailias, at least in India, would have long ago merged in the general body of the Shiahs proper.[61]

While the Preface to the 1946 posthumous reprint edition faithfully announced the inclusion of two new chapters (entitled 'The Apostolical Succession' and 'The Idealistic and Mystical Spirit in Islâm' respectively),[62] the contentious position taken in the 1902 edition on the Ismaili leadership had disappeared producing a bowdlerized version of the section on political divisions and schisms. Such attitudinal shifts as Sir Ameer Ali's draws attention not only to the numerous ambivalences that define the genealogy of any epistemic category, but also to the politics of scholarship, and perhaps also political expediencies. The question of political pragmatism and an ecumenical imagination shall be discussed in the following chapters. However, and on the basis of the ongoing discussion, it will be in order to posit at this point that even as Aga Khan III's Imamate strove to define the contours of an epistemic system, there were other complexities that defined scholarly endeavours among the Muslims, and particularly among the Shia, around the same time.

While the initiatives of the Ismaili Society reflected the growing organized and institutionalized aspect of knowledge networks focused on, and often also involving, the different branches of the Ismailis, certain circulatory character of this knowledge production had already emerged in an earlier phase. The circulatory pattern in reproduction and reuse of customs has been recently highlighted. The case of Muhammad ibn Zayn ul Abidin Khurasani, better known by his *nom de plume* Fidai (Faithful), illustrates the point in the immediate context of the Perso-Indian sphere. Fidai's *Kitab-i hidayat al-muminin al talibin* (c. 1903), as Green argues, was another distinctive product of colonial Bombay's religious economy that sought to recover a glorious Ismaili past while connecting it to the present with re-affirmation of the charismatic authority of the Aga Khans descending from the Alid line, and in the process helping galvanize what Green calls certain neo-Ismaili identity. Fidai's three journeys to meet Aga Khan III between 1896 and 1906, and his subsequent appointment by Aga Khan III as instructor to the Persian Ismailis bring out the circulatory nature of operation of the Ismaili Imamate.[63] The anachronisms and inaccuracies in Fidai's history of the origins of Ismailism and Imams in the post-Alamut period was subsequently corrected and updated to c. 1910 by Musa Khan b. Muhammad Khan Khurasani. Previously in service of Shihab ud-din Shah, he later entered the service of Aga Khan III, and had access to the Aga Khans' private library in Bombay as well as oral sources that bore substantive insights on the community from within.[64] What we have here, therefore, is not only a process of reproduction of customs but also a re-invigorated thrust towards chronicling and carving out, in the process, an Ismaili history that, in the immediate context, became crucial in reconfiguring the position of the religious authority in the wider Perso-Indian world. This circulation of ideas was first discernible in the Perso-Indian sphere. Understandably, this involved movement of preachers, thinkers and scholars related to the Imam's household even as Aga Khan I relocated to Bombay in the 1840s. Howard, for one, took pains to trace a history of connections sustained especially by movement of tithes from western parts of India to Persia, since the late eighteenth century.[65] Much later, and in consonance with this argument of a wide network straddling the Perso-Indian world, Aga Khan III pointed out how his teacher for religious matters – who the Aga Khan thought to be no better than a 'bigoted mullah' – later returned to Tehran and how indeed, he grew up in Bombay listening to, among other things, accounts of travels of their relations and acquaintances to Persia.[66] The picture that emerges is one of lively exchanges and flows.

The history of the Ismailis and Ismailism that we are striving to understand here entered a new phase by the early decades of the twentieth century. It has been thus suggested that the 'reproduction and distribution to Iran of reinvigorated custom and a charisma-based family religious firm' that Fidai's work signified was essentially a product of colonial Bombay's religious economy, and was far removed from the modernist Ismaili project that Aga Khan III came to lead from the early part of the twentieth century from his base in Europe.[67] When Wladimir Ivanow *et al* set out to recover the Ismaili past on the bases of 'Ismaili' source materials, as opposed to prejudiced non-Ismaili (and almost always anti-Ismaili) literature, they were in fact reiterating an earlier intellectual concern that had already seen two entangled phases in its life cycle; first, originating in a specific colonial judicial context and then, second, developing gradually into Imamate-sponsored initiatives that went hand in hand with a reassertion of its religious authority in the Perso-Indian sphere. In other words, in addition to a commitment to excavate Ismaili texts, Howard's project to retrace a web spread across the Perso-Indian sphere provides a key to understanding crucial aspects of both the lines of development that followed, viz., the late nineteenth century efforts at reconnecting Ismailis in a Perso-Indian world, followed by a more vigorous institutionalized project promoted by the Imamate.

It will be ahistorical, though, to situate Howard's efforts to recover an Ismaili history and subsequent Imamate-sponsored institutionalization of scholarship along one linear arc. Interestingly, as already noted, part of the intellectual ventures from the later phase (i.e., post-1866, but pre-dating Aga Khan III's modernist enterprise from the 1910s) survived their immediate context. It may be recalled how the work of Shihab ud-din Shah for instance, ended up being reproduced by the 1940s in the more organized translation and publication projects of the Ismaili Society. This juxtaposition of a nineteenth century intervention alongside a range of medieval Perso-Indic classics is a pointer to the complexities of scholarship institutionalized under the Imamate. It underlines key aspects of the process of canonization that since the Imamate of Aga Khan III came to attach importance to not only the recovery of the 'classics' but also streamlining texts produced in and reflective of colonial Bombay's religious landscape and furthering the Ismaili Imamate's views on theology and religious sensibilities. It shows, furthermore, that the modernist academic cultural endeavour that the Ismaili Society had come to represent under the patronage of Aga Khan III was no passive receptacle. While it was no propagandist or missionary outfit, it emerged nevertheless from the dynamics of the imperatives of scholarship, with all their nuances, that suffused Ismaili cultural life since the latter part of the nineteenth century, with Bombay as the epicentre. The very nature of its venture made it an active mediator in the new organized academic turn that characterized, and also conditioned to an appreciable extent, the understanding of the Ismailis about their varied cultural past from the twentieth century onwards. This chapter has been an effort to unravel their nineteenth century historical context as well as their subsequent ramifications.[68]

Conclusion

Understandably, it has not been our intention to argue for a linear history of what we now see as Ismaili Studies with E. I. Howard's intervention as the entry-point, even though Howard does open up a window into a much complex academic problem. What we have been striving to do is to understand the nature of epistemic implications that Howard bore for the posterity. The very act of preference shown by Howard for the nomenclature 'Ismaili' over 'assassins', for instance, was the first act to recover the moral claims of the Ismailis and reconstruct a cultural past going beyond, and also critiquing, the anti-Ismaili repertoire. Without going into the details of much traversed discursive turn in humanities and social science theory, it is still possible to see with reference to the above example that much of this production and systematization of knowledge about the Ismailis within the rubric of what later came to be labelled as 'Ismaili Studies' emerged out of a range of experiences articulated especially since at least the 1860s. Such experiences were not due to any oppositional relation with the colonial establishment. They developed rather out of a dynamics within the wider rubric of contesting Islamic consciousness and rhetoric, articulated through vocabularies that had come to surface in the politico-legal order that the colonial dispensation brought about in South Asia. This experiential dimension, then, was in essence a dialogic process with (re)conceived cultural past, feeding into an accumulative process of knowledge production, if also critiquing and overturning extant perspectives along the epistemological plane that would later become benchmarks for the posterity. The purpose of this chapter has been to retrace the lineage of this intellectual quest, and the experiential journey within which it was embedded. Beyond the immediate intellectual sphere, the characteristic feature of this Khoja Ismaili identitarian project, as an outcome of internal denominational negotiations connected intricately to the moral argument of public good, informed to a great extent the Imamate's policy under Aga Khan III. Sultan Muhammad Shah Aga Khan III would successfully dovetail his role as the Ismaili Imam with that of a leading political personality championing wider Muslim causes in South Asia in the early part of his career, and gradually and ever so increasingly reaching out to a range of internationalist concerns. This internationalism predicated largely upon his understanding of certain spiritual pan-Islamism which in turn gravitated around an inherent *topos* of religious plurality, and an endeavour to forge a language of ideological pluralism. It is this internationalism that constituted the ideational cornerstone of much of his wide range of religio-political and, not least, social activism, marking at once a significant departure in the format of the Imamate's operations while also setting a new benchmark to emulate.

Endnote

1 Howard, *The Shia School of Islam and its Branches*, 57. (Howard's 'Ismailis' refer to the Khojas of colonial Bombay, with a rich cultural past in Fatimid Egypt; the Mustalis, or the Bohras of South Asia, do not figure in his speech.).

2 Farhad Daftary, *The Ismā'īlis: Their History and Doctrines*, 19 (Cambridge: Cambridge University Press, 1990).

3 For a representative piece of this new scholarship – at once critical of the Orientalist project and refreshingly appreciative of efforts that went on to crystallize what is now known as 'Ismaili Studies' – see, for example the Introduction to Daftary, *The Ismā'īlis*, 1–31; also

see the 'Introduction' to *Medieval Isma'ili History and Thought*, edited by Farhad Daftary, 1–18 (Cambridge: Cambridge University Press, 1996). For a succinct critique of twentieth century and contemporary avatars of such skewed scholarship, as well as depictions in popular media, see Geraldine Heng, 'Sex, Lies, and Paradise: The Assassins, Prester John, and the Fabulation of Civilizational Identities', *differences: A Journal of Feminist Cultural Studies*, 23, 1 (2012): 1-31.

4   Steinberg, *Isma'ili Modern*, 90

5   For a recent analysis of the law case with focus on the arguments of the Plaintiffs, the Defence and the position of the judgement with reference to the colonial state's understanding of the Muslim nature of the Khojas, see Purohit, *The Aga Khan Case*, chapter 2. For specific reference to the Plaintiffs' position in the law court, see ibid., 38–45. Also see her chapter 3 for an examination of *ginan* literature (religious literature of Ismailis of the subcontinent) and the Satpanth in the legal process, and the implications the process bore. As illustrated, our specific emphasis in this chapter on the Defence Counsel's arguments is dictated partly also by the need to situate Howard's speech as a rejoinder to a long trajectory of reformist rhetoric. In other words, the focus here is not so much on the Plaintiffs' speech (well-studied by scholars), but rather the long line of reformist rhetoric of which it was part and which provoked, and even conditioned, the Defence Counsel's polemics, spurring in the process a new socio-religious and intellectual engagement reformulating an Ismaili Khoja identity.

6   Joseph von Hammer-Purgstall, Austrian Orientalist who had spent much of his life in government service working on Turkish and Persian history and culture, and was the author of *Die Geschichte der Assassinen, aus Morgenlandischen Quellen*, (1818), original German edition of *The History of the Assassins, Derived from Oriental Sources*.

7   See M. Ikram Chaghatai, *Hammer-Purgstall and the Muslim India*, 18–21 (Lahore: Iqbal Academy Pakistan, 1998).

8   Writing a decade after Howard, and drawing heavily upon the literature of the 1866 law case, Sir Bartle Frere complained that Hammer-Purgstall (in his English translation which Sir Bartle used) had failed to do justice to 'either the romantic or the political interest of the subject', raising furthermore the question of the lack of appreciation of the diverse forces that led to the 'terrible success of such a hideous system', 'the methods of propaganda', and above all, the question of persecution and the rights of such people within the British judiciary. Sir Bartle was hardly a sympathizer of Howard: but what they had in common was a critique of Hammer-Purgstall and his version of the history of the Nizaris. See Sir Bartle Frere, 'The Khojas: The Disciples of the Old Man of the Mountain, II', *Macmillans Magazine*, XXXIV (1876): 430–38, especially 436–37.

9   Suzanne L. Marchand, *German Orientalism in the Age of Empire: Religion, Race, and Scholarship*, 73, 100, 119–20 (Cambridge and New York: Cambridge University Press, 2013 [2009]). And this was the case despite his thorough training in Oriental languages. Indeed, as has been observed, from the 1820s through the 1870s the German Arabists suffered under the adverse effects of rather 'low levels of public interest and state support' (Ibid.,118).

10 Anon., 'A Voice from India' in Goolamali, *An Appeal*, 1.

11 Ibid., 2.

12 Ibid.,16.

13 Ibid., 9–11.

14 Still later it came to be included in the 1864 tract 'A Voice from India'. A sum of Rupees 2000 was announced as a reward for anyone giving information about the anonymous author of that letter. See Anon., 'A Voice from India' in Goolamali, *An Appeal*, 13–14.

15 Anon., 'A Voice from India' in Goolamali, *An Appeal*, 11.

16 Ibid., 8.

17 Ibid., 15–16.

18 Ibid., 17.

19 Ibid., 12. One cannot help but underscore the community-specific nature of the discourse of 'improvement and progress'. What happened under Aga Khan III in the subsequent period was, however, a systemic expansion of the idea of social responsibility that went hand-in-hand with his project of a spiritual pan-Islamism, which in turn was to reposition the Ismaili denomination within an overwhelming Sunni community. From the early decades of the twentieth century, and increasingly in more recent times, this came to be seen within the rubric of the venture of liberal Islam.

20 The demand was also buttressed with references to specific legal provisions, e.g. the invocation of the State Prisoners' Act of 1859. (Ibid., 12–13; see also, 9, 11, 19).

21 In fact, the extent to which Orientalist constructions of assassin legends received support in governmental circles can be testified to by the letter of C. Forgett, Deputy Commissioner of Police, addressed to late Commissioners of Police. An article in *Times of India* (27 November 1862) notes how concerned Forgett was about what he thought to be utter fanaticism leading to 'deeds of blood', and 'cowardly attack of secret assassins' unleashed by the Aga Khan's followers at the Aga's instance (Ibid. 36).

22 Howard, *The Shia School of Islam and its Branches*, 17.

23 Ibid., 17.

24 Jewish hostility towards Muslims, according to him, had been always much more potent. Sir William Muir, 'Sura V, v. 9 (The Coran)', *The Hebrew Student*, 1, 2 (May 1882): 14. Although a late nineteenth century tract, this nevertheless needs to be seen, in qualified way, in the light of a long series of historical developments supposedly ensuing from around the time of Islam's spread beyond the Arab world when discrepancies between Islam and Jewish or Christian faiths became evident as the latter faiths were accused of distorting the history of the Prophet's life and interpolating events. Interfaith dialogues and a stress on Christian empathy for Islam, under these circumstances, assumed particular importance, especially on account of administrative imperatives of the British Indian Empire.

25 This, according to W. Muir, vitiated the works of Orientalists like Alois Sprenger. William Muir, *The Life of Mahomet: With Introductory Chapters on the Original Sources for the Biography of Mahomet, and on the Pre-Islamite History of Arabia, Vol. I*, iii–iv (London, 1861). Interestingly, however, when some five years before this Alois Sprenger wrote his article on the 'writing of historical facts' among Muslims, he referred to his 1851 book entitled *(The) Life of Mohammad* as the first of its kind that subjected the sources of the Prophet's biography to 'critical enquiry'; Alois Sprenger, 'On the origin and progress of writing down historical facts among the Musalmans' in *Journal of the Asiatic Society*, IV (1856): 303–29, especially 303, and *Journal of the Asiatic Society*, V (1856): 375–81. The question, therefore, was one of interpretation as to what constitutes the right critical method. It is to be noted that Muir himself relied too heavily upon the *Quran* while dismissing the *hadith* as corrupt; the moot

problem, therefore, was identifying the *reliable* threads from the vast corpus of literature. Muir's position was challenged by those influenced by Sprenger, some of whom had been pioneers in 'Islamic modernism', such as Sir Sayyid Ahmad Khan. For a detailed account of this early polemical episode of Islamic modernism see, Daniel Brown, *Rethinking Tradition in Modern Islamic Thought*, 32–42 (Cambridge: Cambridge University Press, 1999 [1996]). In fact, the authenticity of the *hadith*, the reliability of *isnad* (means of assessing the *hadith* traditions on the basis of chain of transmitters) had been brought to question throughout the nineteenth century; Alois Sprenger, William Muir, Ignaz Goldziher, and even Sayyid Ahmad Khan, for all his critique of Muir, were all critical of the *hadith* to varying degrees and in their own ways (Ibid., 36, 81–107). However, Sayyid Ahmad Khan was no less critical of Sprenger either. See Gail Minault, 'Aloys Sprenger: German Orientalism's "Gift" to Delhi College', *South Asia Research*, 31, 7 (2011): 7–23, especially 16–17.

26 Muir, *The Life of Mahomet*, 2.

27 Howard, *The Shia School of Islam and its Branches*, 64–67.

28 Muir, *The Life of Mahomet*, 73.

29 Ibid., 73–74: Drawing upon the *Kitab al Wakhidi* or traditions like *Mishat* Muir went on to demonstrate how Muhammad himself by his life and works countenanced all these four forms of *taqyyia*.

30 Howard, *The Shia School of Islam and its Branches*, 27.

31 Ibid., 28–42.

32 Thus prior to the establishment of the Old Khoja *Masjid* in their burial ground they are said to have no mosque at all. This discourse of Sunni fanaticism is further propped up by reference to Sunni-Parsi riots about two decades earlier or Sunni hostility towards Shia in general as well (Ibid., 61). Elsewhere too, for instance in Sindh circa 1850, Richard F. Burton, *Sindh and the Races that Inhabit the Valley of the Indus, with Notices on the Topography and History of the Province*, 250 (Karachi: Oxford University Press, 1973 [1851]), reported traces of hostility toward the Khojas in the course of his sojourn.

33 Howard, *The Shia School of Islam and its Branches*, 32, 33.

34 See Tomoko Masuzawa, *The Invention of World Religions, Or, How European Universalism Was Preserved in the Language of Pluralism* , chapter 6, especially 187 ff (Chicago and London: University of Chicago Press, 2005.

35 Ibid., 187.

36 Ibid., 188.

37 The most vociferous and prejudiced proponent of this view was perhaps the Dutch Arabist, Abraham Kuenen (1828–91), (Ibid. 192 ff).

38 Ibid., chapter 4; 187. Cf. Marchand, *German Orientalism*, 135–37.

39 See Masuzawa, *The Invention of World Religions*, 197–206.

40 See Stefan Arvidsson, *Aryan Idols: Indo-European Mythology as Ideology and Science* , translated by Sonia Wichmann, 91 ff. (Chicago and London: University of Chicago Press, 2006). Arvidsson, *Aryan Idols*, 63–123, situates the pursuit of the discourse of Aryanism within the larger context of the nineteenth century European quest for a 'religion of light' in the East, an attempt to modernize religious belief by rescuing Christianity from the clutches of odious conservatism. Cf. Marchand, *German Orientalism*,129–30.

41 Thus, Johann Gottfried Herder (1744–1803) envisioned the *Quran* as 'the great national epic of the Arabs'. See Marchand, *German Orientalism*, 26. Importantly though, the idea of the 'national' specific to the Arabs was crucial to this view.

42 Marchand, *German Orientalism*, 329–30.

43 Howard, *The Shia School of Islam and its Branches*, 44, 56.

44 Ibid., 44, 58: Indeed, in many respects as in this Hammer-Purgstall only embodies the reified and generally established (not just Orientalist) scepticisms of his times towards non-conformist strands in society. Thus Hammer-Purgstall, while conceding to the points of differences between the 'Assassins', on the one hand, and the Templars, the Jesuits, and the Illuminati, on the other, nevertheless entered into a comparative study claiming all of them to be 'secret societies'; this theme of commonality was further developed as he placed the history of the 'Assassins' in a common historical tradition that accommodated the Bacchanalia of ancient Rome or the Templars and Jesuits of his times, culminating in his claim that the 'Assassins… a branch of the Ismailites (represented) the proper Illuminati of the east'. See Joseph von Hammer-Purgstall, *The History of the Assassins, Derived from Oriental Sources*, translated by Oswald Charles Wood, 217; see also, especially 105 ff (London: Smith & Elder, 1835).

45 Howard, *The Shia School of Islam and its Branches*, 44.

46 Thus 'religious murder' is shown as the 'rule of all sects' and, 'assassination as a form of war, meeting the sword with the dagger'. Ibid., 55.

47 Ibid., 58–59.

48 Ibid., especially 80 ff.

49 Ibid., 77 ff.

50 Zulfikar Hirji, 'The Socio-Legal Formation of the Nizari Ismailis of East Africa, 1800-1950' in *A Modern History of the Ismailis*, edited by Daftary 129–59 provides a useful study of the rules and regulations and constitutions that from the early decades of the twentieth century systematically redefined the boundaries of the Imami Ismaili community first in East Africa and South Asia and then gradually globally. For further discussions, with reference to recent scholarship, on the process of canonization and its implications for earlier messianic ideas, see Chapter 4 of the present book.

51 Green, *Bombay Islam*, 162–63.

52 Shihabu'd-Din Shah Al-Husayni, *Risala dar Haqiqat-i Din*, translated by Wladimir Ivanow as *True Meaning of Religion*, 42 (Bombay: Thacker & Co. [1933], 1947).

53 Ibid., 43.

54 Ibid., 46.

55 For an overview of developments from the twentieth century onwards, see Daftary, *The Ismā'ilis*, 25 ff.

56 For fuller details, see Farhad Daftary, 'W. Ivanow: A Biographical Notice', *Middle Eastern Studies*, 8, 2 (1972): 241–44.

57 Recent scholarship on the conceptual framework of 'entanglement' thus points to the transnational scholarly and intellectual endeavours since the late nineteenth century amid changing international political scene. Such scholarship shows, moreover, that the

collaborative ventures underlying 'entangled' relationships did not automatically lend itself to dissociation from either power equations, or the specific agendas of collaborators. For a recent and compelling work in this direction see Kris Manjapra, *The Age of Entanglement: German and Indian Intellectuals across Empire* (Cambridge, MA. and London: Harvard University Press, 2014). See especially the Introduction for a conceptual overview.

58 See Wladimir Ivanow, 'Note by the Editor' in his (ed.) *Collectanea (The Ismaili Society's non-periodical collection of articles), Vol. I, 1948* (Leiden: Brill, 1948).

59 Syed Ameer Ali, *The Spirit of Islâm: A History of the Evolution and Ideals of Islâm. With a Life of the Prophet* (London: Christophers, 1946 ed. [1891]), 324 ff. The 1946 edition was a posthumous reprint of an earlier edition from the 1920s although, the first and a much shorter version of the book appeared under a different title in 1891.

60 Ibid., 342.

61 Syed Ameer Ali, *The Spirit of Islâm Or, The Life and Teachings of Mohammed*, 314 (Calcutta: S.K. Lahiri & Co., 1902 ed.).

62 Syed Ameer Ali, *The Spirit of Islâm*, vii (1946 ed.).

63 Green, *Bombay Islam*,164–68. Apparently, Fidai had been instrumental in enabling Aga Khan III reassert the Imamate's authority over the Persian Ismailis in face of stiff opposition from Murad Mirza, who had supported Haji Bibi against Aga Khan III. Murad Mirza's father, Mirza Hasan, was appointed by Aga Khan I to attend to the administering of the Persian Ismailis once Aga Khan I left for India. See Daftary, *The Ismāʿīlis*,535–37.

64 Daftary, *The Ismāʿīlis*, 440.

65 Howard, *The Shia School of Islam and its Branches*, 85 ff.

66 Aga Khan III, *The Memoirs of Aga Khan*, 17, 19.

67 Green, *Bombay Islam*, 165.

68 As already indicated above, the establishment of the Institute of Ismaili Studies in London in 1977, under the patronage of Shah Karim al-Husayni Aga Khan IV, marks a further development in the direction of organized Ismaili Studies. However, it is for the posterity to assess the historical relevance of the institution with reference to any continuities or breaks in the realms of ideational and organizational practices. For an overview of its research and publication programmes see: http://www.iis.ac.uk/view_sorted_articles.asp?catid=86&layout=children&l=en (last accessed 30 November 2015).

3

Pan-Islamism and an Asiatic Spirit

Postnational Subjectivities in an Age of 'Transition'

Political Pan-Islamism had its foundations on sand, and could not endure. There is a right and legitimate Pan-Islamism to which every sincere and believing Mahomedan belongs–that is, the theory of the spiritual brotherhood and unity of the children of the Prophet. It is a deep, perennial element in that Perso-Arabian culture, that great family of civilisation to which we gave the name Islamic in the first chapter. It connotes charity and goodwill toward fellow-believers everywhere from China to Morocco, from the Volga to Singapore. It means an abiding interest in the literature of Islam, in her beautiful arts, in her lovely architecture, in her entrancing poetry. It also means a true reformation–a return to the early and pure simplicity of the faith, to its preaching by persuasion and argument, to the manifestation of a spiritual power in individual lives, to beneficent activity for mankind.[1]

His Highness the Aga Khan, 1918

Compelled on account of a frail health the young Hazir Imam had to stay away from both military service in World War I as well as an active public service in the historic 1919 constitutional reforms.[2] However, this gave him an opportunity for reflection, one which he thought could be best put to use to design a course to serve his country. The outcome was a blueprint for the reconstruction of India. The outcome, somewhat contrasting his own sedentary phase of life, showed the glimpse of a sense of mobility that he thought was propelling India in a new direction. Written amid the negotiations for political reforms in India and on the eve of the conclusion of the World War I, his *India in Transition: A Study in Political Evolution* encompasses this sense of locomotion and flux in a key expression announced in the title itself, viz. 'transition'. World War I was an event that redefined the very nature of modern warfare, and left for the posterity a repertoire of vocabularies – perhaps most importantly, that of right to 'self-determination' – that found way into the mental universe of large parts of the colonized world. Thinkers, activists and revolutionaries from the colonial world would henceforth recurrently invoke, customize and domesticate such idioms to bolster their own anti-colonial projects, and often with remarkable internationalist aspirations. Recent scholarly works thus trace the emergence across large parts of the world of a shared language of anti-colonial nationalist resistance, during and after World War I, as part of a wider global web.[3] This chapter attempts to trace some key aspects of Aga Khan III's notion of 'transition', which elicits an examination of his ideas of community development, national efficiency, federalism, cultural/civilizational exchanges, pan-Islamism and not least pan-Asianism against this larger backdrop of global flows of ideas.

Aga Khan III's 1918 intervention echoes some of these larger internationalist concerns, but it does so not as an uncritical receptacle of dominant narratives of territorial nationalism or revolution. A book in which both the first person singular and the first person plural jostle for the vantage point from which to embark on journeys of self-discovery through making assertions for *India's* hopes, aspirations and prospects, the Aga Khan's *India in Transition* shows an intersection of the different layers of the individual and the community even as the 'nation' emerged as cultural entity with national questions juxtaposed with larger internationalist issues. 'The war', he noted, 'has enormously changed the political and social outlook throughout the world ... strengthening those forces of democracy and national self-determination, of liberty and progress'.[4] The narrator, interestingly, proceeds from no pre-conceived monolithic identitarian framework that had, from around the late 1910s, and especially in the post-World War I period, increasingly come to be structured along stringent 'national' lines in different parts of the globe. For one, the idea of India that Aga Khan III envisioned in his *India in Transition* emerged from a tension between certain national and postnational forces foregrounding, in the process, its formulation in terms of a certain cultural (and/or civilizational, which he uses somewhat interchangeably) entity.[5] Thus, even as ideas of reconstruction of Indian society and administration were writ large in the book, the India he conceptualized as a cultural/civilizational entity also became meaningful increasingly in terms of a burgeoning cultural internationalism that had come to enamour a whole generation of South Asian intellectuals, thinkers, and politicians.

The first section in this chapter examines the Aga Khan's thoughts on India on the eve of the 1919 constitutional reforms. Bulk of the issues he addressed, however, had also engaged the attention of politicians, bureaucrats, administrators, nationalists of different shades, and thinkers and observers for a considerable period of time since the early twentieth century. This cluster of ideas thus had a shared history in some ways, with striking similarities in terms of approach at times. In the second section we proceed to explore the features of his postnational, internationalist imagination. As will become evident in the course of this and the following chapters, it is this idea of the postnational that informed the Imamate's engagement with the Ismailis, and in turn the Ismaili followers, first in the transregional arena of South Asia and the western Indian Ocean world, and then across the globe. In the process it produced a complex grammar of subjectivities, connecting the Ismaili individual to the Ismaili collective as well as the larger Muslim ecumene. It is once again this postnational imagination that precluded the emergence among the Aga Khani Ismailis of any metanarrative of political pan-Islamism, or any overbearing sense of territoriality. The idea of the postnational, therefore, provides a forceful reminder of voices critical of totalizing or homogenizing metanarratives of territoriality and territorial nationalisms without however, as Javed Majeed qualifies, undermining the idea of 'collective polity'.[6] In the third section we illustrate how, in conjunction with the promise of the postnational, the interlacing of pan-Asian and pan-Islamic consciousness forged a crucial complexity in the Aga Khan's thought. We also see how this reflected the larger socio-political and intellectual concerns that defined Muslim history in late colonial South Asia hinting, at the same time, at wider global processes. In the fourth section, and before we move on the concluding section of this chapter, we seek to identify certain key indices of the global reception of the Aga Khan which, given his increasingly internationalist aspirations, will hopefully help us better appreciate his location in the broader intellectual and ideological landscape of the crucial *inter bellum* years. This chapter, among other things, is also an exploration of the early history of these alternative ideas of polities that stem from this postnational imagination – a constellation that has significant repercussions in more recent times, especially for what I call the 'Ismaili international'.

Conceptualizing 'transition': Community development and national efficiency

Nationalist sentiments are often couched in vocabularies of flux and mobility. Thus while Sir Surendranath Banerjea (1848–1925) found India as a *Nation in the Making* other thinkers, by the late 1910s, discovered an India in transition. Indeed, by the first two decades of the twentieth century we see that the rhetoric of transition had gained some currency. Aga Khan III's *India in Transition* was soon followed by another book with the same title but by a different author, that by M. N. Roy (Indian Marxist, and later, Radical Humanist theorist, 1887–1954).[7] The key to understand such idioms, though, lies in unravelling the problems of topicality as well as larger aspirations and visions. Thus, except for their shared disdain for the notion of a static India, the Aga Khan and M. N. Roy were actually professing two very different kinds of 'transition', a fact that only reiterates the multivalence of metaphors and the resultant intricacies in their usages. An excursus exploring the contrastive nature of these respective interpretive positions would perhaps help us better illustrate their range of meanings across the political spectrum of their times.

For one, the Aga Khan's was not only a treatise on 'political evolution' – which it certainly was, and as the book's sub-title announced – but also an unequivocal document of his grand thesis of gradual and holistic progress. Phrased as 'progressive modernization', it hinged on 'co-operation and understanding between the *rulers and the ruled*', which in turn depended on the role of women in 'the great work of national regeneration on a basis of *political equality*' (emphases mine).[8] The invocation of 'political equality' and the specific political argument of enfranchisement that it subsumed, the exhortation for 'national regeneration', women empowerment and 'co-operation and understanding' between the rulers and the ruled betrayed far deeper concerns. We read this narrative of modernization with holistic aspirations in terms of certain gradualist progress.

Roy's *India in Transition*, by contrast, was an essentially Marxist commentary on the Indian conditions with chapters ranging from 'Growth of the Bourgeoisie', through an enquiry into the conditions of the 'rural population' and down to the proletariat question (divided into three chapters) and to political movement (addressed in two chapters). There is a remarkable degree of dismissiveness with which Roy approached the questions gravitating around Islam and Muslim political mobilization in India and elsewhere. Thus, Roy observed, 'till the earlier years of the twentieth century, politically the Muslim intellectuals were less concerned with Indian affairs than with Pan-Islamism'; and when eventually Muslim intellectuals did turn their attention to 'home politics' in India, they did so as a knee-jerk reaction to the disenchantment caused in the course of the Balkan Wars, thanks to the way the Khalifa's call for *jihad* (lit. 'to strive'/holy war) was cold-shouldered by the Islamic world and the British attitude to the episode.[9] However, 'the tendency towards political nationalism in the Muslim community', according to Roy, was spawned by a very different set of factors, thanks primarily to the activities of a vanguard social group that he believed had come into being by the turn of the twentieth century: 'the ideological pioneers of the Muslim bourgeoisie'.[10] Yet the very fact that the bulk of their political activities through the newly-established All India Muslim League was above all overtly dependent on governmental countenance, if not support, as also the leadership and blessings of the 'religious aristocrat' Aga Khan III and the 'official reactionary' Syed Ameer Ali – both allegedly keen to declare Muslim loyalty to the established colonial order – they remained by far rather 'anti-nationalistic than national'.[11] And in this, they were temperamentally not much different from the bulk of the Muslim 'mercantile and industrial class, which had developed quite independent of the religious unity of the Muslim world'; for them, Roy went on, Pan-Islamism was no more than a 'fashionable cult, without vital attachment', and loyalty to the British establishment the be all and end all.[12] It is not clear, though, why Roy chose not to take note of the gradual ascendancy of the young brigade within the Muslim League that compelled the likes of the Aga

Khan to distance themselves from the League's new guards by the 1910s. Roy's was thus essentially a thesis that systematically undermined the Muslim political activism of the time with a repugnance not entirely unlike, ironically, the standard Indian National Congress line. The 'transition' that was expected to come out of the volatile socio-political matrix was thought to be essentially an outcome of the dialectics of social forces and class struggles leading to a much needed revolution; and the Indian case, thanks to its large population and proletarianized intellectual stratum, was ideally suited for that. 'Pan-Islamism', in this discursive framework, was as useless as the Gandhian option; indeed, it was as early as 1922 that Roy had developed a systematic critique of Gandhi's thought as well. For Roy, 'Gandhi's criticism of modern civilization, that is, capitalist society is correct', but the prescribed remedy 'not only wrong but impossible',[13] owing to the religious and spiritual preoccupation that was central to that movement. Roy believed that Gandhian philosophy, with a staunch critique of Western civilization and notions of 'progress', and with wholehearted commitment to the cause of a spiritual civilization, had failed to gauge the redeeming prospects that Western civilization opened up – and 'which', to quote Roy, 'is after all only a certain stage of human development through which every community has to pass'.[14] In short, for Roy, Gandhian philosophy represented 'nothing but petty-bourgeois humanitarianism hopelessly bewildered in the clashes of the staggering forces of human progress'.[15] Critical of both the Muslim League as well as the Gandhian vision, Roy's was thus a discourse of revolutionary 'transition'. We shall see though how this, curiously, also echoed part of the Aga Khan's surreptitious critique of the Gandhian position on Western civilization, and Gandhi's trademark discourse of village-centrism and self-sufficiency.

'Transition', then, had a rather fluid history that had intrigued very different minds across the political spectrum, marking both intersections and divergences, and invoking at once questions of regional, transregional, and global nature. Professing a somewhat gradualist 'transition' as opposed to Roy's revolutionary wave, Aga Khan III, however, offered a remarkable breadth in his *India in Transition* that made it at once an overwhelming and complex narrative. The volume, in his words, was meant to be a 'detailed exposition' of his 'thoughts on India' and his 'hopes and aspirations for the future', that had come to the forefront since Lord Montagu came up with his announcement for 'substantial steps' in the direction of self-governing institutions. Quite understandably, most of the 31 chapters directly or indirectly address the bulk of the administrative issues of the time, ranging from 'reforms', federalism, 'provincial reorganization', the institution of Viceroyalty, local self-government, to the more bureaucratic questions of civil service, police and judiciary. A sizeable part of the volume also addresses issues relating to foreign policy, economy and finance, and pan-Islamic concerns with the latter in particular, as we have noted, opening up a range of identitarian issues that take us to the realm of the postnational. The preoccupation with the overarching administrative concerns provides a backdrop to much of his ideas of society and schemes that can be grouped together under the general rubric of a certain 'developmental imagination'.[16]

A celebration of a federal model became the hallmark of his proposed administrative restructuration. Recent scholarship has underlined the correlated nature of the Aga Khan's notions of minority, federalism, and pan-Islamism. Taking a cue from the principle of weightage under the Morley-Minto Reforms, the Aga Khan sought to escape the constraints imposed on the Muslim minority by their numbers through an invocation of the federal model as well as cultural internationalism related to pan-Islamism.[17] If the essence of this internationalist imagination was a 'South Asiatic Federation', conceived of as one of the dominions of a free union of nations with Britain as the head,[18] its pivot was an India that was thoroughly reconceptualized along a federal model of decentralization. This recent commentary by Faisal Devji on the Aga Khan's thoughts about India's Muslim population with reference to the South Asiatic Federation thus aptly gives us a clue to understand how the very aspirational entity of the federation was expected to become the site for India's Muslims to transcend their minority status. As the Aga Khan noted, the federation was expected to 'contain not only the 66½ millions of Indian Moslems, but the thirty or forty millions more Musulmans inhabiting South Persia, Mesopotamia, Arabia, and Afghanistan'; consequently, there would be 'little danger of the Mahomedans of India' of becoming 'a small minority in the coming federation'.[19] The following chapter argues that this has to be situated against the backdrop of an emerging preoccupation with the 'redistribution' of Muslim population, a theory that was gaining ground after the World War I.

We should emphasize though that this experiment also bears a particular cultural meaning, since in the preceding pages the Aga Khan came to rehearse the decadent fate of Muslim nations, with the last bastion of Ottoman Turkey being 'drawn into the Teutonic orbit', and becoming a 'satrapy of Germany'.[20] Importantly, however, this forms a part of the Aga Khan's engagement with the minority question, given his position as the spiritual leader of a rather small Shia denomination vis-à-vis a predominantly Sunni presence in South Asia's Muslim ecumene. I have elsewhere indicated, and will further discuss in the course of this book, that the Aga Khan's idea of a spiritual pan-Islamism, his endeavour to provide an effective leadership in the Khilafat cause, his sponsorship of the All India Muslim League initiative as well as the educational project in Aligarh were all part of his own way of announcing the important role of the non-Sunni, non-North Indian Muslim in South Asia's Muslim politics.[21] What is equally important though is to disentangle these categories and try to understand them in the light of their wider intellectual backgrounds, kindred ideas, as well as their transregional and or global resonances. In as much as the discourse of federalism came to mark an intersection of ideas about the nation, governance, different aspects of administrative reforms, the minority/majority dynamics in the Aga Khan's thought, it merits a critical engagement. It is to this genealogy of federalism that we now turn in this section.

The Aga Khan's model of federalism had its roots in a plan that he prepared in collaboration with G. K. Gokhale (senior Congress politician, 1866–1915), drawing some attention from the official circles.[22] To be sure, the idea of federalism had a shared history, albeit differing subtly in approaches to it, depending on the political-ideological and socio-intellectual location of its authors and their agenda.[23] For all the differences in the choice of modalities of implementation or ultimately in conceptualizing the nature of the federal units, the idea of federalism was almost inevitably garbed in the idioms of administrative reform addressing far reaching social concerns. Aga Khan III's experiment of wedding administrative and social reformist issues was thus part and parcel of a shared and complex discursive field. Thus, no wonder the last ten chapters, with meticulous and telling titles in particular bring a wide gamut of social issues to sharp relief.[24] Collectively, they form part of a wider discourse of what can be referred to as 'national efficiency' aimed at building strong character of both the individual and the nation that had come to gain considerable traction both in the imperial metropole and in large parts of the colonial world.[25]

For one, this developmental project was premised on a systematic advance of federalism that he expected to facilitate self-government, 'a structure of local autonomy... built up from the municipalities of the great towns down to the smallest village *panchayat* ...'.[26] Interestingly, the theory of local autonomy, and kindred ideas of village improvement and community development were themes common to both nationalist thinkers and statesmen as well as a section of British bureaucrats, albeit with varying implications. Aga Khan III's idea of local autonomy, however, should not be seen as feeding into any larger discourse of self-contained villages, a thesis most notably associated with M. K. Gandhi (1869–1948). Thus, in the Aga Khan's words, such 'economically self-contained and entirely independently administered village community ... would be entirely unsuited for the expanding life of modern India ... stopping the circulation of the blood to any of the various members of the human body'.[27]

If this brings out some aspects of the commonalities as well as complexities in the nationalist *imaginaire*, echoes of such concerns are also discernible in influential bureaucratic circles especially in the interwar and post-World war II years. Thus having served in various parts of the subcontinent and well informed about the philosophical thoughts of economic theorists ranging from Thomas R. Malthus (1766–1834) to John M. Keynes (1883–1946), Sir Malcolm Lyall Darling (1880–1969) elaborated on a sophisticated schema of rural and agricultural development, which was later to crystallize into his coherent 'community development' discourse.[28] The hallmarks of the Darling version of a developmental venture were a keen interest in co-operatives especially in agricultural and banking sectors and an emphasis on education as a working starting point in this journey of 'community development' (reminiscent once again of the Aga Khan's emphasis on the key question of education).[29] Pivotally crucial in this structure was his model of co-operative credit system, although not necessarily of the Communist variety.[30] For Darling, the inspiration for co-operative credit organizations came, at least in part and especially after the World War II, from the Swiss Raiffeisen model: at the same time he also sought to legitimate the very idea of state-supported co-operative ventures along Keynesian lines.[31] Against a larger discursive backdrop of community development, the model of co-operatives in particular marked a further shared area of concern for bureaucrats, nationalist thinkers, and leaders of communities. Aga Khan III, for instance, had lamented already in 1918 about the dismal state of 'banking and co-operative capitalism in India',[32] while Darling later came to note how the Islamic sanctions against banking, for instance, frustrated such initiatives in the course of the 1927 Soodamand Conference in Aligarh.[33] While the Aga Khan's developmental vision thus had a number of shared concerns with enduring relevance for the posterity, the crux of his developmental agenda, however, lay still somewhere else, and one that had bearing especially on his Ismaili followers in their conceptualization of a community. I have in mind here the Aga Khan's bringing the language of the religious in a meaningful conversation with the language of development, with all its fluctuations and varying emphases. In the process, an Ismaili understanding of Islamic norms of conduct, under the aegis of the Imamate, were virtually recast in a modernist framework to shore up projects ranging from co-operative banking through educational and similar other humanitarian activities. As the following pages show, it provided the crucible in which a blueprint for the bulk of Aga Khan III's – and eventually Aga Khan IV's, albeit with significant shifts – development initiatives came to be designed.

At another level, to return to our survey of the ideas in the Indian context in general, the ideas of uplift of 'depressed classes', voluntary social service, and nation building with emphasis on the key issues of education through health and sanitation together marked an equally significant shift towards a language of citizenship as opposed to that of a colonial subject. These intertwined ideas had come to preoccupy thinkers, politicians, activists and statesmen of the stature of M. K. Gandhi through Jawaharlal Nehru (1889–1964) among others. Scholars have, in this connection, stressed the disciplinary strategies deployed by the Indian National Congress during the Swadeshi and Gandhian phases.[34] Moreover, the various Indian associations in the early twentieth century aimed at building strong individual character as well as a nation saw much virtue in the likes of Robert Baden-Powell's (1857–1941) regimented Scout Movement.[35] Aga Khan III's admiration for – and earnest exhortations, echoing Gokhale, to introduce among the Indians – the Swedish P. Henrik Ling's (1776–1839) pioneering drill techniques to combat not only lethal ailments and debilities, but also make a healthier nation with healthy women at par with men has to be seen against the same backdrop.[36] Yet, it will be an oversimplification to say that the argument of 'national efficiency' was necessarily embedded in the discourse of citizenship tied up with unequivocal anticolonial nationalism. As Aga Khan III noted, 'education in the widest sense, and national efficiency as required in the modern world, are impossible ... under an irresponsible and bureaucratic form of government'. What he had in mind was, 'a national system, broadly based on the representation of every class, caste and creed *under the sovereignty of the King-Emperor and within the unity of the Empire*' (my emphasis).[37] Beyond a sense of disenchantment with and resultant critique of the British bureaucracy, which made a surreptitious way into the Aga Khan's *India in Transition*, there was thus also an underlying faith in British trusteeship that turned his language of national efficiency into a language of *training* into citizenship that he envisaged developing within the larger framework set by the constitutional reforms since 1908–09.

The Aga Khan's work then is at best a narrative of ambivalence and ambiguities, with the occasional riposte to the colonial dispensation and its mode of functioning, but not entirely dissociated from an implicit faith in the unity of the Empire. It is important, therefore, that we appreciate his discursive forays – ranging from notions of federalism through experimenting with imperial citizenship – and their wider connotations bearing in mind this intrinsic ambivalence. In the remainder of this section we briefly trace the incipient disillusionment bordering almost on a full-fledged rejoinder of the British administration. The very title of one of the chapters in his *India in Transition*, albeit much later in the book, announces this break. In 'Chapter XXIX: The Limits of British Trusteeship', we see one of the sharpest shifts away from his usual steadfast belief in British governance and tutelage. This can be testified to by a comparative analysis of his 1903 and 1904 budget speeches in the Council of the Governor General on the one hand, and sections of his 1918 volume, *India in Transition*. The critique of British budgetary policy discernible in his budget speeches in the early 1900s was decisively limited in scope, concerning at most problems such as the lack of elementary education and the question of merging contributions from the imperial government and princely states for imperial defence. Oblivious of the overarching concerns of the nationalists and the systematic development of the 'drain theory' – also shared by some English Liberal thinkers and humanitarians of the time[38] – the 1903 speech actually began with a congratulatory note extended to the government for the 'steady though slow progress in the material prosperity of the country' amid various economic problems.[39] The reformist vision was extended in due course over the next decade to incorporate a plethora of issues such as public health and general standard of living.

However, this widening of remits spurred, in the process, a much critical re-appraisal of the moral bases of the British rule, 'principles of justice and rights of [sic] self-determination for nations'.[40] Thus:

> The responsibility such proprietorship (that England enjoyed) connotes has been so vicariously exercised as to devolve normally upon a small circle of men, and more particularly upon a Secretary of State whose continuance in office has been dependent far less on the relative merit and advantage of his services to India than on the exigencies of party convenience, or on the verdict of the electors on subjects having no relation to India ... How many debates, how many critical divisions, how many proposals to share the sacrifice in the battles against cholera and malaria, plague and poverty, do the pages of Hansard record? How often, with what voices, and with what power, has the House of Commons discussed the need for overcoming mass illiteracy in India? In what general elections of Parliament have votes been affected in any appreciable degree by the terrible poverty-famines or poverty-plagues of that distant country?[41]

Again, a couple of pages down the line:

> ... at least 60,000,000 Indians, a number equal to all the white races of the Empire, can afford but a single meal a day, and suffer the pangs of inadequate nourishment from birth to death. Has this mass of poverty ever been an outstanding problem at any British general election? Has it been so much as touched upon in the electoral manifestos of party leaders, or even in the addresses of Ministers from the India Office appealing to their constituents?[42]

This, he added, was further aggravated by the problem of 'a tragic non-comprehension on the part of some conservative elements in England' who had always stubbornly opposed any idea of devolution of authorities from the British electorates to 'the representatives of all the communities of India'.[43] These are languages that present a sharp contrast to the clinically-controlled critique of 1903–04. At the same time, the idioms of the 1918 critique mark an attempt to not only relate to the overarching topicality of the myriad issues that tended to stifle the colonies but also raise much larger questions revolving around political ethics and modalities. Indeed, it is the idea of devolution – systematically worked out in the 1918 treatise on 'transition' – that formed the cornerstone of the Aga Khan's theory of India's reconstruction and answer to a wide range of contemporaneous problems. It is this formula of checks-and-balances, an experiment with federalism customized to the specific Indian needs that constituted the pre-condition for much of his socio-political policies. This, he thought, could gradually create an environment conducive to the realization of the potentials of the individual communities and groups in their way to progress.

India beyond India: 'Transition' and postnational sensibilities

Aga Khan III's pan-Islamic, and ever increasing internationalist, concerns have been studied in connection to a discourse of Asianism that intrigued a large section of Asian political and intellectual elites in the interwar years.[44] However, the imbrication of this pan-Asianism with Indic/Brahmanical and Islamic consciousness produces a far more complex narrative of internationalist aspirations, bordering on the postnational. In the process, one also sees a reconstitution of a moral and cultural geography that necessitate in turn a re-assessment of the very conceptual framework of pan-Islamism with which Aga Khan III operated. Problematizing this specific variant of pan-Islamism enables us to see within this discursive rubric how the racial, religio-cultural and civilizational forces intersected producing a remarkably versatile cultural space rendering, in the process, the idea of a nation-state redundant, and even unwarranted. Thus Aga Khan III's *India in Transition*, with its complex entanglement of pan-Asian and pan-Islamic aspirations, becomes in effect a narrative documenting an engagement with an array of issues of postnational character. The India conceptualized within this larger framework, then, is an India beyond its conventional territorial understanding, a cultural space that transcends the strictures of nation-states.

The opening chapter of *India in Transition* (Chapter I: Social Organization) sets the tone, if at times along somewhat programmatic lines, of this religio-cultural topography. Human progress in 'developed societies', thus, came to be seen along different civilizational (and, as mentioned used interchangeably in Aga Khan's thought, with cultural) lines: 'Western'; 'culture of the Far East'; 'Brahmanical'; 'Islamic, or Mahomedan'.[45] What makes Aga Khan's civilizational thesis intriguing though was the underlying idea of dialogues, historical links and cultural intercourse that made each of these traditions products of much cross-fertilizations, and often miscegenation. Far from archetypical Arabs, the Muslim ecumene is thus acknowledged to be constituted of 'very distinct and different races', from the 'white Berbers of Morocco and Algeria' to the 'Arnauts of Albania (perhaps the purest European race)' to the Serbs of Bosnia and Macedonia, and 'the hundreds of millions of every colour and race in Africa, Arabia, Persia, Central Asia, India, China, and the Malay Archipelago'.[46]

The Muslim ecumene thus outlined was characterized by a remarkable degree of plurality at different levels; and while their diversities were accepted, and even celebrated, what still brought them together was a spiritual quest. We shall have opportunity to elaborate on the lineaments of this spiritual *topos*, but before we do so, it will be pertinent to assess the programmatic dimension of his civilizational schema and the relationship it bore with the India he conceptualized. The India in this narrative is no single monolithic nation, but a country whose culture is defined by the very 'co-existence of the four main surviving streams of human culture', as alluded to above.[47] This valorization of India's cultural catholicity is also wedded to an idea of India's cultural expansion, bordering on and drawing upon the aspirational and the 'historical', both towards Southeast Asia as well as towards the Northwest of the subcontinent.[48] Consider this, for instance:

> Can anyone deny that, if the Mogul Empire had not been dissolved, or if it had been succeeded by a powerful and united Hindu Empire over the whole of India, the lands of the Persian Gulf littoral would long ago have been brought under Indian dominance? ... whatever the flag that may hereafter float over Basra and Bagdad, over Bushire and Muscat, *Indian civilisation, commerce, and emigration must become an increasing power in Mesopotamia, Persia, and Arabia.* This process will add greatly to Mahomedan influence in India itself, while, on the other hand, *by taking Hindu influences into lands hitherto regarded as the preserves of Islam*, it must inevitably lead to a better understanding between the Brahmanical and the Islamic peoples of the peninsula.[49]
>
> (Emphases mine)

Drawing upon this, it has been suggested that it betrays 'an admirably impartial way' to 'embrace contemporary Hindu fantasies of empire' and, in the process, '[the Aga Khan] saw in India's world-historical mission the only real chance for resolving the country's religious rivalries'.[50] To be sure, such imperialist visions formed part of a larger project of imagining what Kalidas Nag (1892–1966) *et al* came to call a 'Greater India', and represented a particular vein in the nationalist project.[51] While taking a cue from the general argument of imperialist ambitions, I would however venture to further suggest that the Aga Khan's underlying idea was far more deep-rooted in a wider civilizational argument. While trying to resolve on the one hand the Muslim minority question in his imagination of a South Asiatic Federation, the Aga Khan eventually flirted with an idea that betrayed and bore significant repercussions beyond the narrow remits of Indian politics. At one level, the Aga Khan's invocation of a South Asiatic Federation might on the surface show some commonalities with the 'Hindu' imperialist/ nationalist complex. At another level, one still sees elements that in effect signify endeavours to relate to critical cultural and civilizational exchanges, bringing both the Hindu and Islamic world-historical imaginings in a dialogue, while recognizing all the while India as the confluence of the four major civilizational streams. Even as a certain 'Perso-Arabian culture' forms the core of the 'Islamic' civilization that the Aga Khan envisaged,[52] to return to the epigraph standing at the head of this chapter, the Islamic sphere so conceptualized as a cultural zone open to the osmotic influence of other civilizational forces was not necessarily tethered to any political venture. How else does one explain the invocation in one breath of ideas of both a 'Hindu Empire' as well as the flow of 'Indian civilization, commerce, and emigration' regardless of the flag that flies in western Asia? Given the transregional and increasingly global stakes of the Ismailis, this language of cultural internationalism bore momentous implications. In other words, the conjunction of a critical cosmopolitan vision, cultural internationalism and postnational aspirations – albeit with varying emphases – animated both Aga Khan III's engagement with the idea of India, and his visions for the Ismaili community. These were, therefore, aspirations for new forms of civilizational and cultural exchanges. The endeavour betrayed at once a degree of ambivalence towards the Arab-centrism of conventional Islamic *weltanschauung*, coupled with endeavours to situating India – itself understood as a somewhat diffuse civilizational/ cultural zone – in a substantially reconstituted Afro-Asian world, hinging on an alternative cultural and religious landscape.

The cosmopolitanism was, moreover, informed by a historical consciousness that championed holistic progress and development. Indeed, the nineteenth century Ottoman administrative and constitutional reforms (*tanẓimat*), according to the Aga Khan, had failed due to a lack of co-ordination and a holistic vision.[53] In his acute awareness of, and critical engagement with, different imperial forms – the Ottoman, as much as the British – and in his conceptualization of a capacious spiritual pan-Islamism critiquing the strictures of the European model of nation-state, the Aga Khan both resonated and critiqued a Muslim cosmopolitanism characteristic of the age of empires. Recent scholarship has located the idea of a Muslim cosmopolis within the rubric of the 'imperial assemblage' of the Ottoman and British empires, as an intellectual and civilizational zone that 'transcended political borders, territorial confines, and cultural particularities', all the while remaining 'neither caliph-centric ... nor entirely anti-British'.[54] The distinguishing feature in the Aga Khan's thought though remains the way he brought his evolving Ismaili denomination, with its own specificities and disparateness, in dialogue with the overarching language of Muslim universality. This he did furthermore by engaging selectively with the symbology of the caliphate and idea of an imperial citizenship, with its promise for shared opportunities, that he thought the British Empire ought to throw open to its Indian subjects. In the process, the Ismaili community was expected to become an important stakeholder in a widening cosmopolitan discourse. And yet, at the same time, in his critique of the *tanẓimat* on account of its alleged incompleteness, and indeed in his engagement with the semiotics of the Caliphate, the Aga Khan also voiced a contemporaneous caveat against a triumphalist narrative of reformism in modern Ottoman history and its larger cosmopolitan appeal.

These experiments with idioms of pluralism and postnationality can be further read at two correlated levels with significant consequences for the very idea of citizenship: first, one in which Aga Khan III sought to address the question of Indians in different parts of the British empire, and second, whereby he addressed his Ismaili and/or Muslim followers more directly. By pointing to the repercussions on the idea of citizenship I intend to draw attention in particular to his concern for a meticulous taxonomization, conceived of within the British imperial framework and systematizing different forms of Indian migration to the other British colonies. There is thus emphasis on differential forms of managing Indian migration to colonies such as South Africa, Canada and Australia depending on whether such Indians went for permanent settlement, for which he recommended 'ordinary rights of citizenship'. As distinct from this were the other forms of migrations:

> [T]ravellers for instruction and pleasure, the commercial representatives of large Indian houses, and such Indians belonging to the liberal professions as desire to make their home in these countries... the would-be emigrants who live on an economically low standard than that of the white man in the labour and lower middle-class markets.[55]

This taxonomization, then, had its roots in the crucible of the British colonial framework following in part the logic of colonial capital and market flows while bringing to the forefront questions of rights and entitlement in the context of emigration. Critically though, central to this argument of citizenship for emigrants of Indian origin was Aga Khan III's emphasis on India's historic connections to Africa, and the direction India can, consequently, give in that continent's progress.[56] The Aga Khan's idea of an Indian leadership in Africa betrays the lineaments of a more widespread phenomenon viz., to borrow Nile Green's words, an 'imperial Islamicate', signifying the emergence in Africa of a sphere in which Indians, especially Muslims, saw themselves as carriers of civilization and progress.[57] In correspondence of more private nature, he took care to balance his argument of loyalty in particular of his Ismaili followers to the Empire, especially in the War years, with an articulate denunciation of any idea that 'the white settlers have been the makers of East Africa, and are entitled in consequence to a dominating voice in the evolution of Kenya to a higher status ... [resulting in] no substantial advance in the political rights of Indians ...'[58] This, then, was part of a wider discourse of 'shared opportunities' that was thought to be one of the British Empire's enduring promises.[59]

Yet, one wonders if for the Aga Khan this meant any outright act of national chauvinism. The Aga Khan's idea of 'India' was, as the ongoing study illustrates, anything but rigid modular nation-state modelled on European lines. In his schema, an India conceptualized at the intersection of diverse cultural and civilizational forces, signifying in effect the core values of 'Asiatic' spirit, was also the epicentre and pivot of a loosely defined entity of the 'South Asiatic Federation'. As an experiment that challenged stringent notions of nation-state and territoriality, this becomes better intelligible in the light of the conceptual rubric of a postnational imagination. As illustrated in the course of this book, this also had significant implications for the community of the Ismailis aspiring an increasingly global cosmopolitan character.

The amalgam of the logic of the colonial dispensation and a transregional cultural order is what makes Aga Khan III's cosmopolitanism particularly intriguing. At one level, conditioned to a great extent by the internal dynamics of the historical matrix, this critical cosmopolitan venture reflects in effect the specificities of the context from which it emerges. The context was, one can barely forget, constrained by the limitations imposed by the colonial order. Thus, while Indian emigration to other parts of the Empire, ranging from Fiji to the Straits Settlement to Ceylon to Africa to Mauritius and the West Indies were all situated within the context of the British imperial framework, the emigration to Africa came to be especially seen as manifesting the 'hopes amongst instructed Indians' to lay the foundations of 'a daughter country on the other side of the Indian Ocean', a vision that subsequently came to be arrested by the imposition of 'restrictions and disabilities among the Indian communities' by the white colonists.[60] Indeed, Aga Khan III's invocation of a pre-colonial history and the idea of historic networks seen on a *longue durée* also provide a riposte to the hegemonic discourses surrounding ideas of borders and territories that, under the colonial order, redefined, selectively facilitated, or severely constricted the nature of Indian migrations.[61]

There is, thus, a critical element in Aga Khan III's thought about the Empire, but rooted nevertheless in the specificities of a colonial context. This predicament of Indians of having to engage with the colonial state even as critiquing its policies, as much in the subcontinental as in diasporic contexts, is also discernible in several other destinations of Indian emigration, such as the Malay world. While the Chinese migrants to Malaya 'maintained transnational connections outside the state' through its own range of 'diasporic social and economic institutions', Tamil emigration went on to create a new vocabulary of political subjecthood within the imperial framework.[62] What makes Aga Khan III's critique particularly interesting, though, is not only this knowledge of the constraints of colonial framework but also a steadfast belief in the possibilities of creating alternative spaces of communication, facilitating community development and activism. There is, therefore, a marked anxiety in the Aga Khan's thought to both conceptualize an imperial citizenship and also transcend the limitations imposed by the colonial order, somewhat akin to the Chinese endeavour in Malaya. For his Ismaili followers in particular, the latter meant efforts at creating religiously underpinned institutions that would condition the profile of an Ismaili community in both the subcontinent as well as in diasporic contexts within a spiritually defined

Muslim world. At another level, the invocation of idioms of older historic networks and transoceanic connections, in conjunction with recast idioms of civilizational order, had significant implications for the cultural identitarian experience of the Indian-origin Khoja Ismailis in the colonial western Indian Ocean world. Subsequently, this also facilitated introspections along the lines of cosmopolitan citizenship which, as we have seen following Andrew Linklater, exhorts individual citizens to engage with, and in fact extend, Kantian morality and ethical aspirations to create what Linklater calls 'universal frameworks of communication'.[63] Institutions formed under the Imamate of Aga Khan III would thus provide a blueprint for subsequent institutional articulation of the Imamate's idea of, first, connecting a global Ismaili ecumene, and graduating eventually into a still grander project of relating its notions of religious normativity with universal values of the Muslim world in general. In short, I should reiterate that the Ismaili case vindicates that ideas of universals are often conditioned in the specifics of historical matrices, intelligible with reference to the dynamics of a group's very own internal socio-religious and political issues. And they do so contrary to views that hinge on a rather slippery binarism of a 'good' universal cosmopolitanism versus 'narrow particularism'.[64]

A recent oeuvre points to another pertinent predicament: viz. in framing the debate in terms of 'a singular dominant abstract universalism versus multiple minor culturally rooted particularisms' we tend to ignore the 'different kinds of cosmopolitanism that exist outside the assimilationist versus pluralist dichotomy'.[65] It is this *appreciation* of cosmopolitanisms located at different planes that holds key to unpack what we generically call the other cosmopolitanisms. Kwame Anthony Appiah's compelling formulation of cosmopolitanism as a sentiment will be perhaps one of the most forceful notions in this cosmopolitan constellation. One might argue that it is this cosmopolitanism as a sentiment that 'celebrates the fact that there are different local human ways of being', that informed the Aga Khan's discursive frames of a pluralism at various levels, and also provided a promise for new cultural combinations.[66] In his aspirations for new cultural formations one sees efforts at penetrating increasingly terrains conventionally held by the nation-states, an aspect already incipient in the postnational imagination. In doing so, as chapter 5 further interrogates, Aga Khan III was in effect anticipating a language of cosmopolitanism that operates through the medium of global assemblages drawing upon both postnational and denationalizing forces.

To conclude this section though, I would like to reiterate one particular point that has surfaced in the present discussion. India was to be the 'pivot and centre' of a vast landmass 'consisting of a vast agglomeration of states, principalities and countries in Asia extending from Aden to Mesopotamia, from the two shores of the Gulf to India proper, from India proper across Burma and including the Malay peninsula' and stretching furthermore from 'Ceylon to the States of Bokhara, and from Tibet to

Singapore'.[67] However, we have noted that the India thus conceptualized was a diffused cultural/civilizational entity. With India at the core of the imagined 'South Asiatic Federation', the Aga Khan both foregrounded his preference for the decentralized model as well as managed to move beyond the standard idea of India as coterminous with the subcontinent, eliciting a much richer engagement with the Islamic world not envisaged in the Hindu imperialist imagination. However, the Aga Khan did so by taking recourse to his trademark language of cross-cultural engagements and deterritorialized religious landscapes, peppered with a rhetoric of trusteeship. These were then historical forces that he felt epitomized India, and rendered her uniquely suited to be the core of a pan-Asian universe.

Pan-Islamism and the quest for an Asiatic ethos: 'Spiritual force', reason and an ethical community

Pan-Islamism, or rather a specific version of it, thus formed one among several other overlapping ideational strands in Aga Khan III's pan-Asian imagination.[68] The pan-Islamism that the Aga Khan spoke of and subsequently developed was declaredly a spiritual-cultural quest that drew more upon vocabularies of ancient and historic connections, and of socio-cultural activism rather than political.[69] Religion, in this view, was more a 'spiritual force' than 'temporal'.[70] There was at the same time, one should reiterate, no privileging of one form of Islam over another. This resulted in the process, often in the face of stiff opposition, in a vigorous defence of mystic Islam: 'The strong mystic influence that permeates Moslem nations cannot be mistaken for any other spiritual force than that of the Koran'.[71] The celebration at once of the spiritual and cultural *topoi*, as opposed to the political, as well as the plurality of voices that it entailed, remained a central element in Aga Khan III's grand narrative of Islamic consciousness.

The following chapter explores in greater detail the political ramifications of his ecumenism. However, I would hasten to add here that it was, once again, this sensitivity to the spiritual and cultural *topoi* that formed the cornerstone of his speeches at the League of Nations in the 1930s, and underwrote his larger critique of nation-states and political boundaries. Perhaps more in his capacity as India's principal delegate than as the League's president, he underscored 'the intimate spiritual, cultural and economic relations' India shared with lands that formed the Kingdom of Iraq,[72] while upon the entry of Afghanistan into the League he noted it as an event that 'no representative of India, no Muslim, no Asiatic' could possibly overlook, and spoke at length of the 'glorious brotherhood of Islam' and the pride India takes in 'her Eastern blood, her Eastern languages, her Eastern cultures'.[73] The invocation of the rhetoric of the 'Asiatic' and of the 'Eastern' cultural *topos* with a particular emphasis on India within that cultural map has to be seen in the context of a language of Asiatic solidarity.

Influential sections within the Indian nationalist ranks, including the Aga Khan himself, however, had been also critical of the League of Nation's Euro-centrism. There had been a strong line of Indian criticism of the League of Nations for its alleged 'lack of universality, the incompleteness of its composition and the tiny representation of Indians in its organization', an argument that the Aga Khan too had to address in his speeches at the League of Nations' platform in Geneva.[74] Evidently, while on the one hand his vision of Asian solidarity subsumed a language of pan-Islamism, his internationalist imagination, on the other, was at the same time critical of the kind of restricted internationalism that the League of Nations championed. Thus, the League of Nations he envisioned was meant to be much more than a mere political platform: it was, above all, meant to be an international forum sensitized to larger cultural questions, both real and aspirational. The Indian disappointment for the League of Nations' failure to address these larger internationalist issues emanated from the deep fissures that underlay the very foundations on which India's relationship with the League of Nations stood. This shaky foundation, in turn, resulted from India's anomalous position within the League of Nations as the only non-self-governing member, albeit a founding one.[75] Using a scalar methodology, recent scholarship has shown how concepts of the 'national' and the 'international' operated at various scales even as India's burgeoning sense of nationhood started to define itself in the international context while international concerns in turn came to inform Indian national politics. However, thanks to India's colonial subjugation, this interplay between the national and the international spurred tensions in matters of governance that raised the fundamental question of sovereignty.[76] For Aga Khan III, however, the quest for an Asiatic spirit and pan-Islamism were in essence interlaced variations of his understanding of a certain cultural internationalism that he accused the League of Nations of overlooking. What he had in common with other nationalists in the colonial world was a critique of the League of Nation's Euro-centrism. Yet, distinctively though he would thence proceed to ground his thesis in a language of cultural/spiritual internationalism. More specifically, and especially in the context of the Islamicate world, his emphasis on a spiritual pan-Islamism was in effect a reification of the idea of an organic unity in Islam.

It will be a blinkered argument, though, to see the Aga Khan's thesis as an insular case. A significant line of this endeavour to figure out the organic bases of Islam was thus crucially important in a certain quest for its 'spirit' and its ethical manifestation. Islam's project for realizing practical morality, compatible with different stages of human progress, vis-à-vis European barbarism was thus a larger intellectual venture that defined, for instance, the core argument of Sir Ameer Ali's 1873 book *A Critical Examination of the Life and Teachings of Mohammed*. This 1873 volume formed the basis of his later seminal intervention, *The Spirit of Islam* (1891), a work whose subtitle changed in subsequent editions and, as we have noted in the previous chapter, so did some of its contents. The emphasis on the centrality of the life and teachings of Prophet Muhammad, as well as the quest for a certain spirit of rationalism as defining religion and propelling progress, have been traced to the influence of Syed Ameer Ali's teacher W. E. H. Lecky (1838–1903), and to the Hegelianism of D. F. Strauss (1808–74) and his major work *Life of Jesus* (1835).[77] It was at the hands of the likes of Sir Ameer Ali that 'Islam', originally an infrequent occurrence in the *Quran*, emerged as a proper noun denoting an entity and/or institution gradually outshining other competing categories such as *iman* (belief) and *mumin* (believer) and facilitating, in the process, its politicization in colonial India.[78] The increasing preference for 'Islam' – first introduced into European languages in the early nineteenth century – to the earlier category of the 'Muhammadan' by the Europeans reflected the Orientalist preoccupation with creating a bounded category of 'religion' like Christianity, and was part of a wider process of the making of world religions like 'Hinduism' and 'Buddhism'. At the same time, the appropriation of 'Islam' by those who now figured within this new-found religious discursive frame as a category oppositional to the 'West' was both a product of, and response to, European colonialism. Indeed, in his pursuit to recover a glorious history of Islam, Ameer Ali himself had a whole chapter dedicated to outlining Islam's 'political spirit' (Ameer Ali, *The Spirit of Islam* [1946 ed.], Chapter VII). The chapter celebrated Islam's constitutionalism leading to establishment of a 'Republic',[79] which could also well be read as a politico-cultural manifesto. Such sweeping historical outlines, however, were often subjected to criticism from contemporaries as well as later scholars. It has been thus noted that Ameer Ali's reconstructed Islam was far removed from the predominant views of *ulama* (theologians), a phenomenon that at once produced a chasm between the traditional and the English-educated elites and fomented a 'sterile narcissism'.[80]

The real significance of such interventions as Ameer Ali's, however, lay in the way such works provoked debates about alternative conceptual frameworks. What Ameer Ali did, moving well beyond the theme of 'political spirit', was to suggest a conceptual base of Islam, an alternative to the traditional understanding of Islam's 'five pillars'. A belief in the unity, power, mercy and supreme love of the Creator; charity and brotherhood; subjugation of the passions; outpouring of a grateful heart to the Giver of all good; and accountability for human actions in another existence formed the bases of this alternative model, an understanding that gestures at an ethical idea of the five pillars of the community rather than a ritualistic one.[81] The inclusion of chapters entitled 'The Apostolical Succession' and 'The Idealistic and Mystical Spirit in Islâm' in later editions of his *magnum opus*, moreover, furthered this project of reconceptualizing a wide encompassing ethical system. The chapter on 'Apostolical Succession', while bringing to the forefront an essentially Shia issue, offered a comparative study of the institutions of Imamate and the Caliphate. Proclaiming that the spiritual tie between the Imam, or the spiritual leader, and the community of believers 'binds the one to the other in the fealty to the Faith' Ameer Ali came up with an essentially personalized view of Islam. His schema underlined at once the absence of any 'priesthood' and, consequently, a 'direct communion' of individuals with God with the Imam functioning as a 'link between the individual worshipper and the evangel of Islâm', providing a 'mystical element' and accounting for the 'remarkable solidarity' of the religion.[82] The argument of centrality of the Imamate to the 'solidarity' of the Muslim ecumene was thus paired with a defence of the mystical strands in Islam, outlined in the chapter entitled 'The Idealistic and Mystical Spirit in Islâm', and echoed much of Aga Khan III's concerns. As we have seen, the Aga Khan saw the mystic in Islam as the *Quran*'s 'spiritual force'.[83] Syed Ameer Ali, likewise, noted:

> The idea among the nobler minds in the world of Islâm, that there is a deeper and more inward sense in the words of the Koran, arose not from the wish to escape from the rigour of "texts and dogmas", but from a profound conviction that these words mean more, or less, than the popular expounders supposed them to convey. This conviction, combined with a deep feeling of Divine pervasion,–a feeling originating from and in perfect accordance with the teachings of the Koran and the instructions of the Prophet, led to the development among the Moslems of that contemplative or idealistic philosophy which has received the name of Sûfism, and the spread of which, among the Mohammedans, was probably assisted by the prevalence of Neo-Platonic ideas.[84]

Evidently, therefore, the idea of Islam as a comprehensive spiritual system, emphasizing mystical experiences and encompassing inter alia spiritual and other notions of progress, had gained some ground by the early decades of the twentieth century in South Asia. These were also ideas that were increasingly employed to understand the very bases of the worldwide Muslim community. Sir Muhammad Iqbal (1877–1938), a contemporary of both Syed Ameer Ali and Aga Khan III, thus sought to recover the conceptual category of *millat*, originally used in the *Quran* to refer to a religious community, as the site to relocate nationhood, and providing in the process an alternative to a European model of nation-states and territorial nationalism.[85] This reformulated Islam became an 'empowering ethic', one that emulated a Nietzschean critique of passivity of religion (Christianity, in Friedrich Nietzsche's [1844–1900] particular case) while asserting a strong view of self-affirmation.[86] Indeed, as has been pointed out, 'In Iqbal, both Khûdî [selfhood] and pan-Islam consist of an oppositional stance combined with self-assertion'.[87] Iqbal showed a remarkable degree of historical insight in outlining first the western origins of the idea of 'pan-Islamism', a European discourse of legitimating aggression in the face of alleged Muslim conspiracies, and then

Jamal ad-Din al-Afghani's (1838–97) thesis of 'defensive measure'. But rather than a political project, by contrast, Iqbal saw pan-Islamism as an essentially social experiment cutting across lines of race or colour.[88] If *khudi* meant an unequivocal assertion of the self, its oppositional category *be-khudi* (roughly, selflessness) ensured the dissolution of the individual selves into the community, an 'organic totality' reminiscent of both the Hegelian *volksgeist* as well as strong Sufi influences.[89] However, notwithstanding the resonance of Sufi ideas and leitmotifs, Iqbal was at the same time critical of Sufism, which he accused of failing to 'provide an empowering intellectual, artistic and spiritual response to the modern age'; his was an exercise to tell 'true' Sufism from the 'false', and has been thus located by scholars squarely in the contested terrain of the twentieth century reformist project of neo-Sufism.[90]

The dynamics between the individual and community, the assertion of the self that formed a shared intellectual concern, albeit with variations,[91] was thus sensitized to both emotive (religio-cultural, across time and space) and rational (compatibility of Islam with 'modernism') aspects that in turn were closely connected to the experience of human progress. The consciousness that we have been discussing here is one that connects individuals to not only the collective but also to what they see as their cultural past(s), their own understanding of universals and specifics, through dialogic processes. This integrative experiential process involved furthermore a continuous cycle of learning, unlearning, identification and internalization – a cycle that in large parts of the colonized world often significantly redefined the very lineaments of authentic 'traditions' vis-à-vis later interpolations. Indeed, the aspirations for the authentic in the larger integrative process emerged as a key prop of socio-intellectual concern for generations of the colonized South Asians in general and, in particular, for all of these thinkers that we are presently discussing. The quest for pristine traditions as opposed to later accretions, at the same time, was also connected to the discourses of reform and revivalism which were, in turn, occasionally equally entangled. The unlearning of later unwarranted accretions and the celebration of pristine traditions, often contested, through institutional action, thus, became a key vehicle of the reformist and/ or revivalist projects. Symptomatic of the grand narrative of 'world religions', the striving for the pristine furthermore appealed to smaller denominations, such as the Ismailis, as well. Located at the intersection of the planes of hermeneutics and praxis the reformist and/ or revivalist endeavours sought to define along lines of organic unity what they saw as the true nature of community.

Such endeavours, furthermore, increasingly came to manifest themselves through the widening waves of ecumenism that characterized Muslim politics in late colonial South Asia. Sir Sayyid Ahmad Khan's Muhammadan Anglo-Oriental College, and later the Aligarh Muslim University, thus emerged as the vanguard reformist educational venture drawing also decisively upon languages of ecumenism along a cultural plane.

Moreover, the vocabularies of ecumenism, for all their limited success, still conjured up an alternative universe of pluralism in Islam in South Asia, and that too with remarkable internationalist aspirations drawing upon an idea of organic cohesion. Yet, neither this accommodative universalism was without its reservations, nor the argument of ecumenism in late colonial South Asia holds good in entirety. Iqbal, for one, saw in the Ahmadiyya Movement of Mirza Ghulam Ahmad (1835–1908) a critical threat to the very structure of Islam. Thanks to its perpetual expectation of the prophet, the Ahmadiyya Movement, according to Iqbal exposed the Islamic community to fragmentation. By contrast the Ismailis, Iqbal noted, did not raise the Aga Khan to the position of the prophet, and hence, was very much part of the Islamic ecumene he idealized.[92] The idioms of ecumenism thus went hand in hand with ideas and praxis of mainstreaming as well as marginalization.

However, it needs to be iterated that the cultural ecumenism drew extensively upon discourses of educational reformism and institutional activism. Consider, for instance, Iqbal's 1934 letter to Sir Ross Masood, Vice Chancellor of the Aligarh Muslim University which refers to a personal correspondence he had with the Aga Khan about reforming the Theology curriculum at the University:

> We have been teaching Theology on old lines with no results. Indeed our teaching has had no reforms, because we have not been doing the right thing. What is wanted is to rebuild our Theology much on the same way as Ghazali and others did in their own times. This is a matter which will largely determine *the future of Islam both in and outside India*. Special steps will have to be taken and special training will have to be given to those who may turn out to be *the future builders of Islamic religious thought*.[93]
>
> (Emphases mine)

The 'future of Islam', both in India and elsewhere, thus came to be directly related – if in somewhat programmatic vein – to educational reform within an institutional framework, which Sir Sayyid had originally intended to model on the lines of Cambridge. The nature of curricular overhaul and the religious consciousness that Iqbal had in mind can be gauged from his historic lectures at Aligarh University held about the same time, and compiled later along-with other lectures delivered at Madras and Hyderabad, in a volume called *The Reconstruction of Religious Thought in Islam*. Iqbal's was a philosophy of activism, one that exhorted to keep the door open for the individual's learned hermeneutics. Thus as he wrote in his lecture entitled 'The Human Ego— His Freedom and Immorality', '... it is surprising to see that the unity of human consciousness which constitutes the centre of human personality never really became a point of interest in the history of Muslim thought'.[94] This, according to him, elicited an independent approach to 'modern knowledge' and to 'appreciate the teachings of Islam in the light of that knowledge'.[95]

It should be reiterated, though, that the new Muslim intellectuals' stress on *ijtihad* (independent reasoning employed to interpret Islamic sources) in opposition to *taqlid* (acceptance of religious ruling coming from higher religious authorities) faced serious challenge from influential circles, such as by the likes of Husayn Ahmad Madani (1879–1957) and the traditional religious authorities.[96] Interestingly, however, as has been pointed out, Iqbal wrote neither a *tafsir* (exegesis) nor a *tarjuman* (interpretation) of the *Quran*.[97] His project of recovering an Islam divested of later influences and accretions both drew upon a set of idioms and operated within an ideational framework of reformism that bore traces of western lineages. Generations of Muslim thinkers, religious leaders, activists – from Sir Sayyid Ahmad Khan through Syed Ameer Ali to Allama Muhammad Iqbal to Aga Khan III, among others – thus defined the contours of what has been called an 'Islamic modernism' in late colonial South Asia drawing upon, as well as qualifying and customizing in crucial ways, a range of philosophical tools from the western repertoire, from British liberalism to neo-Hegelianism. For all the internal differences, variations and fluctuations in their thought, what they all postulated was not an unqualified idea of 'the rational, legal individual of high liberal thought, but the striving semi-divine self of the classical texts', in search for 'an ideal human community' for which 'standard modular nationalism was only a poor, materialistic apology'.[98]

Aga Khan III, in particular, was more direct in arguing for interpretive possibilities in Islam and taking it up at organizational level and at an international scale. Islam, thus, 'is the most rational, most social, of all faiths' and, the general stagnation in large parts of the Islamic world, could only be overcome through the 'task of reinterpreting Islam', however 'offensive and unpleasant it may be to the conservatives'.[99] Along with his Egyptian associate Zaki Ali,[100] he gradually went on to locate his project squarely within the larger schema of 'religious revival' in their jointly-authored book.[101] The programmatic manifesto laid down the contours of a conference of 'the various and numerous peoples of Islam', with delegations from Sunnis as well as the 'Shi'ite sects and sub-sects' to be held at the seat of al-Azhar, Cairo, the cultural and political hub of the Fatimid Caliphate.[102] Combining the internationalist ecumenical project with a glorification of the Fatimid Caliphate – in a tacit preference to the Abbasid – the authors emphasized the need to streamline Muslim law in the light of the contemporaneous 'spiritual and material needs'. After all, 'genuine Islam is in perfect agreement with reason'.[103] They defended their endeavour arguing that:

> according to the principle of *Ijma'* [consensus of the Muslim community, or of the *ulama*] ... the interpretation of the precepts and laws which

regulate the lives of the Faithful, as laid down in the Quran and the Traditions of the Prophet, can be done at any time and for any generation.[104]

Furthermore:

Such an interpretation, by means of the *Ijtihad* which is a personal and living research, can be made, *within the general limits of the Quran and Traditions*. The suppleness of Muslim Law enhances its value, and its broad lines leave room for vigorous growth and adaptation to the changing and unforeseeable circumstances of *international life* … It would be erroneous to assume that the door to interpretation has been shut, because the four leading juridical schools of Muslim orthodoxy had already decided, for all time, as to the prescriptions of Muslim Law. *Even with regard to these four schools (Hanafite, Shafi'ite, Malikite and Hanbalite), an individual is free to choose among them the rules to follow on different points; and to do that, he may not be obliged to strictly adhere to a single school.*[105]

(Emphases mine)

Note in particular the way the hermeneutic programme came to be connected to wider questions of contemporaneity, adaptability as well as internationalism. Also note the emphasis on the freedom of the 'individual' in her/his choice of 'the rules to follow on different points'. One might venture to imagine that this stress on the individual formed part of a wider discourse, one that had already started in the late nineteenth century, whereby the idea of *ijtihad* was gradually splayed out by reformers and theorists such as Sayyid Ahmad Khan, to accommodate the volition of all believers, and not merely that of a select echelon of *mujtahids*.[106]

The experiment, however, had to be carried out 'within the general limits of the *Quran* and Traditions', i.e., within a framework of given structures, invoking also a language of legality with significant interpretive possibilities for larger ethical questions. Indeed, scholars have emphasized the overarching importance of the normative framework of the *Quran* in Aga Khan III's thought, and have argued furthermore that he envisaged the widening of the scope of both classical interpretive approach in Ismailism (*tawil*) as well as a strictly reform-oriented *ijtihad*. This he did, it has been suggested, by conceiving *ijitihad* in line with the reformers of the *islah* (amendment/improvement), invoking a more 'operational and multifunctional concept which made it possible to take account of contemporaneity'.[107] Yet, this hermeneutic project was not without its checks-and-balances, and an emphatic effort to ensure that Islam does not fall prey to 'posterior deviations and infiltrations' in the name of informed volition.[108] The proposed conference, in its organized institutional form, was therefore expected to further 'doctrinal and moral purification' promoting 'moral education' involving, and bringing together, the Sunni and the Shia branches so that the Cairo congress would eventually become, in the absence of the Caliphate since its abolition in Turkey, 'a sort of permanent Muslim Assembly, a sort of Islamic League of Nations concerned with Muslim welfare in all domains'.[109] The model of the League of Nations, divested of its Euro-centrism and territorial nationalist paraphernalia, then, gradually emerged as a template for the Muslim world to figure out its own religio-cultural and ethical universals and specifics. This religious and cultural internationalism, thus, was meant to propagate a pan-Islamism along spiritual lines,[110] reminiscing Aga Khan III's early ruminations that we have already seen above in the course of this chapter.

A question of reception

Even as we have, so far, tried to trace the lineages of some key aspects of Aga Khan III's thought and continue to do so in the following chapters, it will be pertinent to pause for a while to see the nature of reception of his ideas in British administrative as well as other influential circles. This is an important question, given that the fate of liberalism in India in general and that of individuals such as the Ameer Alis and the Sayyid Ahmad Khans in particular have come to be reassessed in terms of the effective reception, or the lack of it, of their ideas.[111] Viewed in this light, one can say, that not all of Aga Khan III's pan-Asian and internationalist aspirations, as well as (arguably, self-declared) mediation between the 'East' and the 'West', was well received. At times, such arguments were accorded scant institutional recognition. My concern though is not so much to harp on the question of individual autonomy since the lack of it in the corridors of political power is quite natural, if not obvious, in a colonized society. Rather, my concern is to explore the nature of alternative possibilities both within and beyond European models, and the vocabularies invoked for their articulation. It is in this politico-intellectual and religio-cultural realm that we see much promise, mostly in the form of aspirations and programmatic claims.

The Aga Khan's nomination for a Nobel Prize twice in the 1920s went without further positive headway on both the occasions. Thanks partly to Aga Khan III's Persian background and cordial relations with the Iranian ruling elites in general, and the efforts of the official nominator Prince Samad Khan of Iran (also a Member of the International Court of Arbitration at The Hague), and not least backed by the resolution of the Upper Chamber of the Indian Legislature in particular, the Aga Khan's name was recommended to the Nobel Committee in Norway in 1924. The 'motivation' emphasized his contributions as an 'Asiatic' to the new process of transition that was supposedly redefining the relations between the West and the Asiatic world that reflected in the post-war peace efforts, and above all in the 'loyalty to the Empire'.[112] Furthermore, Samad Khan's nomination papers included extracts of a letter that he received from the Aga Khan stressing the services that he said he rendered to the cause of peace and preventing conflagrations between the West and Muslim Turkey in the post-World War I scenario.[113] In the interwar years, this language of peace and loyalty to the Empire bore great import.[114] These were years in which, as scholars have shown, internationalist and imperial humanitarian ideals in the aftermath of the World War I entered a complex relation. In the process, through much vicissitudes, conservative endeavours of Empire-wide humanitarian campaigns were gradually replaced by widening internationalist humanitarian activism. Yet, this was no linear shift.[115] In a way, therefore, the emergence of internationalist humanitarianism radiating from the imperial metropole was a complex historical process whereby a certain conservative imperial humanitarianism came to be systematically debated, negotiated and even appropriated by sections of the colonized societies. The case of the Aga Khan's nomination by a Persian prince shows the relevance of services in peace as well as post-war reconstruction efforts in general, and the Aga Khan's connections with other non-European (especially Persian) political elite circles in particular. That the nomination, once vetted and debated in India and Britain, brought up other contentious issues go on to debunk tall claims of a 'unanimously passed' decision made in the Memorandum on the Aga Khan's services. Perhaps not entirely unlike the crosscurrents that sought to circumscribe the Imam's position in the latter part of the nineteenth century, these instances point to the enduring nature of subterranean critiques in the ranks of the British administration. It thus puts to quandary any argument of Aga Khan III's easy relations with the British. For one, there had been serious suspicion in influential circles that the Aga Khan's name was suggested only to counter the nomination of M. K. Gandhi.[116] Furthermore, when the Aga Khan's name actually came up by way of nomination, the Government of India very discreetly distanced itself from the nomination stressing that it came from members of a Legislative Chamber, 'each of them individually qualified to propose a candidate... not a matter in which the Government of India could take part'.[117] Even this official position was, such confidential records show, an outcome of a manufactured consensus, and was not easy to arrive at.[118] The nomination was repeated in 1925, but in both cases went unevaluated by the Nobel Committee.

However, rather than looking at it as a history of slippages, I see this as primarily an exercise in self-fashioning on the part of Aga Khan III – a failed one, for that matter, as his declared aspirations went unrewarded. The crux however lies in the more abstract realm of concepts and vocabularies that characterized this exercise in self-fashioning. I underscore especially the rhetoric of world peace, religious and cultural amity, and cultural relations between the 'East' and the 'West'. These are all allusions of a larger internationalist agenda that constituted an abiding aspect of his thought. Although they did not cut a favourable image with the Nobel Committee, they still continued to define his position at such international platforms as the League of Nations in Geneva in the

1930s. A particular concern for me has been to also trace the genealogy of clusters of some of these ideas, for instance of his quest for an Asiatic ethos, spiritual pan-Islamism, and the postnational imagination, along different planes and in different spheres. We have already indicated, and will further see in greater detail, how they conditioned ideas about first a transregional and then a global Ismaili ecumene vis-à-vis the Muslim world, also defined along spiritual lines instead of any territorial nationalist vein. We also see how such languages were wedded to vocabularies of political ecumenism in the context of late colonial South Asia.

Conclusion

Idioms of self-affirmation, cultural pluralism and organic cohesion thus formed the props of Aga Khan III's spiritual pan-Islamism while the India he envisaged, or more appropriately an 'India in transition' as he said, symbolized the point of intersection of the predominant civilizational/cultural streams that he thought defined the course of human progress. His *India in Transition*, on the one hand, remained first and foremost a treatise on political as well as cultural pluralism, celebrating the idea of federalism. It profiled, moreover, an idea of cultural internationalism with a repositioned India in that map. This idea of pluralism along different axes constituted the bases of his postnational imagination, one that postulated the thesis of India as primarily a cultural/civilizational entity outside the ambit of Euro-centric discourse of territorial nationalism. In the Indian context, the theory of religious and cultural pluralism moreover also mirrored a discourse of secularism with South Asian specificities.

The idea of a spiritual brotherhood of Islam, on the other hand, drew extensively upon an argument of organic cohesion that had informed several key Muslim intellectuals and thinkers of the time. Variants of this thesis, albeit with internal differences, underscored inclusivism of one form or another with significant internationalist and cosmopolitan aspirations with their own contextual specificities. In this chapter we have charted out its cultural lineaments while in the following pages we shall engage with the political dimension that, in particular for Aga Khan III, was combined with a forceful defence of denominational (read Ismaili) specificities. This crucial balance between larger inclusive aspirations along political lines, and denominational particularism becomes intelligible against the backdrop of contending religious nationalisms in South Asia. As well, the discourse of spiritual pan-Islamism once again has to be seen as a trend that tended to move beyond the constricted remits of Euro-centric nationalisms at a broader international arena. Sceptics might be tempted to dub this as a theory of *via media* conditioned by a sense of expediency. However, I endeavour not be sceptical. Rather I intend to appreciate the authorial intent. The authorial intent for Aga Khan III, I suggest, can be problematized at two correlated levels; first, as living Imam of the global Ismaili community, and second as a leading political personality championing Muslim nationalist politics in colonial South Asia. In both cases, though, there were significant internationalist aspects. Besides, one need only reiterate, lineages of pluralism at different planes testify to the fact that the very salience of plurality almost necessarily rest on the precarious balance between the universal and the particular. In the course of this chapter, to summarize, we have attempted to take up some of these issues: exploring the modalities of different forms of identification, assessing the importance of specific vocabularies and relate them to larger intellectual and religio-cultural processes that conditioned the notion of a spiritual pan-Islamism. In the following chapter, we examine the complexities of the Aga Khan's ecumenical endeavour to mediate in South Asia's Muslim politics while also juxtaposing his endeavour to providing spiritual leadership to his Ismaili denomination.

Endnotes

1   His Highness the Aga Khan, *India in Transition: A Study in Political Evolution*, 156–57 (London: Philip Lee Warner, 1918).

2   Aga Khan III offered his military service to the reigning British monarch in the wake of the World War I (Ibid., vii ff).

3   This framework of international origins of anti-colonial resistance marks a compelling effort to reassess nationalist movements in different parts of the colonized world as part of a global history of ideas and activism. See, for a masterly work in this vein, Erez Manela, *The Wilsonian Moment: Self-Determination and the International Origins of Anticolonial Nationalism* (Oxford and New York: Oxford University Press, 2007).

4   Aga Khan, *India in Transition*, x. The argument of self-determination recurred in the course of the book in various contexts, in connection to self-determination of the Arabs in Mesopotamia and Syria; or, the suggestion for restructuration of Egyptian administration along such lines. See, ibid., 149–50, 154. Its specific implications in the Indian context form a major concern in our present study.

5   For a discussion on postnationalism, see Majeed, *Autobiography, Travel and Postnational Identity*, Introduction, especially 3–4. Cf. the Introduction to the present book, the present chapter and discussions that follow.

6   Ibid., 4.

7   The English edition of M. N. Roy's *India in Transition* came out in 1922 with a fictitious Swiss publisher's name, although it was printed in Berlin. For a brief history of this work and another related tract entitled *What Do We Want?*, also published in 1922, see G. D. Parikh's 'Foreword' to the 1971 edition of M. N. Roy, *India in Transition*, 5–12 (Bombay: Nachiketa Publications Limited, 1971).

8   The Aga Khan, *India in Transition*, 263. Women empowerment, it should be underlined, was a central and recurrent theme in the Aga Khan III's progressive model. For an overview, see Zayn R. Kassam, 'Gender Policies of Aga Khan III and Aga Khan IV', in *A Modern History of the Ismailis*, 247–64.

9   Roy, *India in Transition*, 223.

10 Ibid., 224.

11 Ibid., 224–25.

12 Ibid., 224.

13 Ibid., especially 205–10.

14 Ibid., 206.

15 Ibid., 207.

16 Benjamin Zachariah, *Developing India: An Intellectual and Social History, c. 1930-50*, (New Delhi: Oxford University Press, 2012 ed. [2005]), especially the Preface outlines an array of cognate ideas that coalesce together to produce certain 'developmental imagination', as opposed to a statist 'developmentalism'.

17 According to the principle of weightage, 'effective' representations of minorities in councils and legislatures depended not only on their numerical realities but also non-numerical factors such as historical importance of such minorities. See Faisal Devji, *Muslim Zion: Pakistan as a Political Idea*, 68 ff (Cambridge, MA: Harvard University Press, 2013).

18 Aga Khan, *India in Transition*, 13 and 161.

19 Ibid., 24.

20 Ibid., 23, 24.

21 Soumen Mukherjee, 'Being "Ismaili" and "Muslim": Some Observations on the Politico-Religious Career of Aga Khan III', *South Asia: Journal of South Asian Studies*, 34, 2 (2011): 188–207.

22 The Joint Memorandum by the Aga Khan and Gokhale in Correspondence between Freeman Thomas, Marquess of Willingdon and Lord Crewe, 7 March 1915, the Crewe Papers, C.53.1.122, Cambridge University Library, Manuscripts and Archives. Part of the inspiration for the federal model, the Aga Khan claimed, derived from a German connection. Recalling one of his meetings with Herbert von Bismarck (1849–1904), son of the Wilhelmine Reich's chief architect, the Aga Khan went on to narrate how Otto von Bismarck (1815–98) admired the concept of a federal structure. It proposed a structure of independent parliamentary units that the Aga Khan felt, unlike the British or the French, perfectly suited the German case because the German Empire by its very nature was no 'compact geographical unit' but 'a long and scattered dominion', Aga Khan, *India in Transition*, 34. See Sevea, *The Political Philosophy of Muhammad Iqbal*, 192 for the Aga's preoccupation with the German model amid a general fad for confederacies in the early decades of the twentieth century.

23 For instance, in the princely states, the notion promised an idea of full autonomy. Thus for Mokshagundam Visvesvaraya (1860–1962), erstwhile Diwan of Mysore, only a federal system that allows the 'Indian States' (princely states) to have 'a voice adequate to protect their interests and they, as well as the provinces, possess full autonomy' can facilitate the consummation of the 1919 administrative reforms. Mokshagundam Visvesvaraya, *Reconstructing India*, 43 (London: P.S. King & Son Ltd., 1920). For a historical study of local self-government focusing on the case of Madras, see Dharampal, *The Madras Panchayat*

System, Vol II: A General Assessment (Delhi: Impex India, 1972). See the Introduction for specific reference to the Royal Decentralisation Commission (1907) and the administrative experiments of the 1910s and 1920s. For a succinct account of engagements with the federal model and the question of representation by colonial officials such as Herbert Risley (1851–1911) as well as nationalists such as G.K. Gokhale, see Dietmar Rothermund, 'Emancipation or Re-integration' in Idem, *The Phases of Indian Nationalism and Other Essays*, 26–56, esp. 49 ff. (Bombay: Nachiketa Publications Limited, 1970).

24 Sample the titles of the chapters: Chapter XXII: Education for the Masses; Chapter XXIV: Public Health; Chapter XXV: The Depressed Classes; Chapter XXVI: The Status of Women; Chapter XXIX: The Limits of British Trusteeship; Chapter XXXI: Co-ordinated Progress.

25 Carey A. Watt, 'Philanthropy and Civilizing Missions in India c. 1820-1960: States, NGOs and Development' in *Civilizing Missions in Colonial and Postcolonial South Asia: From Improvement to Development*, edited by Carey A. Watt and Michael Mann, 271–316, at 282 (London, New York and Delhi: Anthem, 2012 [2011]) points to the centrality of Herbert Spencer's (1820–1903) notions of social efficiency in 'an Indian movement for "national efficiency" that echoed the concerns of the national efficiency campaign in Britain'.

26 Aga Khan, *India in Transition*, 87.

27 Ibid., 87.

28 This discourse of 'community development' was systematically worked out by Darling over the decades, leading him to note in 1935, after a visit to Tagore-inspired Bratachari Movement in Bengal: 'I am becoming more and more convinced that it is to the village schoolmaster that we must look for improvement in the conditions'. The speech came out in *The Statesman* (25 February 1935). See Item 25, Box I, the Malcolm Darling (hereafter MD) Papers, Centre of South Asian Studies, University of Cambridge (hereafter CSASUC). The esteem in which Darling's version of 'community development' and village improvement was held can be gauged from the fact that even after independence and the Partition, he was invited by the Pakistan Government to contribute towards policy-making in 'Village Agricultural and Industrial Development Programme'. See Darling's Pakistan Report, Item 41, Box XII, the MD Papers, CSASUC. Also see the comments of Sir Gilbert Wiles in late 1930s. Wiles started his career as Assistant Collector and Magistrate of Bombay in 1904, and eventually rose to the position of Chief Secretary to the Government of Bombay by 1938. On a visit to a village in 1937–38 (name not mentioned) to deliver a congratulatory speech on that village's winning the Sykes Village Improvement Shield of 1937, Wiles noted that the 'Government regard Village Improvement work as only next in importance to war ...' See Item 7.6.3, Box I, the Wiles Papers, CSASUC.

29 Thus much like Darling's exhortation to look towards the 'village schoolmaster', central to the Aga Khan's developmental framework too was an unambiguous emphasis on 'universal and improved education'. For Visvesvaraya, moreover, the federal structure had to be replicated at various levels, including that of education, linking up organically the various tiers of such administration, from the village/towns to the provincial levels and giving due weight to both primary-secondary-university education and vocational training; see Visvesvaraya, *Reconstructing India*, 261–69.

30 For all the similarities with the Russian case on the surface, the Darling approach was nevertheless inherently different. Thus the co-operative movement he elaborated on was meant to become 'no mean barrier to Communism', Item 28 (?), n.d., Box I, the MD Papers,

CSASUC. Personnel of the Oxford University Press (OUP) also seem to share the same containing 'the communist "approach"' viewpoint. Letter of R. Goffin (of the Warehouse and Trade Department, OUP) to Sir M. L. Darling, 17 October 1949, Item 42, Box, I, the MD Papers, CSASUC. Zachariah, *Developing India*, 123, however, suggests that Darling was impressed by the Soviet achievements and, indeed, thought in the wake of the wartime alliance with the Soviet Union that some of the 'diverse ideas' relating to the 'education of the peasant' and 'collectivization' (as a tool to facilitate 'economic rather than political democracy') could be 'adapted and incorporated into the imperial vision' and applied to India. Cf. ibid. 106 for Darling's views on progress in education in general in Russia that he thought could be emulated in India. For a useful discussion of the genealogies of Darling's ideas on rural development and peasantry, see ibid. 119 ff. One can still argue though, as we suggest, that Darling's quest for the model co-operative, especially in the post-World War II era, did not necessarily remain restricted to the Soviet example.

31 This is testified to by his interest in the yearly activities of the Verband Schweizerischer Darlehnskassen, or popularly called the Raiffeisen movement, founded in Switzerland in 1899; see, e.g., his notes on the 1947 yearly report: Item 41 (?), Box I, the MD Papers, CSASUC. Darling went on to visit their headquarters in St. Gallen in 1949. See the Recommendation for Sir M.L. Darling by the office authorities, St. Gallen, Item 41, Box I, the MD Papers, CSASUC. For his conversation with John M. Keynes on the questions of state-supported co-operations and state initiatives to raise funds for village reconstruction see Darling's notes of an interview with Keynes, held on 8 February 1934, in Item 28.7.1, Box 1, MD Papers, CSASUC.

32 Aga Khan, *India in Transition*, 194.

33 Item 21, Box XII, the MD Papers, CSASUC

34 See Ranajit Guha, 'Discipline and Mobilize', in *Subaltern Studies, Volume VII: Writings on South Asian History and Society*, edited by Partha Chatterjee and Gyanendra Pandey, 69–120 (New Delhi: Oxford University Press, 2003 ed.).

35 Watt, 'Philanthropy and Civilizing Missions', 284.

36 Aga Khan, *India in Transition*, 233 ff.

37 Ibid., 200.

38 The classic 'drain theory' owes its origin to the works of Dadabhai Naoroji, *Poverty and Un-British Rule in India* (1901) and R.C. Dutt, *The Economic History of India*, in two volumes (1906). Such arguments received support from sections of British thinkers and humanitarians as well, e.g., William Digby, *'Prosperous' British India. A Revelation from Official Records* (London: Unwin, 1901).

39 Budget speeches in the Council of the Governor General, dated 25 March 1903, Calcutta, and 30 March 1904, Calcutta, in *Aga Khan III: Selected Speeches and Writings of Sir Sultan Muhammad Shah, Vol. I, 1902-1928*, edited by K. K. Aziz, 216–32 (London and New York: Routledge, 1998 ed.).

40 The Aga Khan, *India in Transition*, 276.

41 Ibid., 279.

42 Ibid., 281–82.

43 Ibid., 283.

44 See Carolien Stolte and Harald Fischer-Tiné, 'Imagining Asia in India: Nationalism and Internationalism (ca. 1905–1940)', *Comparative Studies in Society and History*, 54, 1 (2012): 65–92; especially 72 ff.

45 Aga Khan, *India in Transition*, chapter I; especially 2; 2–7.

46 Ibid., 6.

47 Ibid., 7.

48 Ibid., 9 ff. The Aga Khan's engagement with this idea of India, thus, can be seen as part of a dynamic historical process in which the 'region', understood as an area of interaction evolving out of evolutionary processes, and 'regionalization', understood as an ideologically-propelled political process that carve out regions, both intersect. For elaborations on these two distinct concepts see, Prasenjit Duara, 'Asia Redux: Conceptualizing a Region for Our Times', *The Journal of Asian Studies* 69, 4 (2010): 963–83.

49 Aga Khan, *India in Transition*, 10–11.

50 Devji, *Muslim Zion*, 74.

51 However, Islam and 'Islamism', in the Calcutta-based Greater India Society's version, smacked of unmistakable foreign traits, that ensured the total downfall of 'the great Hindu colonies of Champa and Cambodge', a force that 'swept over the whole area like a hurricane'. Kalidas Nag, *Greater India (Greater India Society Bulletin No. 1)*, 42 (Calcutta: Greater India Society, 1926), Cf. Stolte and Fischer-Tiné, 'Imagining Asia in India'. Also see, for an overview, Susan Bayly, 'Imaging "Greater India": French and Indian Visions of Colonialism in the Indic Mode', *Modern Asian Studies* 38, 3 (2004):, 703–44.

52 Aga Khan, *India in Transition*, 157.

53 Ibid., 296.

54 Seema Alavi, *Muslim Cosmopolitanism in the Age of Empire*, 6 (Cambridge, MA: Harvard University Press, 2015).

55 Aga Khan III, *India in Transition*, 131–32.

56 The Indians in general and the Muslims and Ismailis in particular were, moreover, urged to propel civilizational progress in the colonies of East Africa and make it their home. Indeed, Chapter XIII in the Aga Khan's *India in Transition*, as though celebrating this civilizational metanarrative, is entitled 'India's Claim to East Africa'. Moreover, such cosmopolitanism – resting as it did on an abiding interest in transregional and international issues and in discourses of India's historic connections straddling the western Indian Ocean – brings to sharp relief the distinctiveness of the Ismaili case in general, and that of Aga Khan III in particular. A contrastive picture emerges in Robert J. Blyth, *The Empire of the Raj: India, Eastern Africa and the Middle East, 1858-1947*, 7 (Basingstoke and New York: Palgrave Macmillan, 2003) when Blyth points to the marginal nature of external affairs, vis-à-vis domestic factors, in the policies of the Indian National Congress which did not establish a separate foreign department until 1936.

57 Nile Green, 'Africa in Indian Ink: Urdu Articulations of Indian settlement in East Africa', *Journal of African History*, 53, 2 (2012): 131–50. For a comparison of the Aga Khan's advocacy of Indian settlement in, and even colonization of, East Africa, the global role of the South Asiatic Federation he conceptualized, and his ideas on early Zionism in which he suggested a Jewish homeland within the Ottoman Empire, see Devji, *Muslim Zion*, 75 ff.

58 See letter dated 3 May 1923 from Aga Khan (London) to Lord Peel, IOR, Public Office Records, 'Files on Political and Constitutional Development, Imperial Conferences (from 1934) and Ecclesiastical Matters: 1916- 1947', L/PO/1/6.

59 Metcalf, *Imperial Connections*, 2, 183 f.

60 Aga Khan III, *India in Transition*, 115, 116.

61 Cf. Sunil S. Amrith, *Migration and Diaspora in Modern Asia*, 1 (Cambridge and New York: Cambridge University Press, 2011), which points out in more general terms, the relevance to explore earlier routes and networks: 'Borders did not pre-date mobility. Many of the routes that Asian migrants followed in the age of mass migration built on much older traditions of circulation …'

62 Sunil Amrith, 'Indians Overseas? Governing Tamil Migration to Malaya, 1870-1941', *Past and Present*, 208, 1 (2010): 231–61, at 243.

63 Linklater, 'Cosmopolitan Citizenship', 24; cf. the introduction to this book.

64 Martha Nussbaum drew upon the Kantian model of cosmopolitanism to overcome 'bad' particularisms while Hilary Putnam, in her rejoinder, suggested the co-existence of multiple particularist traditions open to critiques. See Martha Nussbaum, 'Patriotism and Cosmopolitanism' and Hilary Putnam, 'Must We Choose Between Patriotism and Universal Reason?', in *For Love of Country: Debating the Limits of Patriotism. Martha C. Nussbaum with Respondents*, edited by Joshua Cohen, 2–17; 91–97 respectively (Boston: Beacon Press, 1996).

65 Kris Manjapra, 'Introduction' to *Cosmopolitan Thought Zones*, edited by S. Bose and K. Manjapra, 3.

66 Kwame Anthony Appiah, 'Cosmopolitan Patriots', in *For Love of Country*, edited by Joshua Cohen, 25; for discussions on cosmopolitanism as sentiment, see 23 ff.

67 Aga Khan, *India in Transition*, 13

68 However, the relationship between pan-Islamism and pan-Asian imaginations, in a more general context, was complicated further by the fact that for the better part of the first half of the twentieth century large sections of Muslims in Asia saw Japan, with its ever so vigorous pan-Asian aspirations, as the saviour of Muslim interests in the Islamic world in the face of western aggressions. For an instructive study, see Selçuk Esenbel, 'Japan's Global Claim to Asia and the World of Islam: Transnational Nationalism and World Power, 1900-1945', *The American Historical Review*, 109, 4 (2004): 1140–70.

69 Aga Khan, *India in Transition*, Chapter XVI ('Islamic and Turanian Movements') is one of his earliest comprehensive manifestos valorizing this spiritual-cultural project while documenting, at the same time, the failure of political pan-Islamism .

70 Ibid., 158

71 Ibid., 6: Indeed, mysticism had always been accorded, and it still does, a degree of respect in Ismaili thought. Such ideas are also reflected in curricular materials meant specifically for Ismaili children and the youth, both in contemporaneous and subsequent times. E.g., testifying to the enduring relevance of Aga Khan III's assertion, Abualy A. Aziz, *A Brief History of Ismailism* (Dar es Salam, 1974), a later work 'highly recommended to high school students by the Ismaili Association for Tanzania' as claimed in the title page, 144 ff. traces Islamic mysticism to the ascension of the Prophet and the meditative exercises of Imam Ali.

72 The Aga Khan's Speech in the Assembly of the League of Nations, Geneva, 1932, in the Verbatim Record of the Thirteenth Ordinary Session of the Assembly of the League of Nations (1932), Third Plenary Meeting, 5, The League of Nations (LON) Archives, The United Nations Archives, Geneva (UNAG).

73 The Aga Khan's Speech, Assembly of the League of Nations, Geneva, 1934, in the League of Nations Official Journal, Special Supplement No. 125, Records of the Fifteenth Ordinary Session of the Assembly Meetings, Twelfth Plenary Meeting (1934), 75, LON Archives, UNAG.

74 See The Aga Khan's Speech, Assembly of the League of Nations, Geneva, 1935, in the League of Nations Official Journal, Special Supplement No. 138, Records of the Sixteenth Ordinary Session of the Assembly Meetings, Sixth Plenary Meeting (1935), 66, LON Archives, UNAG. In his 1936 speech he would point to the lack of the League of Nations' flexibility and universality urging to adjust its constitution to the 'changing needs' of the time. See the Verbatim Record of the Seventeenth Ordinary Session of the Assembly of the League of Nations (1936), Tenth Plenary Meeting, 5, LON Archives, UNAG.

75 Manela, *The Wilsonian Moment*, xi, 10–11, thus points to the anxieties of the British administration over the admission of India as one of its founding members, even as nationalist leaders rejoiced in hope. Later, sheer political astuteness urged some, such as David Lloyd George (1863–1945), to discover the gravity of what they had promised by invoking the rhetoric of self-determination in a fit of wartime generosity to muster colonial support in the war efforts. This eventually led him to add a note of qualification to his memoirs specifying a limited applicability of the doctrine, pertaining 'only to Europe and the non-Turkish portions of the Ottoman Empire' (Ibid., 39). Aga Khan, *India in Transition*, 278 too had to remind his readers of Lloyd George's wartime promise adding that the 'British public' had been privy to it.

76 Stephen Legg, 'An International Anomaly? Sovereignty, the League of Nations and India's Princely Geographies', *Journal of Historical Geography*, 43 (2014): 96–110.

77 Peter Hardy, *The Muslims of British India*, 107 (Cambridge and New Delhi: Cambridge University Press, 1998 [1972]).

78 Devji, *Muslim Zion*, 203. Cf. Wilfred Cantwell Smith, 'The Historical Development in Islam of the Concept of Islam as an Historical Development' in Id. *On Understanding Islam: Selected Studies*, 41–77 (The Hague: Mouton Publishers, 1981).

79 See Sevea, *The Political Philosophy of Muhammad Iqbal*, 134.

80 See Hardy, *The Muslims of British India*, 107.

81 See Devji, *Muslim Zion*, 202–03.

82 Syed Ameer Ali, *The Spirit of Islam*, 125 (1946 ed.). Cf. the emphasis, in a text meant essentially for a western audience, on the absence of mediators between man and God and a resultant free agency of man to both act or not to act, in Prince Aga Khan and Zaki Ali, *Glimpses of Islam*, 7 and 9 (Lahore: Sh. Muhammad Ashraf, 1954? [1944]). The 'Islamic principle' is thus defined as 'monorealism rather than monotheism', a point further developed in his memoirs (Ibid., 5), Cf. the epigraph in the 'Concluding Reflections' of the present book.

83 See above, especially n. 71 in the present chapter.

84 Syed Ameer Ali, *The Spirit of Islam*, 456 (1946 ed.).

85 Sevea, *The Political Philosophy of Muhammad Iqbal*, 147 ff. Cf. the re-invigorated interest in the early twentieth century in classical Islamic scholarship to understand the locus of nationality. On the role of Maulana Muhammad Yunus (d. 1923) of the Farangi Mahal in the valorization of Arab tribal formations, morality, and Ibn Khaldun's (1332–1406) notion of *asabiyya* (group solidarity), see Francis Robinson, *The 'Ulama of Farangi Mahall and Islamic Culture in South Asia*, 139 (New Delhi: Permanent Black, 2012 [2001]).

86 Sevea, *The Political Philosophy of Muhammad Iqbal*, especially 102 ff.

87 Javed Majeed, *Muhammad Iqbal: Islam, Aesthetics and Postcolonialism*, 58 (London and New Delhi: Routledge, 2009). For discussions on the interplay between the forces of selfhood and community consciousness as well as pan-Islamism, see especially his chapters 3 and 4.

88 Majeed, *Muhammad Iqbal*, 58–59.

89 G. W. F. Hegel's (1770–1831) *volksgeist* or 'spirit of the people' postulated that 'nothing in a specific human culture can be understood in isolation', so that religion, politics, art etc. everything symbolizes various facets of that spirit, effecting an organic unity. Sevea, *The Political Philosophy of Muhammad Iqbal*, 150.

90 Sevea, *The Political Philosophy of Muhammad Iqbal*, 106 ff.

91 The variations and differences must not be overlooked. Iqbal, as we have noted, was heavily influenced by Friedrich Nietzsche. Not Aga Khan III, though. For the Aga Khan, Nietzsche represented the face of German militarism culminating in Fascism. See Aga Khan, *India in Transition*, 104. Cf. his speech on 'Jinnah and the Making of Pakistan', in *Aga Khan III: Selected Speeches and Writings of Sir Sultan Muhammad Shah, Vol. II: 1928–1955*, edited by K. K. Aziz, 1397 (London and New York: Routledge, 1997 ed.).

92 Sevea, *The Political Philosophy of Muhammad Iqbal*, 121 ff.; 149.

93 Letter from Sir Muhammad Iqbal to Sir Ross Masood, dated 5 March 1935, cited in K. A. Nizami, *History of the Aligarh Muslim University, Vol. 1, 1920-1945*, 179–80 (Delhi: Idara-i Adabiyat-i Delli, 1995). Cf. how Mushirul Hasan, *Legacy of a Divided Nation: India's Muslims since Independence*, 37 (New Delhi: Oxford University Press, 2012 [1997]), draws upon the works of J. L. Nehru and M. N. Roy to suggest a gradual erosion of the high academic standards in Aligarh after the disappearance of its towering 'First Generation'.

94 Mohammad Iqbal, *The Reconstruction of Religious Thought in Islam*, 95–96 (Lahore: Shaikh Muhammad Ashraf, 1960 [1930]).

95 Ibid., 97.

96 However, the defence of *ijtihad* and the rejection of *taqlid* had been a pivotal concern in the reformist endeavours since the eighteenth century, represented by the likes of Shah Wali Allah (1702–62) and Muhammad al-Shawkani (1760–1834), culminating in the Ahl i Hadith movement in colonial South Asia. See Brown, *Rethinking Tradition*, 22 ff. for a succinct treatment. Among the Shia in colonial South Asia, the *mujtahids* (those qualified to perform *ijtihad*) were especially powerful, thanks in particular to the victory of the Usulis over the Akhbaris in the eighteenth century in both West as well as South Asia. In colonial South Asia, their power rested on their public engagements and contributions, and not merely on their scholarship. See Justin Jones, *Sh'ia Islam in Colonial India: Religion,*

Community and Sectarianism (Cambridge and New York: Cambridge University Press, 2012); cf. Francis Robinson, 'Strategies of Authority in Muslim South Asia in the 19th and 20th Centuries' in *Muslim Voices: Community and the Self in South Asia*, edited by Usha Sanyal, David Gilmartin and Sandria B. Freitag , 16–36, at 22–23 (New Delhi: Yoda Press, 2013).

97 Sevea, *The Political Philosophy of Muhammad Iqbal*, 88 ff.

98 Bayly, *Recovering Liberties*, 320–21. It may be noted in this connection that it will be an act of oversimplification to see a linear development of Muslim 'separatism' from an unproblematized minority politics. Thus, Farzana Shaikh, *Community and Consensus in Islam: Muslim Representation in Colonial India, 1860-1947* (Cambridge: Cambridge University Press, 1989) points to the relevance of religious and political authority within the framework of Islamic tradition and its continuous tension with liberal-democratic tradition conditioning, in the process, the nature of Indian Muslim politics in especially the late colonial phase.

99 Aga Khan III's 'Presidential Address to the All India Muhammadan Educational Conference, Rampur, 21 February 1936', in *Aga Khan III, Vol. II*, edited by Aziz, 1117.

100 Zaki Ali had connections with Al-Azhar and enjoyed much confidence of Aga Khan III. Together they wrote another volume, in French, entitled *L'Europe et l'islam* (Genève-Anemasse: Editions du Mont-Blanc, 1945). Personal correspondence with Michel Boivin.

101 Aga Khan and Zaki Ali, *Glimpses of Islam*, 'Chapter III: Religious Revival in Islam'.

102 Ibid., 64.

103 Ibid., 70.

104 Ibid., 65.

105 Ibid., 65–66.

106 Ayesha Jalal, *Partisans of Allah: Jihad in South Asia*, 160 (Cambridge, MA. and London: Harvard University Press, 2008).

107 See Michel Boivin, 'The Reform of Islam in Ismaili Shī'ism from 1885 to 1957' in *Confluence of Cultures: French Contributions to Indo-Persian Studies*, edited by Françoise Delvoye, 197–216, at 206, translated by Rashmi Patni (Delhi: Manohar, 1994).

108 Aga Khan and Zaki Ali, *Glimpses of Islam*, 66.

109 Ibid., 66–67, 69.

110 Ibid., 73.

111 Bayly, *Recovering Liberties* broadly charts out the many lives of liberalism in colonial India. Faisal Devji, 'Apologetic Modernity' in *Modern Intellectual History*, 4, 1 (2007): 61–76 points to the lack of autonomy of the Muslim modernists such as Sayyid Ahmad Khan, a status that precisely gave them the luxury to engage in their modernist ventures. Similarly Martin Forward, 'Syed Ameer Ali: A bridge-builder?', *Islam and Christian-Muslim Relations*, 6, 1 (1995): 45–62 questions if Ameer Ali could, at all, be seen as someone sufficiently qualified to be able to function effectively as an interpreter of Islam between 'East and West'.

112 See 'Memorandum on the Services of H. H. the Aga Khan to the Cause of International Peace' in Papers related to the Nomination of Aga Khan III, Year 1924, No. 2-1, The

Norwegian Nobel Institute (hereafter NNI). Cf. Aga Khan's 1914 speech at a meeting of the Indian Volunteers Committee in London urging Indians to join the Empire's war efforts amid 'India's and the Empire's difficulties'. See *The Times* (2 October 1914), in *Aga Khan III, Volume I*, edited by Aziz, 505–09, at 506.

113 See Samad Khan's letter to Baron Wedel Jarslberg, dated 27 January 1924, and mentioned attachments in Papers related to the Nomination of Aga Khan III, Year 1924, No. 2-1, NNI.

114 The Germans' perceptions and propaganda of the Muslims in South Asia on the eve of, as well as during the war years, as 'leaders of revolution in India' did not help the Muslims cut a peaceable image with the British. However, such a perception represented a grossly-oversimplified idea about Muslims stretching from West Asia to India who the Germans, thanks to their Orientalist idée fixe, expected to pit against the British and succeed. See Kris Manjapra, 'The Illusions of Encounter: Muslim "Minds" and Hindu Revolutionaries in First World War Germany and After', *Journal of Global History*, 1, 3 (2006): 363–82, especially at 374.

115 See, for instance, Emily Baughan, 'The Imperial War Relief Fund and the All British Appeal: Commonwealth, Conflict and Conservatism within the British Humanitarian Movement, 1920-1925', *Journal of Imperial and Commonwealth History*, 40, 5 (2012): 845–61. Baughan suggests that for all their internationalist claims, the widening humanitarian venture of the Save the Children Fund still had to appropriate the imperial rhetoric ('efforts of the dominions and mother country') of the Imperial War Relief Fund, which they sought to displace.

116 Summary of the proceeding of the Council of the State, 8 February 1924, in Papers related to the Nomination of Aga Khan III, Year 1924, No. 2-1, NNI.

117 Letter of J.P. Thompson, Secretary to the Government of India in Foreign and Political Department to the Secretary of the Nobel Committee, dated 11 April 1924, in Papers related to the Nomination of Aga Khan III, Year 1924, No. 2-1, NNI.

118 The Aga Khan figures in the confidential correspondence of the time as a political opportunist ('always anxious to be in the limelight on the side which he thinks is going to win'), dangerously cut-off from his own Muslim fraternity ('he cd. [could] only speak to them [the Muslim troops] through an interpreter and they laughed at him'), busy with his private affairs in the Continent ('concerned mostly with his pleasures, and the sale in Switzerland of his German securities'), and maintaining relations with the 'Indian anarchists'. See IOR, Political and Secret Department Records, 'Papers relating to the recommendation of the Aga Khan for the Nobel Peace Prize, 1924', 1924, L/ PS/ 10/ 588, File 748/ 1916, Pt. 1-date: 1915–25.

4

The Hazir Imam, Ismailism and Islam in Late Colonial South Asia

The example of the Prophet and of Abu Bakr and Omar and Ali should convince these pious people that the first duty of a Moslem is to give his time to the service of nation and not merely to silent prayers.[1]

His Highness Aga Khan III, 1902

The choice of the historical examples cited above is redolent of at least two crucial aspects that defined Muslim history in late colonial South Asia. First, it is reflective in general of the much persuasive rhetoric of an Islamic activism embedded in an Islamic normativity that marked a process of a gradual shift from 'other-worldly' to 'this-worldly' piety. In the process it emphasized the importance of self-affirmation and development of self-consciousness that characterized the history of Islam in South Asia and large parts of the Muslim world in the nineteenth and twentieth centuries.[2] Second, the invocation of the key Sunni figures by the spiritual head of a Shia denomination symptomizes a complex, and somewhat strategically syncretistic, ecumenical venture in late colonial South Asia within the framework of an inclusive Muslim 'nation'. The gradual shift from a certain other-worldly to this-worldly religious experience, as Francis Robinson illustrates, rested upon four conceptual planks: self-instrumentality, self-affirmation, affirmation of ordinary life and a certain inward-turn accompanied by a growth of self-consciousness and reflexivity. In the previous chapter, we have merely gestured at the relevance of these four intertwined themes in Muslim life in the late colonial times with a particular reference to the assertion of human intellect and interpretive possibilities. In this chapter, however, we draw upon the case study of Aga Khan III and discuss one specific aspect of Muslim life in colonial South Asia, viz., the conceptualization of the community in political terms of a 'minority', even as different sectarian and denominational formations sought to reposition themselves within that wider rubric. In doing so we elaborate on the creative possibilities, which both defined and signified the gradual shift towards a 'this-worldly' Islam.

The thematic concerns that propelled the shift towards a this-worldly experience were activated through an invocation of select historical examples, and informed both the ecumenical endeavour as well as the interdenominational dialogues. Thus, the politics of ecumenism, crossconfessional exchanges and 'minority' were closely entwined. This entwinement had bearing on not only South Asia's contending religious nationalist politics in general, but also for the Muslim nationalist politics in particular, given the unmistakable signs of misgivings on the part of a large section of the Shia leaders about both a Sunni as well as a Hindu majoritarianism.[3] The postnational aspect of Aga Khan III's spiritual pan-Islamism and pan-Asianism were, in the painful context of South Asia's colonial reality, circumscribed by a critically-balanced language of ecumenism derived from the nationalist schema that, at the hands of several of the Muslim League's leaders, often went to the other end of the spectrum and acquired a zestful territorial fervour. However, the larger politics of ecumenism was neither without its fluctuations, nor crosscurrents. Indeed, the urgency and the immediacy that underlay the four thematic concerns alluded to above were also almost inextricably connected to the conceptualization of a Muslim 'nation' in South Asia that had to salvage both its inner and outer strength, iron out its various internal differences and devise new languages of connecting the individual to the community in a fast and drastically changing world in the first half of the twentieth century. Aga Khan III's public career stood at the point of intersection of these different strands and, as was noted by the political observer at the Bombay consulate of Wilhelmine Germany as early as in 1913, bore significant political implications. A prince without a country, he was primarily a spiritual leader of a small Muslim denomination of the Khojas, enjoying certain influence among India's Muslims, with the English seeking his support.[4] Here, then, against the backdrop of a project of defining the Muslim modern we have a classic case of development under the stewardship of a spiritual head of a Shiite denomination a religiously-inflected political culture. The political culture so developed drew upon, at one level, a cluster of socio-political idioms in the specific colonial context of South Asia. At another level, far wider pan-Islamic aspirations and postnational sensibilities operating within an essentially religio-cultural space also facilitated a reconfiguration of a global Ismaili community. This mediation then also hinged not insignificantly on the complex politico-religious location of Aga Khan III, as a spiritual head of a small Shiite denomination and as a political personality of a high standing among South Asia's Muslims, rolled into one.[5] In the first part of this chapter, we trace the grammar of leadership, identification, and fashioning. In the following section, we seek to relate the early ecumenical ventures in late colonial Bombay to the question of social reform. In the third part of the chapter, we move on to examine Aga Khan III's intervention in the ecumenical endeavour in the broader South Asian context that both drew upon as well as marked a significant advance on the earlier anticipations from Bombay.

On leadership and languages of identification

'Our identification with our community', as Richard Rorty suggests, '—our society, our political tradition, our intellectual heritage—is heightened when we see this community as *ours* rather than *nature's*, *shaped* rather than *found*, one among many which men have made' (emphasis in original).[6] Implicit in this reiteration of centrality of human agency in the conceptualization of the collective or the community is also an emphasis on the question of 'identification'.[7] We thus realize the need to problematize the *process of identification* in itself, rather than the upshot of *identity*. In so far as contending religious nationalisms in colonial South Asia is concerned, this process of identification has to be seen not only in terms of the 'Muslim' vis-à-vis the 'Hindu' as the two predominant cases, but also in terms of the numerous instances of internal dialogues and negotiations that helped paper the several cracks within each of these categories while bringing out narratives of contesting nationalisms within ostensibly cohesive identitarian framework.[8] Furthermore, a crucial problem often plaguing both state policy and secular academic discourse seems to be a misleading dichotomization of the conceptual categories of 'secular nationalism' as opposed to 'religious communalism'.[9] Thanks to the increasing corpus of thoughtful introspections on the subject, we are now equipped with an impressive repertoire of tools with which to dismantle overtly reductionist narratives both in general conceptual terms as well as those with particular implications for the South Asian context. The pitfalls as well as fault-lines underlying apparently simplistic and linear ecumenical ventures have been thus brought to light.

In this chapter, however, I explore with particular reference to Aga Khan III's public career the process and vocabularies of reconciliation in twentieth century South Asia between his Ismaili denomination and the wider Muslim ecumene. As already hinted, an analysis of the career of Aga Khan III involves engagement with his two *avatars*: the Aga Khan, as the spiritual head of the Khoja Ismailis, and the Aga Khan as the statesman who exhorted for a political accommodation of his followers within South Asia's Muslim *qaum* (nation).[10] It needs to be reiterated that these two aspects of the Aga Khan's political discourse were not mutually exclusive. Neither did he ever suggest any erosion of the denominational traits of his Ismaili followers in general, nor, for that matter, did he ever mean to relinquish, in particular, the spiritual position that his office signified among the Sevener Ismailis across the world. Much of the success of the two *avatars* rolled into one person depended upon the invocation of two different sets of vocabularies: a language of spiritual leadership that scholars have studied within the framework of charisma and messianic authority; and a language of modern political culture drawing upon specific tropes of what one scholar has called 'liberal Islam', a language that also catapulted the Aga Khan to the position of prominent leadership among South Asia's Muslims in the late colonial phase, while also drawing upon significant internationalist aspirations. Recent compelling accounts of the Aga Khan's spiritual position within the framework of charismatic and messianic authority have thus shown how Aga Khan III struck a balance between charismatic authority and secular modernist vocabularies.[11] These recent oeuvres also illustrate interesting nuances in the nature of scholarship on the role of Ismaili Imamate. Socio-economic and political issues have been for decades seen almost exclusively as the propelling forces of changes in modern Ismaili history, and especially that of the Aga Khans' Imamate. However, in a welcome move away from this earlier scholarship's almost parochial focus on socio-economic and political questions in modern Ismailism, recent works have also come to address more critically the persisting nature of conceptual and ideational re-orientations that the Ismaili Imamate witnessed since especially the latter part of the nineteenth century. Marking simultaneously crucial shifts from introspections about Neoplatonic and Christian 'influences' in the conceptualization of the Imamate in early Ismailism,[12] this new spate of scholarship indicates a more enduring nature of conceptual and structural changes that virtually remoulded the Imamate in nineteenth century Bombay. As should be evident, the present book operates within this larger rubric with its own variations and, furthermore, by situating this history against the larger backdrop of the cosmopolitan politico-intellectual milieu of the western Indian Ocean world.

In her recent work Teena Purohit has thus examined the treatment that the medieval Satpanth literature, especially the *Dasavatar*, was subjected to in the crucible of colonial judiciary, as well as contemporaneous scholarship. In the process, the text was split up into discrete and bounded religious classificatory schema resulting in subsequent appropriations in larger identitarian programmes. Drawing upon Giorgio Agamben's conceptual framework of 'messianic time', Purohit has suggested that 'messianic salvation … is a much broader concept that is given significance not in a human incarnation but in a kind of temporal exigency'.[13] Central to her thesis is Agamben's understanding of messianic 'revocation' that facilitated a 'hollowing out' of 'older Indic ideas' in the Satpanth literature – more specifically in the *Dasavatar* – giving post-Vedic concepts such as *karma* and *mukti* (liberation) 'new meaning and exigency with the expectation of the messiah's arrival'.[14] Agamben observes that the '*messianic vocation is the revocation of every vocation*' (italics in original).[15] Furthermore, Paul's *klēsis*, a critically important term in the Pauline messianic diction,

> indicates the particular transformation that every juridical status and worldly condition undergoes because of, and only because of, its relation to the messianic event. It is therefore … [a matter of] change, almost an internal shifting of each and every single worldly condition by virtue of being 'called', forming in the process the core essence of the messianic community.[16]

Purohit sees an immediacy, an exigency of the messianic moment in the *Dasavatar*, although 'the poem's pluralistic notions as well as the messianic imaginary of the *ginān* poetic tradition' underwent a systematic effacement.[17] Accompanied with this was a process of canonization, of which the 'Enthronement Hymn' was a part. The process of canonization provided Aga Khan III 'a theological opening' through which 'to assert his divine intercessory authority' while connecting to, as well as reworking, earlier forms of messianic ideas.[18] The canonization also involved, as Purohit points out in the passing, administrative restructuration through the creation of documents such as the 'Isma'ili Constitution'.[19]

Based on her study of modern Ismailism and to a lesser extent the Swami Narayan tradition, Purohit provides an interesting account of how older ideas and tropes were recast and reworked to shore up projects of redefining religious authority in late colonial South Asia. By contrast, anchoring my present work in case study of the history of Ismailism from the late nineteenth century, I seek to make a more fundamental point about transregional flows and wider intellectual and epistemological concerns that conditioned this history of modern Ismailism. Moreover, we also illustrate how Aga Khan III's activation of the 'messianic time' was, after all, not entirely at the expense of customs and customary traditions. In fact, we have already seen how Aga Khan I's Defence Counsel in the 1866 law case sought to bring the Khoja Ismaili particularities in dialogue with idioms of universality. It can be further suggested that Aga Khan III's project of reconfiguring the community with an emphatic use of the nomenclature of the 'Ismaili' hinged on a critical balance between customs entrenched primarily in the Khoja denominational traditions in South Asia, and perceived discourses of Muslim universality. The latter encapsulated much of his striving to relate to the universality of Islamic religio-cultural sensibilities on the one hand, while also retrieving a pristine Fatimid past on the other. After all, one of the first crucial steps that Aga Khan III took to re-organize the community was to restructure the *jamaat* in a more hierarchic form, and at the same time, customize it considerably to the Imamate's vision of the community. Indeed, as argued above, the triumphalist narrative of religious law as the basis of identitarian projects at the outright expense of customary traits, in the decades immediately following the 1866 law case and predating Aga Khan III's accession to the Imamate, too needs to be re-appraised.

The question of administrative experimentation since the times of Aga Khan III also requires special attention partly because it was no one-off development, and also because the articulation of an Ismaili identity through the constitutional modality was a multisited process that was acutely sensitized to the specificities of the physical and cultural matrices within which it took shape.[20] The earliest phase of this systematization of community protocols – *jamaat* rules and regulations, and constitutions[21] – operated against the backdrop of, and also was occasioned by, the early twentieth century secessionist tendencies in the transregional sphere of East Africa and South Asia.[22] Scholars have also shown how Aga Khan III executed power of attorney to some of his followers to act as his agent arbitrating in property matters in East Africa in the early 1900s, thereby creating a bulwark against the secessionists, but also bringing in its train new sets of complexities.[23] We shall explore the nature of this transregional historical development in the next chapter while, here in this chapter, we intend to restrict our study to an exploration of the public career of Aga Khan III and the import of his dual role. The very question of public career and leadership also brings to the forefront the related issue of the rhetoric of communication and the audience. Moving beyond the charismatic-messianic trope that underpins the Imam's position in the Ismaili telos, we are thus confronted with the need to understand the critically balanced diction as well as practice of political ecumenism, and cultural inclusivism that Aga Khan III promoted.

Charles Kurzman's project to chart out the contours of what he calls certain 'liberal Islam' might give some clue to better understand the mental world of the Aga Khan. Kurzman's thesis of liberal Islam showcases a gallery of no less than three different, although not mutually exclusive, variations of the idea. These are, viz.: the liberal sharia (Islamic law); the silent sharia; the interpreted sharia. While the first of these tropes suggests that the sharia 'requires democracy', the second holds that the sharia 'allows democracy'. The third trope, i.e., 'interpreted Islam', however, admits the divine nature of religion but underscores at the same time the pivotal importance of human intellect, volition and interpretation, opening up in the process the much debated question of plurality of religious traditions in general, and of Islam in particular.[24] The projects of visionaries such as Aga Khan III, with their emphasis on human intellect, exemplify the development of specifically this latter variant of 'liberal Islam'. Moreover, as the Aga Khan's particular case illustrates, there is also a significant degree of critical engagement with the very conceptual bases that sustained the relationship of reason, the scriptures, and *ijtihad*. In the process this complex relationship spawns discussions about the nature of interpretive possibilities and scriptural norms with their bearings on the dynamics of individual and the collective, the latter defined increasingly in terms of an ethical community since the late nineteenth century onwards. In other words, proponents of this third trope could scarcely have ignored the emphasis on an urgency to engage with democratic conventions, and indeed Quranic and hadith emphasis on Muslims following liberal positions within the larger rubric of such norms, an aspect that marks resonances of pluralism and reaches out to Kurzman's first and second tropes with their underlying sharia/democracy dynamics.[25] In the upshot, one observes the complex and often mutually constitutive nature of sharia's relationship with plurality, with the latter conceptualized at once as a pre-requisite, as well as an outcome of interpretive engagements with sharia. The Cairo conference manifesto floated by Aga Khan III and Zaki Ali that we discussed in the previous chapter thus sought to spur dialogues between both different schools of Islamic law and denominations within the larger framework prescribed in the Quranic tradition. In doing so, they were in effect reiterating not only the enduring nature of human endeavour, the contemporaneity of interpretive possibilities but also, more fundamentally, an idea that that is what constitutes the true essence of Islam. There are, then, crucial points of intersections in the analytical frames. What we can argue, though, without having to dwell on this question of concurrences any further, is that the languages of ecumenism – which in the first place conceives of plurality, political, cultural or religious – remain more often than not thoroughly enmeshed, while their invocation or elision are in essence strategic and contingent upon the historical specificities. These historical specificities lead us in turn to the questions revolving around both the individual/collective as well as reason/faith/ethics dynamics that conditioned religious change in modern South Asia, as much as elsewhere.

Much of the historical specificities of identitarian politics in South Asia in colonial times have tended to gravitate around two rival positions, viz., that of elite instrumentality and primordial sensibilities: the so-called 'instrumentalist' school as opposed to a 'primordialist'. Religious nationalist movements thus came to be seen as reflection of either manipulation of supposed symbols of identity by the society's elites (the 'instrumentalist' version), or as extensions of essential – if also understood at an expense of complexities that characterize the *processes* of such essentialization – religio-cultural traits that decisively distinguished one religious community from another (the 'primordialist' approach).[26] However, while the 'instrumentalist' version has been ascribed most consistently to Paul Brass, the analytical framework he developed did not ignore the role of pre-existing cultural values or intergroup attitudes in conditioning the ability of elites to manipulate specific symbols.[27] Furthermore, later scholarship has underscored the pressing need to go beyond the question of pragmatic interests as defining the nature of Muslim 'separatism', an argument that also urges one to re-assess the rather blinkered and narrow framework suggesting minority-to-separatism linearity.[28] Thus, the interrelated aspect of changing historical processes and the role of (politico-religious) leadership in the mediation of such processes has to be accorded due importance. What is also important is to take note of the contesting rhetoric that was invoked to legitimate religious nationalist projects. As has been noted, M. A. Jinnah (1876–1948) and several like-minded All India Muslim League leaders scarcely engaged in any doctrinal discussions of Islam: rather, theirs was an understanding of Islam 'translated into political life only in terms familiar to liberalism: rights, responsibility, and representation'.[29] The united India that senior clerics like Husayn Ahmad Madani of Deoband had in mind, by contrast, was not because of any secular imagination, but because they thought that Islam's work in the Hindu dominated areas would remain incomplete after partition of the subcontinent. Madani's evocative use of Islamic religiosities, matched by M. K. Gandhi's invocation along similar lines in the wake of the Khilafat Movement, then were strikingly different from Jinnah's.[30]

The crux in Aga Khan III's politico-religious thought lies in his addressing both these predicaments relating, furthermore, to a much profound notion of spiritual internationalism defined in Islamic terms and accommodating a plurality of voices. An examination of the public career of Aga Khan III at two different levels, as the Ismaili Imam and as a leading Muslim political figure in South Asia with significant internationalist contemplations, would illustrate the point underlining at once the relevance of studies of not only the persona but also her/his ideational vocabularies or the nature of practical organizational activism. The question of instrumentality of Aga Khan III's leadership, especially the question of duality, is studied here within the analytical framework of 'strategic syncretism', although with certain qualifications. This helps us understand the religio-cultural bases of, as well as the idioms employed in, Aga Khan III's political activism. This activism was further complicated by his efforts to strike a critical balance between internationalism with spiritual pan-Islamic undertones and a burgeoning Muslim religious nationalism that hinged on discourses of territoriality. His was a venture to reconcile these oppositional positions while providing a corrective to the modular nation-state of a clinical European variety in the context of late colonial India. Indeed, for him the very idea of a spiritual Muslim world, subsuming different strands of beliefs and thought, and notions of federalism and confederacy that in turn informed his project of India's reconstruction as well as Muslim ecumenism were no incommensurable categories. In this complex formulation, we have noted, he was part of a much larger intellectual sphere.

'Strategic syncretism' as a concept was employed by Christophe Jaffrelot to study the emergence of Hindu nationalism. Jaffrelot, in turn, was building upon Clifford Geertz's conceptualization of 'ideology' as a 'symbolic strategy', the mechanism of establishing and defending patterns of values, norms and beliefs, upholding specific religious and cultural traditions.[31] In Jaffrelot's formulation nationalism figures as an ideology *par excellence* with emphasis on what he calls the 'manipulative reinterpretations of cultural material' while at the same time with an eye on the 'cultural' aim of the interpreters. Hindu nationalist ideology thus appears as an invented tradition although, he adds, this could also be explained in terms of the sub-category of 'strategic syncretism'. 'Strategic syncretism' as a conceptual framework conceives of a situation where much of the constituent elements of an ideology appear to have been taken from the armoury of antagonistic groups (hence the idea of 'syncretism'); this syncretism is 'strategic' at the same time because it is after all aimed at dominating precisely the 'other' from whose armoury many of the raw materials of conceptualization of that identity have been gleaned.[32] Of crucial importance here is the balance that it strikes between the 'cognitive' and the 'contextual' worlds, i.e. the overarching importance of politico-historical contextuality. The contextuality manifests itself both in terms of providing vocabularies with which the actors equip themselves for articulation and eventual translation of thoughts into actions, or the constraints that it imposes, notwithstanding the agency of the actors.

The difference in the use of this concept in the present study however lies in the fact that the underlying principle here does not hinge upon the identification of any strict ally-enemy binaries as is the case with Jaffrelot's work. By contrast, we proceed from an underlying assumption that tactics of 'strategic syncretism' are not necessarily tactics of disarming an 'enemy'. It could well be employed as a cohesive force with which to coalesce together diverse denominations, sects, worldviews, schools of belief, and thought within a broader ecumenical framework, while at the same time remaining acutely conscious of this plurality. Indeed, much of Aga Khan III's concerns to propel an inclusive ecumenical endeavour papering the diverse fault-lines that underlay the fragmented Muslim community were significantly sensitized to various particularities. The 'strategic' element in this conceptualization of a Muslim community in South Asia thus involved negotiations leading to (re)locating the Khoja Ismailis in that Muslim ecumene. Selective employment of religio-cultural motifs, often symbolic, formed the bases of this political linkage. And yet, the very emphasis on the idea of human volition and activism also necessitates a further qualification, one that brings back the question of human agency, not as an insular factor unrelated to the historical matrix, but as a key vector that is mutually constitutive of historical processes of fashioning. This brings us to the heart of the problem: reviewing the two facets of Aga Khan III's public career.

Ecumenism and the liberal quest I: Reform and identity in Bombay

A recent scholarly work situates Aga Khan III's socio-political programmes within the rubric of a secularism, one in which the progression of the metanarrative of secularization operates in close relationship with the 'dissonant strains' of heterodoxy.[33] Thus, the invocation by Aga Khan III of reformist progressive values of western education, political activism, privatization of religion are all seen as part of a larger colonial public space producing a certain 'secular Islam'. With the secular figuring as an 'empty' category providing leverage for Muslim separatism, Aga Khan III's spiritual leadership among the Ismailis has been argued to manifest a private domain of vernacular devotion and religious practice, which installed the Aga Khan in his charismatic-messianic form, but was also outshone by the secular modernizing projects that the Aga increasingly promoted.[34] While this interesting commentary suggests how the dissonant voices and vernacular traditions were gradually stifled, there is still a predicament that we need to rehearse. For all the erosion of the pre-colonial idioms of devotion ensconced in vernacular structures, the corrosive nature of the Anglo-Muhammadan judicial experiments that conditioned the process in the first place must not be exaggerated. We have seen, for instance, the enduring relevance of customs vis-à-vis colonial efforts at standardizing religious law. If several of pre-colonial Indic vernacular idioms were eroded, other customary practices through, for instance, the mechanism of the *jamaat* still persisted, and were even bowdlerized by the Imamate to govern the community and, since especially Aga Khan III's times, to shore up the community development projects. Besides, the framework of vernacular devotion need not be necessarily seen as coterminous with the South Asian condition either. The nature of scholarly activities in the wake of the 1866 law case, as well as the knowledge networks connecting the transregional Perso-Indian world in the latter part of the nineteenth century have all been alluded to. Finally, Aga Khan III's engagement with spiritual pan-Islamism, Muslim plurality along different axes, and Ismaili denomination within a larger rubric of cosmopolitan internationalism reflects much wider processes aimed at recovering universality of religions (of Ismailism and Islam in his particular case), and their reconceptualization along ethical lines, and hence requires a more focused attention.

The distinctiveness of Aga Khan III thus lay in his effectively negotiating, in his dual capacity, a number of overlapping subjectivities. Such subjectivities emanated, first and foremost, from a Muslim religious nationalist consciousness with political underpinnings within a proposed federal structure in South Asia. Furthermore, they related to an internationalism emerging out of spiritual pan-Islamic quest that was not only invoked symbolically to further the religious nationalist project of South Asia's Muslims, but was also customized in subsequent times to accommodate the postnational sensibilities of the global Ismaili assemblage. Finally, even within the framework of South Asia's Muslim nationalist politics, a further strand in this complex subjectivity was informed by an enduring Ismaili denominationalism with the Aga Khan as the spiritual head. Such denominationalism was, besides, sensitized to the imperatives of both broader Islamic sensibilities and the denomination's trans-regional, and increasingly global character. For this latter strand, the deterritorialized conceptualization of a spiritual pan-Islamism – purged of any political overtones, and valorizing cultural diversity – provided the overarching framework. This involved, on the one hand, a political activism within South Asia that could merge issues of modernization, such as educational development in particular with wider cultural internationalism and discourses of plurality in Islam. On the other hand, more specifically, this process necessitated striking a balance on politico-religious front that could effectively wed certain sectarian specificities to general Islamic religio-cultural ethos leading to a political consensus among the subcontinent's Muslims. Indeed, as we have seen, in the Aga Khan's large corpus of writings, and especially those co-authored with Zaki

Ali, the wider ecumenical project – reflected also in significant internationalist pan-Islamism, albeit divested of the political lineaments – did not come at the expense of the Ismaili denomination's characteristic traits, most importantly the centrality of the Imamate. Rather such a project meant to incorporate these denominational specificities and plural voices through the invocation of idioms of rational interpretations, human intellect and Islam's plural ethos. As early as by November 1918, in addition to the subsequent Khilafat Movement, the Aga Khan had actually come up with a memorial exhorting the British Empire to 'protect Islam in Central Asia'.[35] This was also the year when his *chef-d'oeuvre, India in Transition: A Study in Political Evolution* came out. A treatise on a certain federal experiment, the volume – we have noted – also went on to elaborate on what emerged as the core of his discourse of Islamic consciousness, a spiritual pan-Islamism attuned to the diverse socio-political realities affecting the worldwide Muslim *umma*. In the specific Indian context, the colonial dispensation was urged to maintain a balanced system that would accommodate its subjects of diverse 'religions and races' modelled on the Ottoman Turkish *millat*, a system in which, the Aga Khan argued, 'each would have a fair share in the assembly directly elected', and thus facilitating self-government.[36] By the 1930s, as I argue below, this developed into a comprehensive argument of federalism on the basis of ethno-religious mapping of the subcontinent.

For all the emphasis on the question of devolution, the 'modern State', nevertheless, stands ubiquitous. Thus, the 'modern State, when based on democratic ideals, is not an external body to which its inhabitants go pleading for assistance and amelioration. It is, and ought to be, the concentrated and directing instrument of society as a whole'.[37] One need only reiterate that the idea was expressed in his particular engagement with a post-World War I India with pronounced dynamics between the state and its federal units. More generally though this invocation of the state balanced with a simultaneous distancing from it amounts to what Rajeev Bhargava, in his understanding of secularism, sees as a position of 'principled distance, a flexible but value-based relation that accommodates intervention as well as abstention'.[38] The question of widening enfranchisement and dialogues emerging from below that remained a dominant theme in the Aga Khan's mental world also has contemporary relevance and continues to be re-visited by political philosophers and social scientists. Commenting on the post-colonial predicament in India, it has been thus pointed out that the crisis of secularism is not because of any modernist nature of the imposition, but because it was an imposition in the first place that had scant respect for the diverse forms of intra-community dialogues, and the contextual particularities.[39] Against this larger backdrop, the Aga's insistence on crossconfessional as well as interdenominational dialogues then bears great import.

The pan-Islamic concerns of the Aga were conceptualized along spiritual lines invoking ideas of an organically connected community, though not without their localized political appropriations. However, the language that enabled him to relate the Khoja Ismailis of South Asia to the broader Muslim political entity operated in at least three different but intertwined levels: on the front of social (chiefly educational) reforms, with Aga Khan's involvement in the affairs of the Muslim Educational Conference and the Aligarh Movement; on the political front, where the nascent Muslim nationalist politics took shape by way of foundation of the All India Muslim League;[40] and finally, by way of taking up specific politico-religious issues that bore momentous import at international level and concerned the majority Sunni group in the post-World War I era (e.g., the Khilafat question).[41] The question of social reforms, however, has a longer and complex history, one that dominated the better part of civic consciousness in the nineteenth century colonial India's urban centres. From around the late 1890s, as a recent intervention suggests, debates on the so-called 'social question' led to civic activism in the form of 'social service' and came to pair with this earlier social reformist endeavours. It has been argued that the social reformers primarily focused on 'traditional "indigenous" customs such as prohibitions on female education, child marriage, polygyny, female infanticide, *sati, purdah* and the pitiable state of widows', whereas 'social service' embodied the drive to '"civilize" the urban poor by eradicating "vices" such as drunkenness, gambling and prostitution, and inculcating in them "enlightened" values regarding sanitation and hygiene' feeding to broader concerns for 'the progress of society as a whole'.[42] While the distinction helps us better appreciate the differences in 'objectives and orientations' to sustain 'social improvement' in colonial urban India, there is also a word of caution not to see these two modes as two entirely distinct developments with a clear line of demarcation separating them.[43]

This larger framework buttressed by discourses of social reforms and social service will help us situate the nineteenth century Bombay Khoja Ismaili case better, although we use it with some qualifications. Thus in our efforts to understand 'social service' we try not to restrict it too stringently to a compact and closed model relating essentially to urban phenomena revolving almost exclusively around issues of temperance, health, hygiene and sanitation. The 'social service' we are expatiating on is a wider argument of 'voluntary social service' that Aga Khan III invoked in his 1918 treatise on India, whereby he envisaged to address a wide gamut of social, economic and political issues 'to improve the conditions of life of all the backward elements, whether technically belonging to the depressed classes or not'.[44] This wide encompassing understanding of social service with a strong emphasis on voluntarism, we shall see in the next chapter, was also closely connected to the configurations of first a Khoja Ismaili community in the transregional western Indian Ocean world and eventually the global Ismaili ecumene. Importantly though – and this we need to reiterate lest we run the risk of developing an argument of exceptionalism – the Aga Khan's idea of organized voluntary social service was not really atypical in the wider context of nationalist endeavours in the contemporaneous South Asia within which it developed. As has been underscored, in the early twentieth century 'aristocratic and elite mercantile philanthropy or giving was rechannelled into constructive areas of concern such as modern education'; in addition, 'day-to-day charity of lesser individuals was moving away from personal and largely religious acts to secularized, collective and organized undertakings that were intended to benefit much bigger, transregional groups or "communities"'.[45] As we discuss in chapter 5 in greater detail, this is also a process that gestures at the growing importance of organized religions beyond the confines of individual conduct, and increasingly in shaping wider social processes leading to a gradual deprivatization of religion in crucial ways.[46]

Evidently, the questions of social reform, social service, civic awareness and religious inspiration as well as subjectivities were correlated, albeit in different ways and scales. In the specific context of the Bombay Khojas' tryst with competitive discourses of progress, revisiting the issue of Khoja Ismaili reformism will be pertinent. This is because it was part of a broader maze of dialogues between the city's diverse Muslim communities that emerged in the latter part of the nineteenth century. Connected closely to the western Indian Ocean world, this venture among Bombay's diverse Muslim groups was somewhat removed from the developments in Aligarh when the latter started its journey in the 1870s. This gulf was, however, bridged in the subsequent decades. But in the process it brought, by the early twentieth century, many of the above questions of both ideational and operational nature revolving around social service into sharp relief. Anticipating the subsequent ecumenical ventures that conditioned the scope of Muslim political activism in the twentieth century in its own way, the early phase of reformism in Bombay involved efforts to rechart boundaries of the various Muslim groups in the city. These efforts reflected some of the earliest engagements in intra-denominational exchanges in colonial South Asia, invoking a range of crucial questions, such as those of leadership, social progress and female education. A classic case illustrating such intra-denominational bonhomie comes in the form of a letter that the Daudi Bohra merchant baron, philanthropist and, later, a founding figure of the All India Muslim League, Sir Adamjee Peerbhoy (1846–1913) wrote to the Sulaymani Bohra liberal Muslim Sir Badruddin Tyabji (1844–1906), a leading Indian National Congress politician and a prominent legal practitioner in his own right. In that letter Peerbhoy referred to a correspondence he had had with some 'other gentlemen of *your* (i.e., Sir Badruddin's) *Community* in respect to the erection of a school of the Anjuman Islam', a cause for which, Peerbhoy lamented, they were not willing to contribute. Towards the end of the letter he further requested Sir Badruddin to 'make it convenient personally to see the Chief members of *our Community*' so as to convince them of 'the benefits desirable from the measures which you have in view for ameliorating the condition of *our* long neglected Community' (emphases added). An oscillation between a certain 'your community' vis-à-vis an implicit 'my' community lay at the basis of an 'our community' that Peerbhoy envisioned in the letter.[47] The grand ecumenical endeavour of the South Asian Muslims was yet to arrive. But still, clearly, the rhetoric of 'your' as opposed to 'my' community coalescing into a certain 'our' community, was a language of ecumenism of sorts, albeit in a limited scope within Bombay. The Peerbhoy letter, then, could be seen as a classic instance of intra-denominational negotiations – operating within a broader 'Bohra' rubric – that, in certain piecemeal manner, anticipated the thrust towards the kind of inclusivism that went on to define the larger Muslim religious nationalist identitarian framework in the subsequent decades. Peerbhoy himself later became a leading proponent of this wider ecumenism that acquired a political colour.

The question of education has to be problematized with particular reference to female education, if only to indicate the gaps in principle and practice among South Asia's diverse Muslim communities with divaricating cultural orientations. In other words, female education had been a contentious issue, and one that also brings the specificity of Bombay's different Muslim groups, as opposed to northern India's Muslim reformist initiatives, into sharp relief. This is one sphere where the Sulaimani Bohra Tyabji clan of Bombay made significant contributions that consequently made this denomination stand out amid the mosaic of South Asia's Muslims. As early as 1876, Badruddin Tyabji sent three of his daughters to the first girls' school in Bombay.[48] This was followed by his efforts to promote education among the Bombay Muslims in general (most articulately through the Anjuman i Islam schools), and bringing forth the Muslim 'backwardness' case through his testimony of the 1882 Educational Commission.[49] These initiatives provided Sir Badruddin a site within which to project his general concern for uplift of India's 'backward' Muslims as well as his sympathy and commitment to women's education in particular to an extent that was inconceivable even in Aligarh reformist circles at that time. In fact, it was not until as late as 1896 that the Muhammadan Educational Conference (MEC), Sir Sayyid Ahmad Khan's brain-child, recognized the need to actually do something in line with the kind of social activism, emphasizing women's education, which it had been for long endorsing without making much tangible changes in practice. Yet, not all of these issues were welcomed either. Thus Tyabji's arguments against *purdah* were dismissed by Mohsin ul-Mulk on the grounds that it was a religious issue beyond the purview of the MEC.[50] Thus in emphasizing the importance of organized and active endeavours in female education and, more generally the role of women memorialized in his 1918 intervention, the Aga Khan was in effect taking up a mantle from some of his Bombay peers.

Among the Khoja Ismailis in particular, we have seen, the rhetoric of reformism was invoked in tortuous legal cases almost necessarily gravitating around the idioms of social – especially educational – progress, liberty, enlightenment and in conjunction with questions of identity in colonial religio-legal classificatory terms. Even prior to the legal developments of the 1860s among the Bombay Khojas, and as early as the 1830s, the vocabulary of 'social reforms' with the question of educational progress at its core had emerged as the dominant trope among the self-styled reformists, if also at times providing them with a language with which to masquerade tussles over *jamaat* rights. Kassumbhai Nathubhai, Muhammad Dama and some other rich Khojas of Bombay are thus said to have established a school for Khoja children as early as the 1830s.[51] In the course of the nineteenth century, a thriving associational culture started making ripples in Bombay promoting quintessential reformist programmes expressed through formal agendas and realized through diverse forms of philanthropic initiatives. To sections of the city's Muslims, this meant an arena within which to engage in mutual dialogues negotiating the kind of cohesive inclusivism that the likes of Peerbhoy upheld. Yet, this was by no means ever complete and definitive, marking a triumphalist progression to a modernist reformist ecumenical venture. Peerbhoy, as shown above, had his own share of disappointment, and we shall shortly expatiate on the other aspects of this incomplete reformism. Nor was this the only form of social activism as, to borrow Nile Green's expression, there had been at the same time the kin-based 'family business model' championing a certain 'Customary Islam', and still other ventures sponsoring 'Counter Reformist Islam'. While presenting a complex texture of pluralization of Islam – or more appropriately, 'Islams', as he suggests – in maritime colonial Bombay, Green, however, cautions that these labels should not be reified as coherent 'movements', but should be seen as merely heuristic devices 'to designate widespread but often quite disparate and internally competing "trends" within the [religious] market'.[52] This caveat urging not to take these labels as strict well-demarcated categories hermetically sealed off against each other is something that is further driven home in our present study. The languages of modern 'reformist' associational activism on the one hand, and of associations, which appropriated the reformist model of functioning to promote, one the other, almost exclusively religious programmes along denominational lines, somewhat echoing Green's 'Customary' traits, often remained very closely related and even enmeshed. We have already seen, for instance, how prior to Aga Khan III's restructuration of the Imamate framework, Aga Khans I and II functioned more in the vein of what Green labels as a 'family firm'. Besides, even Aga Khan III's restructuration was coupled with a canonization enterprise that was animated with zealous invocation of certain messianic rhetoric.

What characterized the burgeoning reformist project – which was also selectively appropriated by sections from the customary traditions – was a new-found fervour in associational activism. In effect then, even as such associations opened up new spaces for engagements for these different groups, it never really diluted their old kinship traits. Rather, these associations often also ended up becoming new sites of negotiations and contestations. It will be ahistorical therefore to say that such negotiations often necessarily meant a linear march towards inclusivism and an ecumenical ideal. Representative of the reformist endeavour of the city's Muslim groups was, for instance, the (Bombay) Anjuman i Islam. Thanks largely to the way the institution remained captive of old kin-based diatribes, by the early decades of the twentieth century its dismal fate became apparent. The institution was established with support of men such as the Konkani merchant prince Mohammad Ali Roghay, Sir Badruddin Tyabji *et al.*[53] A school for the Anjuman, with its preference for Urdu as opposed to Gujarati and promoting Anglo-Urdu education, was set up in September 1880. While this signified an endeavour to connect the Muslims of western India with the general *qaum* in the subcontinent, this was in sharp contrast to some earlier trends when the role of Gujarati as a language that bound the various 'Gujarati-speaking trading classes' (for all their internal conflicts and differences, chiefly religious), used to be invoked. Such evocative moments of Gujarati mercantile solidarity came, most prominently, in certain moments of crisis that hampered British-Indian relations.[54] The shift towards Urdu that characterized much of the post-1870s Muslim campaigns for educational reforms marked Muslim life on not only the subcontinent but also in the Indian diasporas elsewhere in the colonies. Thus the disparate Indian Muslim groups of Natal colony in South Africa are also said to have embraced Urdu as an 'Islamic' language, thanks to the efforts of Ghulam Muhammad 'Sufi Sahib', thus marking the passage to a new-found 'Muslim' identity.[55]

Yet, from the very start the Bombay Anjuman had to struggle to convince the city's Muslims of its reformist and philanthropic objectives, part of which has been already referred to with reference to Peerbhoy's 1885 letter to Sir Badruddin. Interestingly, the Bohra presence was quite pronounced in the Anjuman i Islam school. Thus, by December 1884, the school had 595 pupils, of whom 156 were Bohras, compared to only 12 Khojas.[56] The general lukewarm attitude of the majority of the city's Muslims was compounded by the fact that the government's support to the Anjuman was often hedged around with punctilious conditions. A correspondence in connection with the working and management of a boarding house attached to the Anjuman brings out this classic dilemma. Commenting upon a letter from the Director of Public Instruction (dated 19 July 1902), the Acting Secretary to Government Educational Department pointed out that of the 20 occupants of the said boarding house only six had been students of the Anjuman's schools, and the rest were from other institutions, which allegedly flouted the principle on which the Anjuman asked for financial support from the government. The Anjuman's reply (dated 9 September 1902) was virtually a restatement of its declared and implicit foundational agenda: it emphasized that other students were admitted not at the expense of Anjuman's own students; that the aim of the Anjuman was to provide, in addition to 'primary and middle education...

facilities to *Mahomedan* students who join Colleges with a view to obtain Degrees and Diplomas', as also helping poorer students financially (emphasis added).[57] Yet this claim for inclusivism sounds more like an essentially putative rhetoric. In addition to the government's scepticism, to make matters worse still, endemic and internecine factionalism along lines of sectarian differences affected the institution. By 1920–21 the Bombay Anjuman i Islam was losing its importance due not only to the nonchalance of those important in the Home Rule League, but also due to hostility from the Khoja group who had failed to get one of their nominees from their denomination elected for the post of President; furthermore, it was noted that the education system required reorganization.[58]

Ecumenism and the liberal quest II: Aga Khan III and a Muslim identity in South Asia

By contrast to the Anjuman's dismal fate, monies were increasingly flowing towards the Aligarh initiative that, along with the All India Muslim League, suffused and sustained the Indian Muslims' political project with a cultural agenda. Eventually, the Aligarh Muslim University campaign became an enterprise that further led to the crystallization of a specific cultural definition while carving out an all-India Muslim constituency at the same time.[59] Furthermore, both the Aligarh as well as the Muslim League ventures were propelled to a considerable extent by leaders who had been, until then, operating somewhat at the fringes of the Muslim sphere in northern India. The first annual session of the Muslim League (1907) thus enjoyed the blessings of Aga Khan III, who had by then started frequenting political and cultural circles outside Bombay, and was moreover chaired by Sir Adamjee Peerbhoy, an event that also marked significant paradigmatic shifts in his mental world. Yet, the crystallization of an all-India Muslim constituency with Aligarh as the symbolic epicentre was far from a linear development. The student-strength at the fund-starved fledgling institution had been dwindling sharply since 1895. An embezzlement scandal around the same time, and factional bickering following Sir Sayyid Ahmad Khan's death (1898) compounded further the troubled situation. Cumulatively they threatened to jeopardize prospects of the Mahomedan Anglo-Oriental College, the kernel of the future university.[60] Yet, at the level of an abstract ecumenical appeal, what characterized this movement was a degree of commitment to a shared 'Muslim' reformist cause that brought together individuals, albeit with their own divaricating agenda, across the political spectrum. Invoking a language of ecumenism the Congressman Sir Badruddin Tyabji (also leading member of the Muhammadan Educational Conference, but a critic of Sir Sayyid), eventually came to contribute Rupees 2,000.[61] While the chunk of the financial contributions came from the Nawab of Rampur, leaders from these smaller

Shia denominations had actually emerged as champions of this widening enterprise of propagating 'Muslim education' and bailed the project out of the quagmire of scandals, financial distress, and factional fights.[62] In 1906, Sir Adamjee Peerbhoy donated Rupees 110,000 for the establishment of a science college at Aligarh.[63] Even prior to this, Aga Khan III had already come up with his exhortations to promote education among India's Muslims, and subsequently in 1911 organized a substantial collection for Aligarh University. These contributions were all the more crucial considering that the Aligarh Movement did not find uncritical acceptance among all sections of the Shia everywhere. Indeed, in the crude world of power relations and interdenominational equations, it also accentuated the cleavages between the Shia and Sunni, sometimes in places geographically not very far from Aligarh itself. Thus, in Amroha, public debates not only went on to question Aligarh's universalistic Sunni reformist project, but actually came to establish a series of organizations to undermine the Aligarh version of reformist agenda, financially supporting Shia students and promoting parallel structures of modern vocational education.[64]

The politics of cultural inclusivism, understandably, was not without misgivings, and nor did they go unmediated in specific localized contexts. A somewhat related case in point is the Khilafat Movement that, propelled by a spirit for ecumenism emerged as a syncretistic programme signifying, in semiotic terms, the larger cultural/civilizational and spiritual *topos* that Aga Khan III outlined in his *India in Transition*. Moreover, this syncretism couched in a language of an emotive identification not only buttressed the larger inclusive project, but also in the process helped reposition within the broader Muslim world in South Asia the smaller denominations ensuring a leading position for the Aga Khan among South Asia's Muslims at the same time. It was a project that marked not only a high watermark in the ecumenical endeavour among the Muslims in South Asia, but also attracted considerable involvement and co-operation from the Indian National Congress under the stewardship of M. K. Gandhi. The Khilafat Movement that ensued has been studied at length with special reference to the question of leadership, and their systematic use of 'Islamic symbols' to rally a following for India's nationalist cause.[65] However, what interests us here in particular is the language of religio-cultural ecumenism that was not confined within the strict boundaries of a derivative, and often reductionist, politically inflected nationalism. In the deputation that went to London in defence of the Khilafat there were thus no less than two key Shia Muslim figures: the Shia Ismaili Imam Aga Khan III and Syed Ameer Ali (Ithna Ashari Shia), bringing to the forefront this wider cultural concern, albeit not without utter indifference from different quarters, if not hostile critiques. Thus, Edwin Samuel Montagu (1879–1924), Secretary of State for India, noted in the wake of the post-World War I developments and the Khilafat agitation that the Aga Khan was nevertheless 'a loyal and very moderate Mohamedan, far more moderate than the orthodox'; Montague added further that Indians after all did 'have a right to a predominant voice in this question, not only because it affects the peace and security of their country, but because they played a predominant part in the context of Turkey'.[66] It can be recalled in the passing that the question of loyalty to the British was an important desideratum in all negotiations with London.[67] Montagu's Prime Minister, David Lloyd George (1863–1945), was not particularly enthused, however. Nor was Syed Ameer Ali's interpretation of the Khilafat as Imamate endowed with 'spiritual leadership' accepted by all Shia clerics. They accused Ameer Ali of factual inaccuracy and flawed explication of spiritual presence and attributes of the Imam.[68] Thus, it has been aptly argued that pan-Islamism in northern India, right from its earliest stages, was scarcely a part of any galvanized project aimed at ecumenical Muslim identity with a harmonized Shia-Sunni political opinion.[69]

Indeed, who knew better about the poverty of political ecumenism on a global scale than the Aga Khan himself when he noted the relevance of a spiritual pan-Islamism pointing out how facile, in contrast, political pan-Islamism was.[70] Critical about the legitimacy of political pan-Islamism, and hence an ecumenism on an international plane based on a political language, Aga Khan III in effect translated the ecumenical endeavour into a language of incorporative spiritual ethos within the framework of an Islam celebrating its cultural diversity. He did so, furthermore, without stoking any intricate theological engagement. Recent scholarship shows how Sunni thinkers in colonial India took up a 'depoliticized model of Muslim society' developed by the Shia who, having suffered military defeat at the hands of the Sunnis in the early history of Islam, 'witnessed the establishment of a political order separated from a religious authority... vested in a messianic future'. Furthermore, the Shia elegy of the martyrdom of its early Imams emerged as a key trope for the larger Muslim narrative in colonial India – beginning with Altaf Hussain Hali – producing out of 'such disparate sources' the *umma* as a 'kind of historical subject', a global society transcending the 'bounds of any state'.[71] It is within this larger religio-cultural project that figures such as Aga Khan III has to be situated, albeit with significant variations and reservations when matters boiled down to the contending religious nationalist politics in late colonial India. Moving along the conceptual plane of the Muslim *umma* as a global community Aga Khan III envisioned a community with remarkable inner strength and a promising future. Yet, this envisioning sequence was also punctuated by the occasional elegiac moment – such as the defeat of Turkey in World War I resulting in the abolition of the Khilafat – that he thought could be employed to facilitate further the development of a language of Muslim universality, a language punctiliously divested of political idioms.

As distinct from this language of spiritual/cultural universality of Islam and the *umma*, was the language of Muslim religious nationalism in South Asia that drew upon an array of cognate socio-political issues; from socio-cultural concerns to the political, asserting its presence through electoral politics. Christopher Bayly has sought to explain the apparent contradiction between a distaste for 'modular nationalism' and the programme of carving out Muslim states in accordance with Muslim League model in Sir Muhammad Iqbal's thought by underlining the fluidity of the idea of 'state' as late as the 1930s and even up to the mid-1940s. Emphasizing a freedom of choice, rather than straightjacketed territorial nationalism, Iqbal, according to Bayly, meant to have a 'domain within a wider Indian empire' where Muslims would be free to follow the pristine Islamic way of life. However, since a pan-Islamic union was out of question after 1918, it would have necessitated some 'redistribution' of Muslim population.[72] Bayly sees a more articulate version of this thesis in Aga Khan III's correspondence with the Punjab Muslim leader Sir Fazli Hussain (1877–1936) in 1935. Bayly thus highlights the way Aga Khan III came to see the northern and the eastern parts of South Asia as the home of the subcontinent's Muslim majority, where Muslims from other parts of India could gradually migrate. It was high time, furthermore, that the Muslims realized that the power of the Hindus was on the rise, supplanting the British; otherwise, their fate would be akin to the Jews' in contemporaneous Germany.[73]

Written on the eve of his visit to Geneva to represent the Indian delegation at the League of Nations Assembly, the letter in question offers instructive insights on a number of other issues, and therefore elicits some further attention. First, while arguing for a piecemeal Muslim migration, it also expresses disenchantment with models and mechanisms previously highly regarded: thus, 'separate electorates, weightage are all… artificial'.[74] Second, one sees in the letter traces of some of his earlier ideas as well as an advance on them. Thus the federal plan outlined in *India in Transition* was taken up once again with more emphatic argument in favour of autonomy of the provinces creating, in the process, a 'United States of Southern Asia', or a 'United States of India rather than an imperial and united India'. The degree of autonomy thus envisioned can be gauged from the Aga Khan's exhortation to 'territorialize' the 'Indian Army' vesting the provinces with the crucial responsibility of defence.[75] On the eve of independence and partition of the subcontinent, with dreams whittled down by the crude realities of political vicissitudes, the idea was subsequently recast in the language of a confederation, meant to include India and Pakistan in what the Aga Khan called 'Hindustan-Pakistan Con[federation] or alliance or Dual Realms', proposing the Nawab of Bhopal's name as the principal negotiator.[76] Finally, and more importantly perhaps, the 1935 letter also suggested a blueprint of what the Aga Khan called a 'moderate State socialism' that he thought would help the poor Muslims and, above all, the 'Depressed Classes'. Indeed, 'there must be keenest religious and secular education and we must open our arms as wide as possible to adopt members of the depressed classes'. Again, as he summed up towards the end of the letter: '[There is a need to promote] Intensive teaching of child welfare and conversion of such members of depressed classes as are willing to come – to be worked out through our religious leaders'.[77] This position is somewhat in contrast to the one he took in 1918 when he was stressing the state's intervention even as charting out the contours of certain voluntary activism. Unlike 1935, in 1918 there was a careful attempt not to invoke the rhetoric of 'missions', thanks to the proselytizing character with which they were often associated.[78] It needs to be perhaps reiterated that the shift by 1935 towards certain voluntary conversions of the 'depressed classes' has to be seen against the backdrop of not only a competitive politics of social uplift but also of reclamation that came to preoccupy leaders ranging from M.K. Gandhi through B.R. Ambedkar (1891–1956) to Aga Khan III himself.[79] The 1935 letter, then, documents the changing contours of some of Aga Khan III's earlier ideas about minorities, the nature of state, and indeed a rich panoply of the federal model that he had been toying with for a number of decades.

At another level, contrasting, furthermore, the emotive aspect of ecumenism, the question of political representation never went uncontested. Take for instance the landmark case of the Muslim Deputation of October 1906 to Lord Minto at his Simla residence, an event of momentous import in the history of campaign for separate electorates for Muslims, and indeed the political culture of the then soon-to-be-established All India Muslim League.[80] The critique came from none other than Muhammad Ali Jinnah, then very much in the thrall of moderate Congress politics. Jinnah's critique was two-fold: to what extent was the Deputation 'representative'; and the very object of the Deputation.[81] Furthermore, there had been opposition to the very foundation of a central association like the All India Muslim League. An organization such as this, it was thought, might dismantle the structure of local associations, or challenge the Aligarh leadership. Besides, Aga Khan III's suggestion that the Simla Deputation be turned into a permanent committee (as opposed to any direct popular movement) so as to materialize the Deputation's demands was also partly conditioned by his not-so-smooth relation with Nawab Salimullah, who was much more devoted to the Bengal Partition issue.[82] However, once established the All India Muslim League proved to be a sufficiently broad forum that had among its key leaders the Aga Khan as well, who too could entrench his position in a remarkably short time, thanks partly to his sponsoring the cause of the Aligarh Movement, along with his larger project of championing Muslim cultural universalism.

By the 1930s, Sir Fazli was assiduously updating the Aga Khan of political developments in India while the latter was constantly on the move. Sir Fazli's letters were punctuated with notes of congratulation to the Aga Khan, on one occasion, for keeping in some sort of order an essentially heterogeneous lot of people,[83] while welcoming on another occasion his intervention to 'cement various schools of thought'.[84] It was this nuanced understanding of cultural universalism wedded to denominational particularism and plural voices, that account for the distinctiveness of the Imami Ismaili social identity. Thus, against the immediate backdrop of the Imami Khoja/Ithna Ashari Khoja split in the 1900s, while the Aga Khani Ismailis were prohibited to enter any social relations (e.g., marriages or sharing meals with Ithna Ashariyas) or constitute any place of worship other than the *jamaatkhana*, and burying in burial grounds of other denominations in contrast to nineteenth century practices, it was laid down nevertheless that 'professional dealings' with non-Aga Khanis were permissible.[85] Subsequently much of the intra- and interdenominational exchanges were revived and scrupulously celebrated by Aga Khan III. While the Shia clerics in Amroha had their misgivings about Aligarh, the Aga Khan and some like-minded Shia leaders chose a different path: viz., in taking active part in the Muslim League and Aligarh endeavours, and striving in the process to work out some kind of commensurability between a language of political ecumenism and denominational specificities. Thus special care was taken to fine tune these denominational particularities, bringing them in consonance with the overarching cultural and spiritual values of Islam stoking up, for instance, larger religio-cultural imageries as the one embodied in the quotation that stands at the epigraph of this chapter. If a South Asian Ismaili was exhorted to identify with this larger universalism at one level, (s)he was also asked to be part of sweeping endeavours of self-affirmation in India that virtually redefined the boundaries of the Muslim community. 'Aligarh', he noted in his Reply to the Address from the Trustees of the MAO College in January 1910, 'should not only turn out learned and capable men but good Musalmans' who should at the same time not hesitate to imbibe the European spirit of self-sacrifice.[86] If the question of 'converted Muslim' came up in connection to South Asia's Khojas, as they often did and at times buttressed with the colonial classificatory literature, the Aga Khan would unequivocally point to the differences between the Hindus and Muslims in the subcontinent. Such differences, according to him, were not only 'religious', but also historical and physical.[87] I have elsewhere suggested that the reference to the question of proselytes is no innocuous passing comment on the unity among Muslims of South Asia: it is a crucial sub-text appended to a political schema that sought to place his followers, many of whom had been converted probably just a few centuries back, at par with the bulk of the Muslim population.[88] Memorializing the plurality within Islam coupled with a language of spiritual universalism was thus meant to obviate any sectarian fallout, while relocating by great tact the diverse and splintered – part of them converted – Muslim groups within that rubric. In the context of colonial India it gave meaning, moreover, to the programmatic statement to facilitate voluntary conversions as the Aga Khan ruminated in the 1930s. In the international arena, it rendered the idioms of territorial nationalism and statism redundant and made possible a successful accommodation of Ismailis from diverse ethic-cultural backgrounds, each of them a cosmopolitan citizen under the guidance of the Imamate's religio-cultural programme, and conversing between themselves in a critical cosmopolitan language. The evolution of this global Ismaili ecumene, or what I have called the Ismaili international, is what we elaborate on in the next chapter.

Conclusion

For Aga Khan III, the balance of formulating a 'Muslim' identity cutting across the sectarian walls lay in negotiations at different planes: viz., engaging with issues ranging from the denominational to political ecumenism, within the matrix of Muslim religious nationalism, to spiritual pan-Islamism with both global and local ramifications. For the Ismailis spread across South Asia to East and South Africa to Central Asia (and also to the global North in contemporary times, thanks to the secondary-migration of the Ismailis largely from Africa) and following the Aga Khan as the Imam of the time, this, however, meant a constant exercise in re-adjustments and adaptions to critically different historical, socio-cultural and political contexts. Aga Khan III was the first of the living Imams in modern times to have toured extensively mediating in, and facilitating, this acutely context-specific religio-cultural process(es). Standing at the nexus of these different planes, the Imamate (currently under Aga Khan IV) strives to promote through its system of protocols and its message of community service a language of postnational subjectivities in an essentially deterritorialized cultural space. The system of protocols – along-side the symbolic royal title reserved for the Imam, and gradually incorporating other apparitions of the state such as an anthem, a flag, and not least the diplomatic status that the Imam and his legates are accorded to in several countries in contemporary times – conjures up no less than a state-like form of the Imamate with significant semiotic implications emulating, as has been pointed out, a British model of indirect rule.[89] More specifically, for the bulk of the Ismailis spread across the globe, this model of governance produces a religio-cultural matrix within which to learn to live like an Ismaili. Given the globally spread nature of the community in contemporary times, realizing the importance of being Imami Ismaili rests to a great extent on the narrative of internationalism, and the successful customization of the core discourse of spiritual pan-Islamism in different contexts. In other words, the Ismaili individual identifies with the globally spread Ismaili ecumene by drawing upon not only conceptual tools specific to the community, but also invoking larger internationalist aspirations, a set of universals, that crystallized gradually from the times of Aga Khan III. Sensitized to the varied politico-cultural contexts, they are realized essentially within a sphere of praxis along a deterritorialized plane. In the following chapter we discuss the ideational lineaments, operational modalities and ramifications of the global Ismaili assemblage, the earliest experiments for which were carried out in the transregional arena of South Asia and East Africa, gradually developing different pathways across the world while also remaining centripetally related to the Imamate at the core.

Endnotes

1 Furthermore, according to Aga Khan III, this was important not least because the time and money spent on such prayers and pilgrimages or celebrations of martyrdoms had more often than not vitiated the fraternal bonds of the *umma* exposing it to sectarianism. See Aga Khan III's Presidential Address to the All India Muslim Educational Conference, 1902, Delhi in *Aga Khan III, Volume I*, edited by K. K. Aziz, 210.

2 See Francis Robinson, 'Religious Change and the Self in Muslim South Asia since 1800', in idem, *Islam and Muslim History in South Asia*, 105–21 (New Delhi: Oxford University Press, 2012 [2000]). Also, idem, 'Other-Worldly and This-Worldly Islam and Islamic Revival: A Memorial Lecture for Wilfred Cantwell Smith', *Journal of the Royal Asiatic Society*, Series 3, 14, 1 (2004): 47–58.

3 Devji, *Muslim Zion*, 66 points out that 'the minority protection sought by the [All India Muslim] League's Shia leaders had to do with the fear of a Sunni majority as much as a Hindu one'. More generally, Aamir Mufti, *Enlightenment in the Colony: The Jewish Question and the Crisis of Postcolonial Culture*, 12–13 (Princeton: Princeton University Press, 2007) reminds one of the centrality of the nationalist project in the process of 'minoritization'.

4 'Der Aga Khan dagegen ist eine Fuerst ohne Land, nur geistliches Oberhaupt, und die Sekte, die ihm folgt, die Khojas, unmfasst nur einen kleinen Prozentstaz der Muhamedaner Indiens … Bei seinem Glaubensgenossen gilt er etwas, weil ihm die regierung haelt, und die Englaender ihrerseits suchen seine Unterstuetzung, weil sie ihm Einfluss auf die Massen zutrauen' (translation mine). See the despatch dated 21 February 1913 from the German General Consulate in Bombay to Chancellor of the German Empire, Theobald von Bethmann-Hollweg in Politisches Archiv des Auswärtigen Amts, Abteilung A, Englische Besitzungen in Asien, No. 2, Britische Indien, Bd. 49, vom 1 März 1912 bis 15 April 1913 (R 19350). However, given the scepticism of the English – from roughly around the same time and especially in the course of the war years – regarding the influence the Aga Khan arguably held among the masses and the Muslims in particular, this German appraisal of British belief in his popularity with the masses seems debatable. See chapter 3, in particular where I discuss the debates around his nomination for a Nobel Prize in the post-World War I years, for a sense of the general and persistent scepticism in influential circles in the British administration.

5 For an earlier formulation of this argument, see my 'Being "Ismaili" and "Muslim"'.

6 Richard Rorty, *Consequences of Pragmatism*, 166 (Minneapolis: University of Minnesota Press, 2003 [1982]).

7 This emphasis on 'identification', as distinct from exclusive discussions about 'identity', invokes the idea of a two-way *process* whereby 'groups, movements, institutions try to locate us … construct us within symbolic boundaries' and in turn 'we try to manipulate or respond to it' so as to 'exist within that kind of symbolic framework'. Stuart Hall, 'Politics of identity' in *Culture, Identity and Politics: Ethnic Minorities in Britain*, edited by Terence Ranger, Yunas Samad and Ossie Stuart, 129–35, at 130 (Aldershot: Avebury, 1996).

8 M.T. Titus, *Islam in India and Pakistan: A Religious History of Islam in India and Pakistan*, 87–115, 170–79 (Calcutta: YMCA Press, 1959) underscored the sectarian differences and the ramifications of Islam's tryst with non-Islamic environment in South Asia. *Caste and Social Stratification among the Muslim*, edited by Imtiaz Ahmad, (Delhi: Manohar Book Service,

1973), among others, is an ambitious project to identify the specific 'Indian' elements of Islam in the subcontinent. Ayesha Jalal, *Self and Sovereignty: Individual and Community in South Asian Islam since 1850* (London and New York: Routledge, 2000), encompasses the variables of individual, regional, class and cultural differences that went into forging an Islamic identity in South Asia.

9   See for instance, Ayesha Jalal, 'Exploding Communalism: The Politics of Muslim Identity in South Asia' in *Nationalism, Democracy and Development: State and Politics in India*, edited by Sugata Bose and Ayesha Jalal, 76–103 (Delhi: Oxford University Press, 1998) for a critical engagement. A further problem is the very expression 'communalism', purporting to an apparent 'illegitimacy' of religious nationalism. See Gyanendra Pandey, *The Construction of Communalism in Colonial North India*, 8–9 (Delhi: Oxford University Press, 1990). It is precisely because of the delegitimizing aspect of the term 'communalism' that, taking cue from Peter van der Veer, *Religious Nationalism: Hindus and Muslims in India* (Berkeley: University of California Press, 1994) among others for instance, I use the expression 'religious nationalism' in the present study.

10 Cf. *umma* (people/ community). The different modes of conceptualizing *umma* and the different resultant imports have been dealt with at length in academic works. For instance, seen primarily as a group of people bearing common characteristics, *umma* is also said to denote the different units which form a community, and can consequently imply, 'a people, a society, a nation, a tribe, a culture, a multi-social, multi-cultural community in the sense it is used to describe Muslim civilization.' Merryl Wyn Davies, *Knowing One Another: Shaping an Islamic Anthropology*, 128–30; see especially 107–08 (London and New York: Mansell, 1988).

11 See Teena Purohit, *The Aga Khan Case: Religion and Identity in Colonial India* (Cambridge, MA: Harvard University Press, 2012). See esp. 125 ff. Cf. Idem, 'Identity Politics Revisited: Secular and "Dissonant" Islam in Colonial South Asia', *Modern Asian Studies*, 45, 3 (2011): 709–33. For the framework of 'liberal Islam' see *Liberal Islam: A Sourcebook*, edited by Charles Kurzman, (Oxford and New York: Oxford University Press, 1998), especially the Introduction. Also see, idem, 'Liberal Islam: Prospects and Challenges', *Middle East Review of International Affairs*, 3, 3 (1999): 11–19.

12 For succinct overviews exploring the nature of Imam in Batini thought, with reference to Christian ideas, see Sami Makarem, 'The Philosophical Significance of the Imām in Ismāʿīlism', *Studia Islamica*, 27 (1967): 41–53. For the theory that the idea of the Nizari Imam owed its origin to Plato's model 'Philosopher King' and cognate Neoplatonic discourses, see Sami G. Hajjar and Steven J. Brzeznski, 'The Nizārī Ismāʿīli Imam and Plato's Philosopher King', *Islamic Studies*, 16, 1 (1977): 303–16.

13 Purohit, *The Aga Khan Case*, 125.

14 Ibid., 127.

15 Giorgio Agamben, *The Time That Remains: A Commentary on the Letter to the Romans*, 23 (Stanford: Stanford University Press, 2005).

16 Ibid., 22.

17 Purohit, *The Aga Khan Case*, 129.

18 Ibid., 131.

19 Ibid., 129.

20 See Hirji, 'The socio-legal formation of the Nizari Ismailis of East Africa, 1800–1950', in *A Modern History of the Ismailis*, edited by Daftary. Drawing upon a case study of the Ismailis in Tanzania, Rose M. Kadende-Kaiser and Paul J. Kaiser, 'Identity, Citizenship, and Transnationalism: Ismailis in Tanzania and Burundians in the Diaspora', *Africa Today*, 45, 3–4 (1998): 461–80, show how the 'Ismaili constitution serves as the framework for a dual citizenship that coexists with, and transcends, the traditional boundaries of the nation-state' (ibid., 462).

21 It is important to note the terminological shift from 'rules and regulations' to 'constitutions', because it is only as late as 1946 that the word 'constitution' first appears in the title alongside 'rules and regulations'. Furthermore, only in 1962, under Aga Khan IV was the word 'constitution' used in the title while the expression 'rules and regulations' was dropped (ibid., 146–47).

22 The translocal/transregional dimension of the early developments in the formation of a bounded Aga Khani Ismaili community and its earliest experiments in social service have been highlighted in Mukherjee, 'Universalizing Aspirations'. It should be reiterated, however, that the defence of each of the contending parties had always had a strong connection to, and underpinned with idioms of, the competing strands of the faith they claimed to profess. More importantly, such languages were often invoked in defence against what they sometimes saw as intrusion on the part of the colonial establishment. Thus a serious opposition came from the Sunni Khojas in matters of participation in the Melvill commission that was constituted by Sir Richard Temple's government in Bombay to enquire whether the Khojas – that expression being still dominant in administrative lexicon – should be included under the Hindu Wills Act (Act XXI of 1870). We have already seen, in Chapter 1, the nature of opposition the Aga Khan's camp offered. However, the Sunni party argued that it was their very faith that was in danger: as the Khoja community 'profess themselves to be Musalmáns' following 'Muhammadan law of inheritance contained in the *Holy Korán* and *Hádis*', any new law that upset this made the Khojas virtually 'infidel', as had been the case with Ahmedbhoy Hubeebbhoy for reason of his association with the Commission. See Petition of Abdullah Haji Alarukhia and 12 other Sunni Khojas, IOR, Public and Judicial Department Records, 'Papers Relating to the Khoja Succession Bill', 1886, L/PJ/6/169, File 235.

23 H. S. Morris, 'The Divine Kingship of the Aga Khan: A Study of Theocracy in East Africa', *Southwestern Journal of Anthropology*, 14, 4 (1958): 454–72, especially 464 ff.

24 Kurzman, 'Liberal Islam: Prospects and Challenges', especially 12–13. Cf. Bayly, *Recovering Liberties*, 231: 'Muslims who accepted rational interpretations of the Koran are also sometimes loosely called "liberals"'.

25 Kurzman, 'Liberal Islam: Prospects and Challenges', 11.

26 This debate about elite manipulation among South Asia's Hindus and Muslims is encapsulated in the Brass-Robinson debate. This gravitates around the question of elite agency, often *allegedly* going to the extent of circumventing contextuality, as upheld by Paul Brass, *Language, Religion and Politics in North India*, 119–81 (Cambridge: Cambridge University Press, 1974); Brass, 'Elite Groups, Symbol Manipulation and Ethnic Identity among the Muslims of South Asia' in *Political Identity in South Asia*, edited by David Taylor and Malcolm Yapp, 35–77 (London and Dublin: Curzon Press, 1979); Brass, *Ethnicity and Nationalism: Theory and Comparison*, 69–118 (New Delhi: Sage, 1991). Opposed to this is

Francis Robinson, 'Islam and Muslim Separatism' in *Political Identity in South Asia*, edited by Taylor and Yapp, 78–112; and also, 'Nation Formation: The Brass Thesis and Muslim Separatism' in Idem, *Islam and Muslim History in South Asia*, 156–76 (New Delhi: Oxford University Press, 2012 [2000]), where the historical significance of the socio-religious and cultural movements and the general politico-historical contextuality are underscored. However Robinson, *Islam and Muslim History*,13 is not very comfortable with the label 'primordialist' either.

27　See e.g., Brass, *Ethnicity and Nationalism*, 76–77; Cf., for a theoretical outline, Quentin Skinner, 'Some Problems in the Analysis of Political Thought and Action', *Political Theory*, 2, 3 (1974): 277–303, at 289–301, underlining the dynamic relationship between 'professed principles and actual practices of political life'.

28　Shaikh, *Community and Consensus*; Cf. Bayly, *Recovering Liberties*, 232, where he suggests that the so-called 'Muslim separatism' should be seen as 'a principled position, rather than a simple reflection of the community's minority status'.

29　Faisal Devji, 'The Minority as Political Form' in *From the Colonial to the Postcolonial: India and Pakistan in Transition*, edited by Dipesh Chakrabarty, Rochona Majumdar and Andrew Sartori, 85–95, at 86 (New Delhi: Oxford University Press, 2007).

30　Ibid., 86–87.

31　Christophe Jaffrelot, 'Hindu Nationalism: Strategic Syncretism in Ideology Building', *Economic and Political Weekly*, XXVIII, 12–13 (March 1993): 517–24. See also, Clifford Geertz, *The Interpretation of Cultures*, 193–254 (New York: Basic Books, 1973).

32　Jaffrelot, 'Hindu Nationalism',517; Cf., how Jaffrelot somewhat revised and recast his argument when he preferred the 'invention of tradition' model (where many of the components of Hindu nationalism were depicted as alien to any 'traditional xenology' of the Indians) to that of 'strategic syncretism' arguing that the latter is more relevant in studies of socio-religious reform movements like the Brahmo Samaj that aimed at 'cultural synthesis'. See Christophe Jaffrelot, *The Hindu Nationalist Movement and Indian Politics, 1925 to the 1990s: Strategies of Identity Building, Implantation and Mobilisation (with special reference to Central India)*, Translation of the 1993 French edition, 6, fn 23 (London: Hurst & Company, 1996).

33　Purohit, 'Identity Politics Revisited'. Gauri Viswanathan, 'Secularism in the Framework of Heterodoxy', *Publications of the Modern Language Association*, 123, 2 (2008): 466–76, suggests a reappraisal of the role of heterodoxy in world religions to better appreciate the secular. Viswanathan is careful not to equate secularism with heterodoxy, although, she adds that the field of literary studies had somewhat appropriated the secularization model while expunging its religious origins (ibid., 466–67, 476).

34　Purohit, 'Identity Politics Revisited'.

35　Interestingly, the British officials came to locate this Memorial in the provocative discursive tradition regarding the nature of the British Empire as 'the greatest Muslim power in the world'. See IOR, Political and Secret Department Records, 'Memorandum by H. H. the Aga Khan: suggestion that the policy of Great Britain should be to protect Islam in Central Asia', 1918/L/PS/11/141, Subject P 5169/ 1918.

36　Aga Khan, *India in Transition*, 49. Originally meaning religious community, the *millat* emerged as an important administrative term in the Ottoman Empire referring to a system whereby the non-Muslim subjects were guaranteed autonomy in their 'internal religious, social and communal affairs while retaining their protected status'. See Azim Nanji, *'Millet'* in Idem, *The Penguin Dictionary of Islam*, 115 (London: Penguin, 2008).

37 Aga Khan, *India in Transition*, 299.

38 Bhargava, *Secularism and its Critics*, 7.

39 Akeel Bilgrami, 'Secularism: Its Content and Context', *Economic and Political Weekly*, XLVII, 4 (2012): 89–100. Bilgrami's call for a reconceptualization is in effect also a strong critique of Ashis Nandy's anti-modernist stance that romanticizes the non-West and the traditional past; Nandy, 'The Politics of Secularism' in *Secularism and its Critics*, edited by Bhargava, 321–44. For a concise overview of the literature and recent debates, see Mohita Bhatia, 'Secularism and Secularisation: A Bibliographical Essay', *Economic and Political Weekly*, XLVIII, 50 (December 2013): 103–10; Cf. the sceptic concerns in Shabnum Tejani, *Indian Secularism: A Social and Intellectual History* (New Delhi/ Ranikhet: Permanent Black, 2014 [2007]). Tejani sees the emergence of secularism in India as a liberal democratic tool appropriated by the 'overwhelmingly middle-class, upper-caste Hindu men' to provide a 'counterpoint to the challenges posed from margins by the Muslim and Dalit communities'. Thus 'Indian secularism' has to be seen as a 'relational category' emerging at the nexus of 'community and caste, nationalism and communalism, liberalism and democracy' (ibid., 15).

40 These were, however, mutually constitutive aspects. In fact, it was in 1909 that it was decided that the All India Muslim League and the Muslim Educational Conference should be separated. See David Lelyveld, *Aligarh's First Generation: Muslim Solidarity in British India*, 339 (Delhi: Oxford University Press, 1996 [1978]).

41 Mukherjee, 'Being "Ismaili" and "Muslim"', 199 ff.

42 Prashant Kidambi, 'From "Social Reform" to "Social Service": Indian Civic Activism and the Civilizing Mission in Colonial Bombay c. 1900-1920' in *Civilizing Missions in Colonial and Postcolonial South Asia*, edited by Carey A. Watt and Michael Mann, 217–239, at 217–18 (London, New York and Delhi: Anthem, 2012 [2011]).

43 Ibid., 218.

44 Aga Khan, *India in Transition*, 250.

45 Carey Anthony Watt, *Serving the Nation: Cultures of Service, Association, and Citizenship*, 65 (New Delhi: Oxford University Press, 2005). Watt thus illustrates how older Hindu ideals of *dana* (donations) and *seva* (service) were remodelled along lines of social service, thanks to the active intervention of social service associations; Cf. Gwilym Beckerlegge, *Swami Vivekananda's Legacy of Service: A Study of the Ramakrishna Math and Mission*, especially chapter 5 (New Delhi: Oxford University Press, 2000). For more elaborate exposition of the Ramakrishna Mission's discourse of social service, with reference to its social profile and intellectual lineage and not least implications, see idem, *The Ramakrishna Mission: The Making of a Modern Hindu Movement* (New Delhi: Oxford University Press, 2006).

46 José Casanova, *Public Religions in the Modern World* (Chicago and London: University of Chicago Press, 1994), a position re-assessed and re-asserted in idem, 'Public Religions Revisited' in *Religion: Beyond the Concept*, edited by Hent de Vries, 101–19 (New York: Fordham University Press, 2008).

47 See Adamjee Peerbhoy to Sir Badruddin Tyabji, 12 August 1885, Bombay. The Tyabji Papers, Volume 1, Serial Number 24, NAI.

48 The other great feat of the Tyabji clan, in comparison with the Daudi Bohras, had been their success in curbing the Sulaimani religious head's objections to exogamy. The increasing hypergamous connections in turn, facilitated an organic Islamization, and often certain 'ashrafization' (for many of such matrimonial relations were with older 'ashraf' families from northern India) that went hand in hand with 'Urduization'. See Theodore P. Wright Jr., 'Muslim Kinship and Modernization: The Tyabji Clan of Bombay' in *Family, Kinship and Marriage among Muslims in India*, edited by Imtiaz Ahmad, 217–38, especially, 223, 226–30 (Delhi: Manohar, 1976). These efforts represented some of the earliest moves on the part of families from such smaller Muslim sub-sects to new challenges like opening up to exogamous practices. Curiously, however, it was observed that even while the Sulaimanis emerged as pioneers in these experiments, for all their diverse similarities they hardly entered into matrimonial relations with the Daudi Bohras. See *Gazetteer of the Bombay Presidency, Volume IX, Part 2, 1899*, 33, edited by James A Campbell. In contrast, the strong endogamous tradition of the Daudis even after the turn of the century is pointed out. See *Gazetteer of the Province of Sind, Volume 'A'*, edited by E. H. Aitken, 176 (Karachi: Mercantile Steam Press, 1907).

49 Sir Badruddin Tyabji's evidence before the 1882 Education Commission was in line with the 'Muslim backwardness' thesis. See 'The Education Commission 1882: Badruddin Tyabji's Evidence and Anjuman-i-Islam Memorial', chapter VII, the Tyabji Papers, Volume 26, Serial No. 992, NAI. The memorial also documented at length the service the Bombay Anjuman i Islam came to render in the field of education, 'notwithstanding persistent efforts to injure it and depreciate its advantages ...'; see 21.

50 Gail Minault, *Secluded Scholars: Women's Education and Muslim Social Reform in Colonial India*, 190 (New Delhi: Oxford University Press, 1998). Tyabji's Indian National Congress connections might help explain his rather late participation in the MEC affairs in 1903, by which time the social and educational objectives of the MEC had been made much clearer. For a comparison of Tyabji's stance with that of Sayyid Ahmad Khan, see ibid.,183–85. Sir Sayyid's criticism of the *purdah*, or his recognition of the need for women's education, was however not matched by any systematic plan to carry forward such visions.

51 Dobbin, *Urban Leadership in Western India*, 115.

52 Green, *Bombay Islam*, 20. See 16 ff. for a general overview of the different trends he refers to.

53 The original Trustees of the Bombay Anjuman thus included: Sir Badruddin Tyabji, Currimbhoy Ebrahim, Fatehali Shaikh Ahmed, Sulleman Abdool Wahed, and Dawoodbhoy Moosabhoy. Subsequent Trustees also included key figures from the Khoja Reformist Movement, e.g. the Sunni Khoja Ahmedbhoy Habibhoy. Most of these names are clearly suggestive of a strong Bohra and Khoja presence in the ranks of the association's leadership. See 'Distribution of printed copies of the deed for the boarding house in connection with the Anjuman i Islam', Educational Department, Building Grants, No. 395, Vol. 17, 1906, Maharashtra State Archives (MSA).

54 Thus in the early 1830s as protest to municipal decision to slaughter stray dogs that hurt Parsi religious sentiments, the Parsis were joined by Hindus, Jains, and Muslims (particularly 'Ismaili Muslims') showing the power of the Gujarati-speaking coterie. Jesse S. Palsetia, 'Mad Dogs and Parsis: The Bombay Dog Riots of 1832', *Journal of the Royal Asiatic Society*, Series 3, 11, 1 (2001): 13–30; especially at 18–19.

55 Nile Green, 'Islam for the Indentured Indian: a Muslim Missionary in Colonial South Africa', *Bulletin of School of Oriental and African Studies*, 71, 3 (2008): 529–53; at 531–32.

While Urdu certainly did have a rich cultural heritage shared by both Hindus and Muslims, it nevertheless emerged as a rallying point around which communities were redrawn to a decisive extent in the wake of competing religious nationalist politics since the late nineteenth century. See Brass, *Language, Religion and Politics*,127–38; Brass, 'Elite Groups, Symbol Manipulation and Ethnic Identity among the Muslims of South Asia', 48–52; Brass, *Ethnicity and Nationalism*, 83–86.

56 Dobbin, *Urban Leadership in Western India*, 236; See ibid., 232 ff. for an overview on the difficulties the institution faced. Commenting more generally on trends in western India, Kenneth Ballhatchet, *Social Policy and Social Change in Western India, 1817–1830*, 248–50 (London: Oxford University Press, 1957), points to a disdain of religious leaders in accepting Western education on account of what they suspected to be ulterior missionary as well as Utilitarian designs of conversion programmes.

57 See 'Application for the payment of the grant proposed by Government towards the construction of the boarding house in connection with the Anjuman i Islam', Educational Department, Building Grants, Vol. 13, 1902, MSA.

58 'List of Political, Quasi-Political & Religious Societies, Sabhas, Anjumans & Labour Unions in the Bombay Presidency & Sind for the year ending June 1920', Home Department, (Special), File 355 (74)- II/ 1921, 13–14, MSA. And this, in any case, was no aberration in large parts of the African colonies either. For the better part of the colonial period denominational differences among the Indian Muslim population doggedly resisted any effort at standardization of religious education in key sites in East Africa, such as Zanzibar. See Roman Loimeier, *Between Social Skills and Marketable Skills: The Politics of Islamic Education in 20th Century Zanzibar* (Leiden and Boston: Brill, 2009), 224 ff.

59 Gail Minault and David Lelyveld, 'The Campaign for a Muslim University, 1898-1920', *Modern Asian Studies*, 8, 2 (1974): 145–89.

60 Ibid.,146–48.

61 Ibid., 149. Part of this urgency – which Sir Badruddin shared with Sir Sayyid – was directly connected to genuine concerns to uplift the social conditions of a *qaum* seriously discredited by critiques of alleged backwardness in government circles. This is largely attributed to W. W. Hunter, *The Indian Musalmans* (New Delhi: Rupa & Co., 2004 [1871]), though Hunter himself was quite categorical about the limited nature of his sources, which he derived from Bengal. Curiously, though, this was subsequently applied in the pan-Indian context to explain 'Muslim separatism'.

62 Mukherjee, 'Being "Ismaili" and "Muslim"', 202.

63 *Foundations of Pakistan: All India Muslim League Documents, 1906-1947: Volume I, 1906-1924*, 16, edited by Syed Sharifuddin Pirzada (Karachi and Dacca: National Publishing House Limited, 1969).

64 Justin Jones, 'The Local Experience of Reformist Islam in a "Muslim" Town in Colonial India: The Case of Amroha', *Modern Asian Studies*, 43, 4 (2009): 871–908, especially 889–96. This argument of the Shia specificities of Amroha is further developed in idem., *Sh'ia Islam in Colonial India*, especially chapter 4.

65 The classic study of the Khilafat Movement in this vein still remains Gail Minault, *The Khilafat Movement: Religious Symbolism and Political Mobilization in India* (New York: Columbia University Press, 1982).

66 Edwin Montagu's Note, 13 January 1920 (commenting on the Aga Khan's letter dated 8

January 1920 and the Turkish peace), the UK Parliamentary Archives, Lloyd George Papers (LG)/ F/ 172/ 1/ 11 (d).

67　Thus as early as 1914, in a speech at a meeting of the Indian Volunteers Committee (of which M. K. Gandhi was the Chairman) in London on 1 October 1914, the Aga Khan connected the question of Muslim loyalty to the broader Muslim aspirations, dubbing Germany as the most dangerous enemy of Turkey and other Moslem countries, enjoining Indians to shoulder Britain's war efforts while also rebuking D. Lloyd George's (then Chancellor of the Exchequer) alleged flippant comparison of the German Kaiser with the Prophet Muhammad. See *The Times* (2 October 1914), in *Aga Khan III, Volume I*, edited by Aziz, 505–09.

68　Jones, *Sh'ia Islam in Colonial India*, 174.

69　Ibid., 174 ff. Indeed, an ideological critique of the Khilafat agitation developed across a wide political spectrum. Cf., e.g., Ian Bryant Wells, *Ambassador of Hindu Muslim Unity: Jinnah's Early Politics*, 110–30 (New Delhi: Permanent Black, 2005), where we see a Muhammad A. Jinnah busy in what Wells calls 'the backrooms of politics', negotiating and manipulating his way back to the political platform. Far from 'years of wilderness', thus, Wells sees the period between 1920 and 1923 to be of momentous political importance for Jinnah. The Congress veteran M. A. Ansari also later resigned from the Central Khilafat Committee on ground of the communal, retrograde politics of the Committee. M.A. Ansari to Shaukat Ali, 16 July 1926, Delhi, in *Muslims and the Congress: Select Correspondence of Dr. M.A. Ansari 1912–1935*, edited by Mushirul Hasan, 19 (New Delhi: Manohar, 1979).

70　In 1916, he was to suggest in a confidential note, the need to 'knock out' Turkey; the reasons cited were the unholy hobnobbing of the ruling Turkish echelons with the Germans that allegedly hurt Muslim sentiments; drawing a line between this 'modern' Turkish ruling group and general Muslim interests, he went on advocating displacing the government and opting for a separate peace with Turkey. The letter was thought to be 'interesting', but was not passed on to the King because it was suspected to be part of his old machinations for a separate peace treaty with the Turks, despised in influential sections of the British government. IOR, Political and Secret Department Records, 'The War: importance of "knocking out" Turkey: views of the Aga Khan', 1916, L/ PS/ 11/ 111, (Register No. P 4306/ 1916).

71　Devji, 'The Language of Muslim Universality', at 40.

72　Cf. The discussion in chapter 3 about Aga Khan III's idea of a South Asiatic Federation with India at the centre as a tool to enable India's Muslims to transcend their minority status by way of incorporating Muslims from other parts of the federation.

73　Bayly, *Recovering Liberties*, 322–24.

74　Letter dated 13 August 1935 from Aga Khan (Paris) to Sir Fazli Husein in Sir Fazli Hussain Collection, IOR MSS Eur E 352/ 19, Box 3. The sentence originally ran with the twin adjectives of 'unnatural and artificial', but the expression 'unnatural' was struck out.

75　Ibid.

76　See the letter dated 9 March 1947, from Aga Khan to M.A. Jinnah, Bombay, Document Number 106 (F. 327/ 1-2), in *Quaid-i-Azam Mohammad Ali Jinnah Papers: Prelude to Pakistan 20 February-2 June 1947, First Series, Vol. I, Part 1*, edited by Z. H. Zaidi, 210–11 (Islamabad and Lahore: National Archives of Pakistan/ Ferozons Pvt. Ltd., 1993). For an outline of his early views on the 'Army and Navy', see Aga Khan, *India in Transition*, chapter XVIII, 173–85.

77　Letter dated 13 August 1935 from Aga Khan (Paris) to Sir Fazli Husein in Sir Fazli Hussain Collection, IOR MSS Eur E 352/ 19, Box 3.

78 Aga Khan, *India in Transition*, 250-251. Thus Muslims and Hindus should all work together for the welfare of the depressed classes through what he calls 'mutual help associations on a national scale' relying on voluntary service (ibid., 251).

79 Tejani, *Indian Secularism*, 202, 219, points out that as early as 1906 Aga Khan III expressed his reservations about including the 'Depressed Classes' within the Hindu folds and later, along with M.A. Jinnah, argued for separate electorates. The 1935 position, then, must have had a longer history that only gradually crystallized into an assertive political project in the 1930s.

80 The importance of this event has been underscored by generations of commentators, politicians and historians alike. Aga Khan III, the leader of the deputation, himself noted it as 'the starting point of the recognition of the principle that the important Muslim minority in this country should have fair and legitimate share in the administration of the country'. Inaugural Address of the Aga Khan, Third Session of the All India Muslim League, Delhi, 29–30 January, 1910; see *Foundations of Pakistan: Volume I*, edited by Pirzada, 94. Similarly, retrospective scholarly works such as Matiur Rahman, *From Consultation to Confrontation: A Study of the Muslim League in British Indian Politics, 1906-1912*, 8 (London: Luzac & Company Ltd., 1970), have hailed the Simla Deputation as 'unique in that the Muslims of India were ... anxious to take their full share in the political activities of the country as a distinct identity.' Lelyveld, *Aligarh's First Generation*, 337, however, argues that the deputation was essentially an act of the 'Aligarh elders' and the Aga Khan was nothing more than a titular leader. The crux, nevertheless, lay in the *elders' choice* of the Aga Khan as the leader of the deputation, which at once promoted him to the much aspired position of leadership of South Asia's Muslims (although obviously not uncontested) vis-à-vis the Congress claims of representing Muslims.

81 This came in the form a letter published in the *Gujarati* (Mumbai, 7 October 1906). See *The Collected Works of Quaid-e-Azam Mohammad Ali Jinnah, Vol. I, 1906- 1921*, edited by Syed Sharifuddin Pirzada, 1 (Karachi: East and West Publishing Company, 1984).

82 Rahman, *From Consultation to Confrontation*, 28–30, suggests a much nuanced power struggle between Aga Khan III and Nawab Salimullah. The All India Muslim League was nevertheless established, thanks to the concatenation of different forces: that of the increasing tide of Hindu nationalism, the ostensible failure of the Simla Deputation, and above all the role of Syed Ameer Ali, Salimullah, and Mohsin-ul-Mulk among others (ibid., 32–34).

83 Letter dated 23 May 1931, from Sir Fazli Husein to the Aga Khan in Sir Fazli Hussain Collection, IOR MSS Eur E 352/ 19.

84 Letter dated 6 July 1931, from Sir Fazli Husein to the Aga Khan in Sir Fazli Hussain Collection, IOR MSS Eur E 352/ 19.

85 *The Khoja Shia Imami Ismaili Council, Poona: Rules and Regulations*, 39–41, 43 (Poona: The Khoja Shia Imami Ismaili Council, 1913).

86 This reply came out in *The Times of India* (27 January 1910, Bombay). See *Aga Khan III, Volume I*, edited by Aziz, 325–27.

87 See his interview with *The Times* (14 February 1909); cited in *Aga Khan III, Volume I*, edited by Aziz, 288–93.

88 Mukherjee, 'Being "Ismaili" and "Muslim"', 204.

89 Devji, 'Preface' to van Grondelle, *The Ismailis in the Colonial Era*, xiii.

5

The Importance of Being Ismaili

Religious Normativity and the Ismaili International in the Age of Global Assemblages

The headship of a religious community spread over a considerable part of the world surface—from Cape Town to Kashgar, from Syria to Singapore—cannot be sustained in accordance with any cut-and-dried system. Moral conditions, material facilities, national aspirations and outlook, and profoundly differing historical backgrounds have to be borne vastly in mind, and necessary mental adjustments made …

Syria, Iran, and the North-west Frontier Province of Pakistan are all countries with their strongly marked individuality, historical background, and traditions. These historical variations over centuries, and the accessibility, or lack of it, of many of the more isolated communities, and the development of communications between my family and my followers have all had their effect …

The correspondence which I maintain with all these far-scattered communities is affected by local circumstances.[1]

His Highness Aga Khan III, 1954

Writing in 1954 in a fast decolonizing post-World War II context, Aga Khan III thus went on to elaborate what he thought to be the distinctive feature of his Ismaili community. Elaborating on the protean nature of the community, the above observation thus expatiates on his general notion of fluidity of Ismailism that we have cited in the epigraph of the 'Introduction' to this book. The Aga Khan further added that the system of administration sustaining this global community had also been commensurately fluid, ranging from 'a highly developed and civilized administrative system of councils' in 'the British, Portuguese and French colonies of East Africa, Uganda, Portuguese East Africa, Madagascar, Natal and Cape Colony', administering a wide gamut of educational, property, executive and judicial matters. In India,

Pakistan, Burma and Malaya, a similar structure holds the community together, while in Central Asia, Afghanistan, parts of Russia and Chinese Turkestan, certain families, or sometimes even hereditary chieftains or secular rulers (but themselves Ismaili) such as in Hunza, function as the Imam's representatives and administrators connecting the myriad localities to the Imamate.[2]

Understandably, the importance of being Imami Ismaili is premised first and foremost on the basis of a belief in the spiritual guidance of the Imam of the time drawing upon an essentially pluralized and dynamic understanding of Islam, sensitized at once to the postnational subjectivities as well as the variegated administrative structures, which stem from the global locations of the community.[3] We have seen that in its early formative phase and in the context of late colonial – and in the early decades of postcolonial – East Africa this functioned through an oppositional mechanism whereby the Indian Muslims in general, and Ismailis in particular, were hailed by Aga Khan III as the carriers of civilizational progress. There was at the same time a systematic erosion of ethnic boundaries, anticipating the future forging of a global Ismaili ecumene out of a range of disparate cultural entities.[4] In its spirit, then, the skeins connecting ideationally the global Ismaili assemblage are reflective in large part of the cultural internationalism that informed Aga Khan III's pan-Islamic imagination. In more tangible terms though, the ideational model thrives on a materialization of a religiously inflected language of voluntary activism and social service or, as a recent commentator says, especially in the early diasporic context of the Ismailis in Africa, on a notion of 'welfare' giving direction to 'the process of connecting subjects through service'.[5] Evidently, therefore, the idea of cosmopolitanism that we are invoking here becomes intelligible first and foremost through the internal historical processes with particular reference to the social world as opposed to the political. In doing so, we are trying to relate to a line of scholarship that expresses a discomfort with the stratospheric abstractions sometimes associated with Kantian political cosmopolitanism or the cultural cosmopolitanism of the intellectuals.[6] This idea of critical cosmopolitanism is based on the premise that 'the very notion of cosmopolitanism compels the recognition of multiple kinds of cosmopolitanism ... which cannot be explained in terms of a single western notion of modernity or in terms of globalization'; moreover, instead of conceiving of cosmopolitanism as 'a particular or singular condition' it should be seen as 'a cultural medium of societal transformation'.[7] While this summarizes effectively a sociological approach to cosmopolitanism in the recent years, it also echoes academic concerns to understand the cosmopolitan imagination not by denying but very much with reference to inherited traditions beyond the classic normative Enlightenment framework of the 'West'.[8] We are, furthermore, invoking the idea of the cosmopolitan in yet another sense. I have in mind Andrew Linklater's notion of cosmopolitan citizenship as a conceptual model within which to situate 'efforts to create universal frameworks of communication'.[9] The Imamate's idea of an Ismaili subjectivity has to be situated at the intersection of these two conceptual planes.

The individual Imami Ismaili's identification with the community rests on the ideational planks that stem from the community's denominational characteristics, coupled with an understanding of Islam mediated by the Imamate. At the same time such identification had always been part of processes of negotiations. In the process it is being continuously worked out, in the sphere of praxis, at once drawing upon as well as facilitating the community's adaptation to the varied politico-cultural and historical contexts across the world where the community is spread. This sphere of praxis, therefore, constitutes a site where one sees the development, within the cultural geometry of Bourdieuian 'habitus', of an array of religious, cultural and normative subjectivities that are specific to the Ismailis but, importantly, also suffused with wider Islamic sensibilities.[10] It is within this larger framework of habitus that both textual and practical aspects enter a dialectic process, working out in line with an Ismaili normativity, and manifesting itself *inter alia* through a system of canonized protocols in the form of the Imam's *farmans* and schooling. This dialectic between forces of normativity and orthopraxy, it can be further argued, in the upshot becomes intelligible in terms of a specific Ismaili pattern for acquiring 'potentiality'.[11] The early phase of this exercise in religious normativity, both ideationally as well as in terms of practice, is documented by the history of the evolving community in the late colonial period in the western Indian Ocean world of East Africa and western parts of India. Moreover, in order for us to better appreciate the gradual emergence from within this transregional crucible of a language of deterritorialized postnationality characteristic of the burgeoning global Ismaili formations, it is important that we also explore crucial aspects of the analytical framework of what some recent scholars have called 'religious internationals'. This chapter interrogates the history of this transition by focusing first on the early experiments with normativity in the community's largely nineteenth century socio-religious life, and then proceeding to examine the carriers of the normative visions. Finally, the chapter proceeds to conceptualize what we may, following on the idea of 'religious internationals', call an 'Ismaili international'. In doing so the chapter seeks to shed light on the more recent history of the global community, its engagement at once with notions of Ismaili and Islamic normativity, and its cultural past. Furthermore, in as much as we study in this chapter the outreach of the Ismaili Imamate-sponsored institutions catering to both denominational as well as non-denominational interests, such as in the spheres of humanitarian and developmental ventures, we also underscore in the process some of the complexities of religiously-underpinned international bodies, and the modalities of their operation.[12]

Conferring on normativity: Ismailism and Islam in the twentieth century

Studies to understand the nature of theological/religious normativity have tended to oscillate between two ends of a spectrum: one with reference to social context(s) within which such normativity operates, and the other, a rather abstract idea of transcendent normativity independent of the question of contextuality. A preponderant thrust in scholarship has been to exemplify the above strands with reference to developments in Christian societies and their encounters with non-Christian cultures. The very idea of inculturation, whereby Christian societies adapt their liturgical formations to diverse non-Christian socio-cultural contexts across the globe while also locating the Gospel centrally in the project, also raises an array of conceptual and empirical complexities. Such complexities range from the question of adaptability on the one hand, to the (re)definition of the core of Christian faith on the other. At the same time, for all the possible pathways that the question of adaptability elicits, no Christian society undergoing or exposed to the process of inculturation could possibly relinquish the claims to what it sees as its pristine religious core.[13] Such dynamics between the forces of adaptability and normativity is, naturally, not restricted only to Christian societies. Our enquiry into the variegated cultural experiences of the Ismailis presents a similar set of academic questions. Furthermore, and as the abiding concern underpinning the present study illustrates, any effort to go beyond merely *narrating* the evolution of an Ismaili normativity will inevitably lead us to explore the idioms invoked in the process, with reference to their implications and deontological possibilities. Such idioms had always been, and still are, all fundamentally correlated to larger questions of community identity – itself a fluid conceptual category, as already shown – and specific interpretation of Islam, and pan-Islamic perceptions.[14]

In the preceding chapters we have seen how the discourse of an Ismaili normativity was shaped in consonance with, and indeed as part of, an essentially pluralized understanding of Islam. This discursive venture involved, furthermore, a mediation of the Imamate which, under Aga Khan III, brought about systematic restructuration of the community's organizations and institutions even as the community spread globally, and Aga Khan III had to play different roles in both national and international arenas. To begin with, however, the Ismaili discourse of normativity that emerged from the late nineteenth century Bombay – before and roughly corresponding to the early years of Aga Khan III's Imamate – met with strong competition from different sections of Bombay's religious and cultural actors. The Imami Ismaili/Ithna Ashari Ismaili split in Bombay, thus, had a remarkable impact in so far as early orthopractic initiatives were concerned. Such initiatives drew upon the new culture of associational activism that had since the latter part of the nineteenth century conditioned civic consciousness in almost all the Presidency towns. Thus, the Mahfil-i-Asna Ashari was established in

1878 with a view to imparting 'Arabic and religious education to the Khoja children of the Asna [Ithna] Ashari community and to hold religious meetings'. One of the earliest associations (*Mehfel*), it was financially supported by the Ithna Ashariya Khoja merchant Ibrahim Hasham. Founded with the active support of Ithna Ashariya landed proprietors and merchants with limited financial means, almost all these associations – for instance, the Mahfil-i-Panjtan established in 1887, the Khoja Mahfil-i-Huasin (sic) established in 1888, the Khoja Shia Asna Ashari Volunteer Corps established in 1919 – had rather limited scope of activities, viz. propagating Ithna Ashariya Khoja religious beliefs. In the records of the colonial state they had all gone down as religious associations of hardly any importance. Barring the Khoja Shia Asna Ashari Volunteer Corps, comprising Ithna Ashariya Khoja youths dedicated to 'keep order at political meetings and processions' and probably reflecting the general spirit of self-help groups of the time, scarcely any of the above organizations had any links with political activism of the times.[15] Writing against the backdrop of this thriving associational life, the self-declared 'reformists' argued with an implicit stereotypical civilizational binarism that the progressive civic culture of the times that they said they voiced was in essence at odds with the Imamate. Ironically, the extent to which the reformists of the early twentieth century drew upon the predominant nineteenth century Orientalist tropes to discredit the Imamate is quite remarkable. The 1901 Northcote Memorial thus recorded that the reformist associations, styled as '*Mehfels*' modelled on 'modern clubs, came to represent the 'advance party'. By contrast, the pro-Aga Khani associational activism came to be denigrated as a deadly group of '*Fidavis*' or 'gangs' with memberships ranging from 50 to 300 persons. According to the writers of the Northcote Memorial the various 'gangs' – the 'Panjebhais' ('Brothers united by the *Panja* or palm of the hand'), the 'gangs' named after the days on which they used to meet, such as the 'Sukarwadias' (those meeting on Fridays), the 'Saniwarias' (those meeting on Saturdays), and other associations sponsored by the Imamate, which also included female '*Fidavis*' – all had in the common the overarching aim to stifle any reformist voice.[16] This bitterness in the language employed by the reformist camp, in a way, betrays the enduring nature of the civilizational normativity that had captured the reformist imagination in the nineteenth century, and which we have seen Aga Khan I's Defence Counsel was impelled to address meticulously before he could re-inscribe the Imamate's history.

The programme of canonization in conjunction with organizational restructuration that Aga Khan III brought about from the early 1900s, thus, becomes intelligible against this larger backdrop of reformist ventures and heightened tension, signalling the onset of a complex historical process that went on to redefine the very contours of an Ismaili identity. Its success in both articulating and translating into actuality a language of community, however, lay in its being dovetailed with a language of an ethical religion. Also significant is the way this idiom of ethical religion, and of social service underpinned with a discourse of voluntarism, came to be customized to diverse socio-cultural and political milieus. And it is precisely this widening process – entailing an array of complexities that stemmed from its inculturation in non-Ismaili contexts beyond the framework of the national – that also sets apart the Imami Ismaili case from the experience of the other identical groups. While the canonized protocols and the Imam's *farmans* to the Ismaili believers gradually started to (re)shape the ideational core of the Ismaili normative universe, the organizational endeavours ranging from management of general community affairs to developing educational programmes have all, over the decades, emerged as vehicles through which to translate the normative claims into actuality. The project of setting an ideal code of conduct for the Ismailis, thus, ranges from normative advice on orthopractic issues in the quotidian life to a systematic institutionalization of mechanisms of instruction to address the needs of the Ismailis.[17] A language of religious and social welfare of the (Ismaili) community thus underwrites the panoply of the Imamate's didactic tools, such as the rules and regulations and constitutions. A cognate set of vocabularies discernible within the same conceptual constellation are the idioms of the community's (i.e. the Ismailis') progress and prosperity.[18] Together, these vocabularies, gleaned from the community's records from the postcolonial times in Africa and Pakistan, signify their continuing relevance in a world in which the language of community and development – intersecting as they had always been, but more importantly than ever in the fast changing decolonizing world – came to re-invent themselves in new forms. Indeed, this has to be seen as part of a larger process even as the project of social service and welfare widened almost incessantly, albeit with the occasional minor halts. In the process, significant adaptations were made in largely non-Ismaili environments, while they had also come to address a wide gamut of non-Ismaili interests taking the developmental *imaginaire*, with specific Ismaili claims, to the non-Ismaili world.

Carriers of normativity: Visions and institutions

Evidently, a language of Ismaili community welfare – in both social and religious terms – co-exists with a larger concern to take the discourse of Ismaili ethics of social service beyond the Ismaili community. A contemporary organizational manifestation of this endeavour to reach a much larger target audience and relate to a universalist language of social justice comes in the form of the Aga Khan Development Network (AKDN).[19] The 'development network' thus named marks the consummation of a prolonged process of institutionalized social service since the Imamate of Aga Khan III. In its current form – invoking at once an idea of a holistic 'development' as well as a degree of flux and fluidity encapsulated in the expression 'network' – the organization emerged in the 1980s reflecting a larger historical process of Imamate-sponsored institutionalization.

Indeed, the 1980s have been seen by scholars as a watershed in history when 'religion showed its Janus face, as the carrier of not only exclusive, particularist, and primordial identities but also of inclusive, universalist and transcending ones'.[20] And yet, as this present study illustrates, this was not always so much a narrative of abrupt rupture in essence or spirit, but rather a shift in modes of articulation and operation, and in emphases. At one level, the AKDN thus consolidated and/or subsumed earlier bodies, such as the Aga Khan Foundation (AKF, established in 1967), which was originally designed to sponsor the Imamate's early developmental programmes. At another level, the AKDN also brought in its train a widening in both the nature of its scope, in line with larger ethical questions, as well as its target audience even as non-Ismailis across the globe came to increasingly benefit from its programmes.

The AKDN's component bodies thus operate with a wide spectrum of mandates and include the Aga Khan Academies (AKA), Aga Khan Education Services (AKES), Aga Khan Foundation (AKF), Aga Khan Agency for Microfinance (AKAM), Aga Khan Fund for Economic Development (AKFED), Aga Khan Health Services (AKHS), Aga Khan Rural Support Programme (AKRSP), Aga Khan Trust for Culture (AKTC), Aga Khan Planning and Building Services (AKPBS), FOCUS (Focus Humanitarian Assistance) etc. Understandably, the idea of 'development' with which the AKDN functions is one that is not restricted to the rather narrowly confined understanding of the concept that is sometimes argued to have emerged only as late as in 1945 in response to the specific humanitarian needs of the post-World War II era, a somewhat skewed model that predominates contemporary Development Studies.[21] Furthermore, the non-denominational character that the AKDN professes is due not only to the wide audience it caters to but also its mode of operations in which various national governments, government organizations and private institutions are partners. Thus, a substantial part of the AKDN's funding also comes from various national governments, multilateral institutions and private-sector partners.[22] The nature of the AKDN's functioning, then, betrays a curious ambiguity that international organizations with claims to promoting universalizing agenda have historically confronted: a commitment to transcend the strictures of the nation-state and territoriality, while at the same time having to take the pragmatic course of engaging with the nation and its institutional manifestations by way of collaborative endeavours. This brings us back to one of our basic premises laid down in the Introduction to this book, viz., critiques of any triumphalist and/or totalizing discourse of nationalism and nation need not be seen as outright denial of the very existence of the framework of the 'national'. Rather, such critiques tend to instantiate at once beyond the rubric of the national, within it, as well as at the interstices from which the nation, or for that matter the state, often withdraws itself. Moreover, such endeavours are very often rooted in the politico-cultural locations of the agent. For Aga Khan III this meant in essence a conceptual model within which to situate a community, while taking it beyond the confines set by the nation-state, an internationalism that helped sustain the very idea of a transregional and global Ismaili ecumene. The host of the community's contemporary institutions have both historically emerged out of this process and, as they have proliferated, tended to facilitate this notion of deterritorialization further. This is also where Saskia Sassen's terminology of the 'denationalized' contra – but not necessarily independent of – the 'postnational' becomes relevant. Together the trajectories of the postnational and the denationalized – which Sassen sees as not necessarily mutually exclusive – have emerged as potent forces in the contemporary world conditioning ideas of citizenship. Such ideas of citizenship tend to operate both beyond as well as within the framework of the national, while the very nature of the denationalized formations in turn involve fundamental changes in ideas of the national state.[23]

International organizations with religious underpinnings typically betray an additional trait, one that concerns self-depiction and taxonomization, viz., for all their religious inspiration, a preponderant reluctance on their part to be identified as religious non-governmental organizations (RNGOs) or faith-based organizations (FBOs) nevertheless.[24] This adds, furthermore, to the pressing need to look beyond constricted analytical categories and underline the pertinence of exploring the transformative nature of the religious experience(s) in the modern world. Thus the literature of the AKDN in its efforts to outline the organization's ethical foundations invokes a distinctively religiously-inspired normative argument to 'realise the social conscience of Islam through institutional action',[25] only to cautiously add its non-denominational outlook in terms of operational modalities as well as target audience, as mentioned above.[26] Furthermore, its initiatives are taken forward by the global Ismaili community with its 'tradition of philanthropy, voluntary service and self-reliance, and the leadership and material underwriting of the hereditary Imam and Imamat resources'.[27] But significantly, as the official literature critically adds, 'religious leaders not only interpret the faith but also have a responsibility to help improve the quality of life *in their community and in the societies amongst which they live*' (emphasis mine).[28] The centrality of the Imam's guidance in 'a liberating, enabling framework for an individual's quest for meaning and for solutions to the problems of life',[29] coupled with efforts at refashioning the Imamate in corporate style are,[30] then, reminders to a much complex but pertinent understanding of both the religious *imaginaire* as well as secularism. Such an understanding of secularism as we have noted in the Introduction with reference to Talal Asad's masterly formulation – one that impels new ideas of 'religion', 'ethics' and politics and new imperatives[31] – helps one better appreciate the critical balance between religiously inflected languages of normativity and activism and of universal idioms of social service and welfare that the developmental vision of organizations such as the AKDN encapsulate.

The continued relevance of the religio-cultural *topos*, though often in re-invented forms, in contemporary developmental endeavours necessitate, furthermore, that we critically engage with this complex entwinement with reference to their mutually constitutive relationship.[32] We have also seen how this mutually constitutive relationship evolved out of the Imamate's persistent efforts, from the times of Aga Khan III in particular. The emphases on human intellect, voluntary activism and organized social service endeavours, mediated by the Imamate for primarily a community spread across the transregional arena of the western Indian Ocean world and then increasingly on a global scale, provided the blueprint for the contemporary development ventures. Thus, the East African Muslim Welfare Society (EAMWS), established in 1945 in Mombasa by Aga Khan III, sought to propagate a more organic idea of unity among the Muslims on the continent through funding the establishment of mosques, schools, scholarships, and catering also to the needs of Africans by way of construction programmes, such as that of the Vasini Island Water Reservoir. The Aga Khan usually matched all contributions made by the non-Ismailis.[33] This idea of matching contributions bore special importance in the sphere of educational experiments that the Ismailis engaged with since the early part of the twentieth century in both South Asia and East Africa. Thus the AKES traces its history to the schools that the Imamate under Aga Khan III started in the early 1900s in Mundra and Gwadur in the western parts of India and in Zanzibar about the same time, followed by those in Kenya, Tanzania and Uganda.[34]

While on the subcontinent the educational experiments of Aga Khan III increasingly assumed a larger ecumenical dimension, ranging from sponsorship of the Anjuman i Islam to the Aligarh venture, there were also parallel efforts where the community of the Ismailis in particular were enjoined to take a leading role. In such ventures as the ones in Gwadur and Mundra in India, and those in East Africa, the Aga Khan thus made the bulk of the contributions, although as the community grew prosperous he expected them to match his contributions. It can be argued that such financial policy of matching grants in educational administration became a crucial vehicle of instilling a sense of active belonging among the community members rather than remaining merely passive receivers.[35] At times, especially as the twentieth century progressed, this meant gradual incorporation of a whole spectrum of non-Ismaili clientele resulting, in the process, in a complex experience of inculturation. We shall have the opportunity in the following section to return to the complexities of these educational initiatives with specific Ismaili imprint, and the role they played in the (re)conceptualization of the community's boundaries over the twentieth century with their more recent ramifications. Thus in tandem with the Imamate's more recent and wider range of developmental initiatives, and amid a widening process of inculturation, earlier traditional networks, with all their cultural specificities have come to be formalized creating further props of institutionalization. It is important to note, however, that this endeavour of inculturation projects itself through a language of universalist visions of sustainable development and progress, which is perhaps also the reason that it has by and large peaceably found in the process allies in different state and non-state actors. While this does not necessarily mean a seamless translation of avowed Ismaili ethics, the general impression one gathers nevertheless is one of relative success in AKDN-led initiatives seeking peaceable solutions to a wide gamut of endemic societal problems.[36] In addition to the widening process of inculturation discussed above, we shall further see in the following pages the centrality of the developmental imagination in the Imamate's mediation between the present and a pristine cultural past. This engagement with the past, we need to foreground, is closely related to another dimension of universality that have historically informed Khoja Ismaili experiences since especially the times of Aga Khan III, viz., the denomination's tryst with a wider Islamic consciousness, or more tangibly, a spiritually bound Islamic community.

I would like to emphasize at this juncture, however, that it is at this realm of praxis that the bulk of the normative prescriptions for the Ismailis coming in the form of the Imam's *farmans* as well as community's codes of conduct were – and still are – discussed, deliberated, and implemented training in the process Ismaili children across the world in Ismaili ethics customized to the diverse cultural particularities, while also centripetally connecting the global Ismaili formations to the Imamate at the core. The very structure of the Ismaili educational system, serving the Ismaili ecumene in different parts of the world, signifies this critical balance whereby local Ismaili formations are, for all their individualities, still administered through a centralized organization with remarkable flexibility. A volume from 1977–78 commemorating 60 years of 'Ismaili education' in Kenya, and indeed symptomatic of general trends in East Africa, as well as other parts of the continent, thus illustrates the point. One thus learns how until 1905 school teachers in towns and villages were all answerable to the *jamaat* treasurer, the *mukhi* who, as our late twentieth century commemorative text suggests, also acted as the leader of the *jamaat*. With the introduction of the first set of rules and regulations in East Africa in 1905, school committees, while still answerable to the *mukhi*, took over the administration. Local Education Boards supervised by the local Ismailia Councils were constituted in the rural areas, while in the urban areas Provincial Education Boards under the supervision of the Ismailia Provincial Council were established.[37] With an overhaul of the system in 1937, in the wake of Aga Khan III's golden jubilee celebrations, it is further argued, 'for the first time education administration became a specialised function within the community', a trend that also signified growing hierarchical structuration. In each of the territories of East Africa, Central Education Board(s) consisting of officers appointed by the Hazir Imam, came to administer educational matters in their respective territories. The educational bodies were made independent of their erstwhile controllers and were, instead, made part of a hierarchical structure with the Central Education Board at the top, bolstered by the Provincial Education Board, Local Education Board and the Village School Committee through the middle down to the bottom of the pyramid.[38] In the post-World War II scenario, the Central Education Boards were replaced by Educational Administrators with full discretionary powers for each of the four East African territories, viz., Kenya, Uganda, Tanganyika and Zanzibar, responsible directly to the Hazir Imam. In addition there were two further Educational Administrators for South Africa and Madagascar. It is this structure, we are told, that 'gave the impetus for the policymakers to develop the system of Ismaili education in the next three decades'.[39]

The problem of adaptability that both the AKDN in general and the Ismaili educational venture in particular came to signify, had never been, however, independent of this larger question of centralized structuration. It is a model of centripetal forces coupled with a remarkable degree of adaptability, a model powerful enough to connect a transregional community cutting across the lines of nations, states, and territories. Dovetailed with a language of reciprocity they inform as well as define more recent and contemporary Ismaili experiences across the globe. It is a holistic endeavour that marks intersections of didactic instructions, administered through a framework set by the Imamate, in both languages of universal ethical questions and Ismaili religio-cultural values, questions of identity, their practical aspects and, moreover, active participation in a process that promises remarkable possibilities of inculturation. In other words, the educational sphere thus acts as the crucial site in which the worldwide Ismailis – and especially Ismaili children – receive both general ethical as well as particular didactic and organizational instruction evoking at the same time active participation and a language of reciprocity, as documented through the comprehensive *talim* programme with a specific Ismaili imprint.[40]

This language of active participation and reciprocity, furthermore, informs the developmental *imaginaire* of the AKDN which in turn is premised on the state-of-art discourse of sustainability. Thus such development efforts of the Imamate become meaningful only when reciprocated by those who are the very targets of the development initiatives, Ismailis and non-Ismailis alike. As the present Imam Aga Khan IV notes:

> *Development is sustainable only if the beneficiaries become, in a gradual manner, the masters of the process.* This means that initiatives cannot be contemplated exclusively in terms of economics, but rather as an integrated programme that encompasses social and cultural dimensions as well.[41]

(Emphasis mine)

Often originating in the specific circumstances of alleviative humanitarian interventions, much of the Imamate's development ventures have thus tended to gradually expand into larger endeavours towards capacity-building and more fundamental infrastructural development which, in certain ways, reminds one of the Spencerian idioms of social efficiency.[42] The cutting edge of the AKDN, and its precursors in limited scale, then, lay – in a large part – in their evoking arguments of sustainability and capacity-building in the multiple locations of the Ismaili ecumene without having to necessarily engage with the paradigm of the national at the *ideational* plane. The nation and/or the state is thus a potential collaborator, a dovetailed appendage, but not a sine qua non. A holistic understanding of development, in line with the AKDN's vision, thus, becomes a key vehicle to carry this language of postnationalism with an Ismaili imprint. In other words, the AKDN's developmental vision becomes meaningful in terms of its fruitful appropriation by an essentially religiously inspired organization that had managed to successfully wed its religious sensibilities to the universalizing language of social justice realized in a postnational universe. And yet, in so doing, it also has to engage, in the realm of *praxis*, with the denationalizing effects within the framework of the national through its engagement with mechanisms of partnerships and collaboration, even as the very idea of the national changes. Thus a combination of languages of the universalizing values of social justice and postnational imagination both conditions and defines the nature of what we have identified as the 'Ismaili international', while its institutional articulation tends to bring itself out through the idioms of the denationalized. It is this complex intertwined relationship that we try to elucidate in the following section.

Conceptualizing an Ismaili international

Our use of the nomenclature of the 'Ismaili international', evidently, is an effort to understand, within the larger rubric of Islamic consciousness, an avowed Ismaili religio-cultural core while also indicating the possibility of different pathways of Ismaili inculturation across the world. An array of denominational issues that defines its religio-cultural core revolving around the pivotal importance of the Ismaili Imamate's leadership then informs this idea of an Ismaili universalism, and its efforts to engage with a perceived Islamic universality. Within the wider space of its habitus, and through its didactic apparatuses, the Imamate has thus historically sought to produce an Ismaili subjectivity, at once underscoring the importance of voluntary affiliation responsive to inherited traditions and structures entrenched in specific religio-cultural experiences and also engaging with universalizing values, ethical codes, and aspirations. This re-invigorated emphasis on higher ethical aspirations beyond a confined political life, then, is also reflective of the Imamate's efforts to create alternative spaces of communication. In the process, the Imamate strives to forge a cosmopolitan citizenship both beyond and, if necessary in more practical operational realms, in dialogue with the national. While in this line of scholarship a Kantian imagination looms large,[43] I am, evidently, invoking it in a qualified manner underlining in particular the idea of a moral community with its own notion of ethical codes that is not necessarily predicated on involvement of the state and the state's various structures.

There is, however, another way in which the Imamate engages with the idea of the state, viz., the way in which the Imamate invokes the state's various apparitions through a complex process of domestication with significant semiotic bearings. As a key vehicle carrying forward the Ismaili Imamate's commitment to universalist project of social progress and human development, the AKDN thus seeks to create a communication community beyond the confines of, but not necessarily entirely dissociated from, the nation and the state. In certain ways, the AKDN, as a non-state actor, illustrates much wider global processes. Thus more generally, based on his case study of various voluntary Islamic organizations and associations in Muslim societies and/or Islamic states, John L. Esposito points to their role in not only providing a critique to the governments' inability to make a positive mark in the domain of social welfare, but also in reinforcing 'a sense of community identity', involving 'spiritual and moral renewal', and bringing to the forefront, in the process, larger ethical questions.[44] As indicated, the subtle difference with the AKDN though is that the nation and the state, if necessary, are also viable partners in its moral projects. In turn, such moral projects are, however, motivated in the first place by religious inspiration.

The question of religious inspiration, as must be clear from our discussions, has its own complexities. In as much as the normative Ismaili subjectivity is what the Imamate envisions it to be, locating it at the intersection of a denominationally specific Ismailism and a larger Islamic *topos* with an underlying idea of compatibility, one has to almost invariably address the question as to how these two streams of fashioning, and more concretely identity, are actually bridged. At one level, the Bourdieuian habitus is where, we have noted, these forces enter dynamic relationships to fashion such subjectivity. At another level, the universalizing rhetoric of social progress and human development propelled by the Ismaili Imamate reaches new heights when seen in conjunction with the inflected idioms of culture and cultural heritage with which the Imamate functions, and which we shall shortly discuss. In so far as the Ismaili international, partly through its ancillary vehicle viz. the AKDN, reaches out to new cultural formations, penetrates new terrains and engages with different ethno/national categories incorporating them in the expanding Ismaili ecumene, the dyad of the postnational/cosmopolitanism bear special significance. The Ismaili educational initiatives in East Africa since the middle of the last century provide a classic case in point. It has been thus noted how an Ismaili community exclusiveness gave way to gradual incorporation of non-Ismaili, especially Swahili-speaking Africans and, in the process, resulting in 'expanding Ismaili conceptions of community beyond their traditional communal orientation'.[45] Closer to our times, the Madrasa Early Childhood Development Programme – launched in the early 1980s, and benefitting over 54,000 children in Mombasa (Kenya), Kampala (Uganda) and Zanzibar (Tanzania), and training over 5,000 teachers and 2,500 school committee members – furthers this process.[46] Its success, we are told, depended crucially on a steadfast support of the Sunni imams, who had to be convinced that the system would be compatible with the Swahili cultural sensibilities.[47] Much of these contemporary or recent developments, then, mark a significant advance on a process traceable to the early, and more particularly mid, twentieth century.

It has been observed that in large parts of the Muslim world in the colonial period there occurred a 'transformation of the Muslim community, the *umma*, from a community of believers to a community of opinion'.[48] While earlier forms of 'knowledge networks of ulama and Sufis persisted', this 'much larger complex of Muslim connectedness', it is further argued, had 'little to do with religion per se'.[49] While the latter statement has to be seen with reference to the momentous forces unleashed by the colonial experience, it need not be seen as an historical process independent of the religious *imaginaire*. This, to reiterate a truism perhaps, is especially so since the triumphalist argument of an inexorable progress of the 'secular' at the expense of the 'religious' runs a precipitous risk of oversimplification. The skeins that connect the contemporary global Ismaili community, our case study, foreground the relevance of the 'new connectedness' that Francis Robinson refers to, and yet, they do not necessarily displace earlier forms and structures in entirety. What is crucially important for us is to see how an apex religious authority (read, the Imamate) mediates didactically through both *farmans* and modern constitutional mechanisms, to engage with an expanding community across the globe. It does so while recasting itself through palpably 'secular' idioms, evoking postnational aspirations, manifesting itself through denationalized modalities, and making interventions in zones once restricted only to states.

It is also important that we bear in mind the variegated nature of the institutional bases that had historically sustained the Ismaili community across nations and cultures. Thus, instances attesting the Aga Khan's statements on cultural particularities about close to a 100 years ago only drive home an argument of a historical continuum. We thus see that in 1869 – i.e., in less than five years after the Aga Khan Case of 1866 that drove an almost irrevocable wedge in the Bombay Khoja circles – a deputation under Sir Douglas Forsyth sent to Yarkand by Viceroy Lord Mayo discovered large number of people in Turkistan, Afghanistan, Chitral, Gilgit, the Pamirs, and the valleys of Kafirstan and Badakhasan who regarded the Aga Khan as their spiritual head and were quite happy to send their regular religious dues through the Aga Khan's agent in Kashmir.[50] Instead of highly structured *jamaats*, a family line of *Pirs* (styled '*Maulais*' in Chitral and '*Muftadis*' in Afghanistan) ensured the Aga Khan's position in these areas. These areas were 'roughly divided among a number of *Pirs*', whose office was hereditary, and all of whom enjoyed great respect receiving immense offerings from the inhabitants mostly in kinds: part of these offerings were converted into coins and were sent to the Aga Khan in Bombay through agents.[51] This complex of conduits thus had a long history that predated Aga Khan III's constitutional experiments from the early 1900s. The system, protean as it was, had had its share of vicissitudes as well, albeit facilitating networks connecting the Imam to his community amid changing political circumstances. Thus, it has been pointed out that in parts of Afghanistan due to hostilities of the Sunnis towards the Ismailis, Aga Khan III could not meet his followers in that country. This was further compounded by British efforts to use the Aga Khan's influence with his followers in Afghanistan to contain the Indian revolutionary Raja Mahendra Pratap (1886–1979), who found asylum in Afghanistan and had a warm relation with King Amanullah Khan (1892–1960). Nevertheless, the Aga could still make use of existing networks to send his agent, Pir Sabz Ali (b. 1871) to Badakhshan in 1923 to confer with the local *pirs*, collect tithes, and send them along to Bombay.[52] Such networks, then, have a long history. Co-existing with constitutional experimentation of the subsequent times, these networks went on to condition much of the Imamate's policies, and its relationship with the transregional – and increasingly global – Ismaili community, as Aga Khan III himself indicated in the middle of the twentieth century (see the quotation from his *Memoirs* at the beginning of this chapter). The pervasive language of cosmopolitanism that we now see running centrally through the worldwide Ismaili community, then, is also a language derived from an historical entanglement. It has to be seen in the light of age-old kinship patterns, administrative (re)structurations consummating in contemporary corporatization of social and religious institutions, forces of spiritual pan-Islamism, and not least the overarching project of the Muslim modern intelligible in terms of a wide gamut of cultural specificities with all its diverse implications.

It will be pertinent here to explicate in greater details some key aspects of the language of Muslim modernity in general, and its use by the essentially religious institution of the Ismaili Imamate in particular. These features, generally speaking, had come to reflect discourses of the Muslim modern in large parts of the Muslim – and indeed, also Islamicate – world since the late nineteenth century while in the more specific context of our case study had, since the times of Aga Khan III, informed the Ismaili Imamate's understanding of Islam as well as its social service ventures. For one, scholars have argued that, ideologically, 'pan-Islamism intersected with the more intellectual discourse of Islamic modernism' while 'the Arabic term for pan-Islamism, *al-jami'a al-islamiyya*, could also be translated as Islamic solidarity across political lines …'.[53] Moreover, in what constitutes the crucial features of this project of the Muslim modern, we are told, both *jihad* and *ijtihad* acquired immense significance. Amira K. Bennison thus points to their common root in Arabic, *j-h-d*, denoting effort and striving. The former could be taken to mean what she calls 'greater jihad', i.e. 'the individual's struggle against his or her baser desires' as well as 'lesser jihad', viz., 'public actions on behalf of religion which include jihad of the tongue, the pen and the sword'.[54] She further notes how *ijtihad*, 'the legal technique of using independent reasoning to derive legal opinions', had historically been a crucial aspect of the Shia thought, although it gradually gained significant traction among the Sunni reformers in their modernist quest, displacing *taqlid* (blind adherence) and *bida* (deviant innovations).[55] The vocabulary of *jihad*, with all its complexities, bore momentous significance for generations of nationalist Muslim thinkers and activists across the Muslim and/or Islamicate world, linking at once languages of anti-colonial resistance and self-strengthening nationalist projects to larger internationalist aspirations of the Muslim *umma*.[56] But the very polysemic nature of the expression also meant that in order to address it meaningfully with reference to its larger ethical implications it has to be seen more as a kindred coordinate of *ijtihad* than a contrastive model. Thus for Sir Muhammad Iqbal, '*Ijtihad*, the jihad of the mind, was the moving principle of Islam'.[57]

It is this understanding of *ijtihad* as a part of a constellation of ethical issues, with a remarkable degree of emphasis on the question of human agency and intellect, that underwrites the didactic mediation of the Imamate and informs the Ismaili ethical ethos. We have thus already seen Aga Khan III developing, along with Zaki Ali, a version of *ijtihad* evoking the role of the individual while also sensitized to the larger questions of Islamic jurisprudence within the remits of 'the Quran and Traditions'. In contemporary times, the AKDN's literature on the Imamate – which serves no less a role in its public outreach – furthermore points to the centrality of 'intellect' in Shiite traditions while also underscoring its complementariness with 'individual conscience', a combination that informs 'the Ismaili tradition of tolerance' and underlines the correlated nature of reason and revelation in Shia thought.[58] Moreover, it is further argued, in 'Shia Islam, the role of the intellect has never been perceived within a confrontational mode of revelation versus reason... [and] the teachings of Imams Ali and Jafar as-Sadiq, emphasizes the complementarity between revelation and intellectual reflection', while closer to our times, 'Aga Khan III describes Islam as a natural religion, which values intellect, logic and empirical experience'.[59] This idea of complementariness thus emerges as a recurrent theme in the thoughts of both Aga Khan III and Aga Khan IV, providing the bedrock of a universal language of reason, faith, and ethics while, more specifically for the Ismailis, the pivotal importance and 'authoritative guidance' of the Imam.[60] Importantly therefore, the idea of the 'faith' – along with its characteristic 'norms and ethics' – invoked here involves a constant oscillation between Islam and Ismailism, a constant dialogic exercise between interwoven idioms of universality and specificities mediated by the Imamate.

We have already underscored in the preceding section the relevance of the overarching context(s) within which these norms and ethics of the faith, howsoever conceptualized, operate. Thus, taking a cue from Aga Khan IV, we are reminded that the 'tendency to restrict academic inquiry to the study of past accomplishments was at variance with the belief in the timeless relevance of the Islamic message'.[61] This exhortation to transcend the limits imposed by one specific place and one particular point of time, in effect, lends itself at once to a complex language of universality and diversity. In conjunction with this interwoven narrative of universality/diversity, the idea of an Ismaili community under the aegis of the Imam of the time enjoining the followers to exercise their intellect and will under his guidance also streamlines human creativity in specific channels. The didactic tools to tutor the Ismailis across cultures and nations in different parts of the world range from the Imamate's constitutional framework through the Imam's *farmans*, to educational initiatives. Their manifestations come, albeit with varied emphases and thrusts, in the shape of the various mandates of the AKDN and its auxiliary organs, as well as the varied Ismaili/Jamati institutions catering specifically to the global Ismaili community's socio-religious needs. These are also precisely the forces that sustain the Ismaili community, indeed hold together the assemblage that we have named 'Ismaili international', which functions after all as much as a community of opinion as a community of believers.

As outlined above, the *talim* educational programme works as the vehicle to inculcate among the worldwide Ismaili children this discourse of an Ismaili ethics acting, thereby, as a cohesive force cutting across barriers of language, ethnicity, and nationality. Likewise, specific professional programmes such as the Secondary Teacher Education Programme (STEP) aims at grooming prospective teachers who want to work within the wider Aga Khan network of institutions, or more specifically Ismaili Religious Education Centres (RECs).[62] An essentially composite globally-spread Ismaili ecumene is thus brought under an overarching umbrella evoking a range of issues that have now emerged as important foci in the history of education. Recent interventions in the field of history of education thus emphasize the pressing need to go outside the confines of the nation-state, stressing instead 'educational transfers in different cultural settings, focusing on local-level transformations and reinventions of meanings and forms of colonialism'.[63] The reference to colonialism need not deter us to explore the postcolonial ramifications of these forces. Undoubtedly, a dynamics of these forces have been crucial in carving out a realm of praxis in large parts of the postcolonial world no less than they did in the colonial times. Yet, scarcely have scholars been in agreement when it comes to explore a global (or transnational, as the aforementioned intervention suggests) history of education. Two main strands have been identified in this field. The first has been referred to as the 'diffusionist' model, one that stresses the spread of education, pedagogic ideas and practices beyond the national boundaries, and more often than not, 'from Western metropolitan centres to less developed countries in the peripheries'. The other has been called the 'aggregative' approach, implying an adding up of the discrete national histories into an aggregative global whole.[64] Proponents of the first strand, it has been lamented, hardly ever look into questions of strategies and methods of such diffusion whereas, advisors of the second approach, have very often failed to illustrate how exactly the discrete national histories combine in an integrative process to arrive at a global plane. The pertinent questions, therefore, that have been raised are:

> Can a focus on issues that are inherently universalist and transnational lead to a point of entry into the global history of education? Can we identify, as one such issue in the history of ideas, the theme of interface between civilizations and its role in the educational discourse of civilizations facing each other?[65]

This is clearly a project to engage with first a colonial educational paradigm in South Asia, then a nationalist reaction to the it, followed by a universalist reconciliation between what the so-called 'two civilizations', viz., 'European' and 'Indian'.[66] Implicit in this formulation is a certain civilizational dichotomy that still has a potential to evolve into a dialogue, and even work out adaptive strategies in its quest for the 'universalist'. While this work is ensconced within the specificities of the colonial South Asian context, the question that it raises at a higher conceptual plane about 'a focus on issues that are inherently universalist and transnational' to understand a 'global history of education' bears great significance. These are also issues that have been central to the evolution of an Ismaili knowledge community since the late colonial times. The key traits of the educational system that hold together the global Ismaili community are precisely an array of universalizing forces ranging from spiritual universality to religious ideals and ethics, all mediated by the Imamate in an immensely diverse cosmopolitan universe. Conversely, the language of religious and ethical universality articulates itself through an educational mechanism that both informs the community of its cultural past against the larger backdrop of Islamic consciousness as well as promotes its distinctiveness. This it does even as adapting its restructured organizational bases to the politico-cultural specificities of the terrains within which they operate. This then is a history of educational experiment regulated by a centralized Imamate and yet sensitized to the cultural particularities and disparateness that the global Ismaili community exemplifies.

We have seen, as well, how this involves engagement along both the postnational and denationalized planes. It will be in order, however, to identify here certain key aspects of the production of the community's cultural past, taken forward by the AKES and the AKTC catering to and co-sustained by both the Ismailis and the non-Ismailis, as well as the so-called Ismaili/Jamati institutions specific to the community. Such engagements too mark an intersection of Ismaili distinctiveness and larger Islamic universality, and are being systematically worked out by organs under the auspices of the Ismaili Imamate. Crucially important in this endeavour is a certain portmanteau language of cultural heritage, invoked by the AKTC. Indeed, the language that the Ismaili Imamate invokes in its engagement in social, religious and cultural spheres, also have larger semiotic implications. The notion of culture and cultural heritage that the Imamate works with, thus, has significant implications for its larger idea of development. In his foreword to the information brochure of the AKTC, the 'cultural agency' of the AKDN, Aga Khan IV thus suggests that 'culture can be a catalyst for development' and that 'conservation and revitalisation of the cultural heritage—in many cases the only asset at the disposal of the community—can provide a springboard for social development'.[67] There is here, on the one hand, an emphasis on the relevance of cultural asset, often in societies deficit in other resources. On the other hand, conservation of cultural heritage is also conceptually located in a much complex web. Thus AKTC endeavours such as the 'Historic Cities Programme', in the process, go well beyond 'mere restoration of monuments' and trigger off forces of 'adaptive reuse, contextual urban planning and the improvement of housing, infrastructure and public spaces'.[68] Conversely, wider developmental arguments are wedded to an insistence on cultural specificities, 'supporting and validating traditional culture in the face of a homogenising world', as Aga Khan IV puts it.[69] While this elicits a language of cultural custodianship, the AKTC, through its various programmes, also seeks to (re)inscribe its own version of Islamic history: through, for instance, the Aga Khan Program for Islamic Architecture whose objective is evident from its title; or, even more specifically, through restoration of heritage sites such as the Umm al Sultan Shabaan mosque and the Khayrebek complex in Cairo which Aga Khan IV saw as facilitating a bridge with the city's Fatimid past, and the Fatimid Caliphs, 'who founded Cairo and who laid its physical and cultural foundations 1000 years ago'.[70] In each of the cases, cultural particularities and diversity in societies in the face of 'a homogenising world' are promoted, and a cultural *imaginaire* beyond both territorial nationalism and totalizing globalization processes valorized.

Thus the developmental imagination once again provides these institutions a mechanism through which to bring the present in a dialogue with the past, with imaginings about the future hovering in horizon. Seminal interventions in the fields of aesthetics, hermeneutics, and art history have pointed to the importance of the 'present' in, and a resultant potential incompleteness of, any restoration endeavour. Thus:

> Reconstructing the original circumstances, like all restoration, is a futile undertaking in view of the historicity of our being. What is reconstructed, a life brought back from the lost past, is not the original.

In its continuance in an estranged state it acquires only a derivative, cultural existence.[71]

While this is an important reminder of the general fact that in every restoration the restorer inserts her/his own cultural self, or at best the cultural predilections of the society of which she/he is part, architectural forms, however, present an interesting contrast by virtue of their command over a space and embracing 'other forms of representation':

> If a building is a work of art, then it is not only the artistic solution to a building problem posed by the contexts of purpose and life to which it originally belongs, but somehow preserves them, so that they are visibly present even though the building's present appearance is completely alienated from its original purpose. Something in it point back to the original.[72]

Much of the Ismaili cultural initiatives carried out under the rubric of the AKTC hinge on an understanding of an indelible nature of aesthetic consciousness of such architectural forms, and their adaptability to the present, and present societal needs. Consider, for instance, this synoptic view of urban rehabilitation that underpins the Aga Khan Historic Cities Programme (AKHCP):

> ... proper urban rehabilitation must rely on a dual approach: In physical terms, the urban shell needs to be repaired, restored, partly reconstructed and adapted to contemporary needs while remaining faithful to the basic cultural and morphological principles that have presided over its growth... In social and economic terms, the living conditions of residents must be improved in the areas of health, education, services, employment, income, etc ...[73]

Funded and implemented by the AKTC with financial support from a range of governmental and private donors,[74] the AKHCP thus draws upon regional and/ or local expertise and support in its holistic venture of 'integrated socio-economic development'.[75] Coupled with a pivotal importance ascribed to the developmental imagination, projects of restoration or reconstructions are also simultaneously freed from any exclusive temporal straightjackets of artistic experience. Thus, a view of cross-temporal adaptability of architectural forms involving an engagement between the past and the present also enter a dialogue with imaginings of the future. The specific contribution of the present Imamate to this language of culture and heritage is the way it seeks to inflect the idea, or for that matter the constellation of ideas associated with it, through an invocation of the concept of sustainable development and aspirations about the future.

Conclusion

It has been aptly pointed out that the AKDN signifies 'an explicit fusion of liberal modernism and Islamic ideologies', a fusion that thrives in close association with capitalist systems.[76] Without rehearsing in detail what has been already discussed in the ongoing work, as well as elsewhere, we should perhaps still underline that much of these more recent manifestations characteristic of the global Ismaili community has to be seen against the backdrop of the history of the community in late colonial South Asia. This history brings to the forefront an array of interwoven critical questions, such as those gravitating around notions of the religious/secular dichotomy, sectarian versus ecumenical aspirations, of nation and territoriality, and of internationalism of different hues and nature. This present chapter, by focusing on an understanding of a cosmopolitan Ismaili international, has also sought to reiterate the relevance of the charismatic religious authority of the Imamate, even as the Imamate under Aga Khans III and IV has been virtually re-invented invoking, ever so increasingly, a wide gamut of 'secular' responsibilities and idioms. Our present work also suggests how important it is to explore the historical lineaments of each of these issues, even as they change shades, emphases, acquire new meanings, and are (re)used or discarded in more recent practices.

Endnotes

1 Aga Khan III, *The Memoirs of the Aga Khan*, 184.

2 Ibid.,184.

3 Ethnographic narratives in more recent times, e.g., Steinberg, *Isma'ili Modern*, 101–02, however, suggest a more complex situation, one in which there are tensions and resentment among sections of the Himalayan Nizaris due to alleged institutional endeavours to standardize religious practices and customs according to predominantly Khoja norms.

4 Cultural assimilation through social intercourse and marriage networks has historical antecedents. In the context of the diasporic Ismaili population in East Africa, for instance, Amiji, 'Some Notes on Religious Dissent' attributes the 'paucity of females of the Khoja caste' as the major force behind marriage with local women, ibid., at 606. For more on the Aga Khan's exhortations to adapt Ismaili denominationalism to local African socio-cultural realities, see Mukherjee, 'Universalising Aspirations', 442–45. Cf. n. 32 in the Introduction. In the light of these nuances, the statement that the Khojas – unlike the Hindus – 'migrated with their families in Muscat and Zanzibar', as Goswami, *The Call of the Sea*, 33 seems to be somewhat too generalized and simplistic.

5 Steinberg, *Isma'ili Modern*, 46. Commenting on the Ismailis in the late colonial-early postcolonial East African scenario, H. S. Morris, *Indians in Uganda*, 34 (London: Weidenfeld & Nicolson, 1968) used the expression 'corporate community' that he argued worked as 'a kind of "pace-making" group in the growth of other caste and sectarian communities'.

6 Delanty, 'The Cosmopolitan Imagination', 26.

7 Ibid., 27.

8   It may be recalled that this is the underlying argument in Bose, 'Different Universalisms, Colorful Cosmopolitanisms', 97–111, as noted in the Introduction.

9   Linklater, 'Cosmopolitan Citizenship', 24.

10 Pierre Bourdieu, *The Logic of Practice*, translated by Richard Nice, 54 (Stanford: Stanford University Press, 1990), sees 'habitus' as a 'product of history' producing in its turn 'individual and collective practices – more history – in accordance with the schemes generated by history'. Our particular concern here is to explore in greater details what this emphasis on practicalities might have meant for the Ismailis, and the historical imagination(s) involved in the process.

11 Saba Mahmood, *Politics of Piety: The Islamic Revival and the Feminist Subject*, 147 (Princeton, NJ: Princeton University Press, 2005), takes cue from the Aristotelian meaning of 'potentiality' to suggest a path of 'training and knowledge', and not any implicit understanding of a 'generic faculty or power'. Therefore, the emphasis here is on the practical aspects of 'a teleological program of volitional training that presupposes an exemplary path to knowledge–knowledge that one comes to acquire through assiduous schooling and practice'.

12 Akira Iriye, *Global Community: The Role of International Organizations in the Making of the Contemporary World* (Berkeley, Los Angeles: University of California Press, 2002) makes a strong case for looking at international organizations as units of analysis to understand modern world history, but stays clear of voluntary religious organizations unless they are involved in 'secular' activities such as 'humanitarian relief and cultural exchange', ibid., 2. Cf. Green and Viaene, 'Introduction', 4.

13 See Dreyer, 'Theological Normativity', especially 5 ff. Dreyer takes cue from Paul Ricoeur's theory of cultural and/or social imagination, to investigate the dialectics of inculturation and normativity.

14 Lewis, 'On the role of normativity', 170 thus enjoins academics to 'bring the norms themselves into debate and subject them to critical enquiry', thereby shifting the attention to exploring 'the justification offered for particular norms'.

15 'List of Political, Quasi-Political & Religious Societies, Sabhas, Anjumans & Labour Unions in the Bombay Presidency & Sind for the year ending June 1920', Home Department, (Special), File 355 (74)- II/ 1921,15–17, MSA.

16 In Goolamali, *An Appeal*, 70–73.

17 For example the Aga Khan Social Welfare Board – one among several similar bodies – is thus responsible for an array of social matters affecting the Ismaili community.

18 See *The Constitution of the Khoja Imami Ismailis in Africa* (Nairobi: His Highness the Aga Khan Supreme Shia Imami Ismailia Council for Africa, 1962) for the recurrent theme of religious and social welfare. Cf. *The Constitution of the Councils and Jamats of Shia Imami Ismaili Muslims of Pakistan* (Karachi: H.R.H. Prince Aga Khan Ismailia Federal Council for Pakistan, 1962) for the rhetoric of progress and prosperity. For instructive comments in this direction, with particular reference to the Ismailis in Tanzania, see Kaiser and Kaiser, 'Identity, Citizenship, and Transnationalism', 466–69.

19 For all the religious underpinnings, the AKDN still declares itself to be 'non-denominational'. See http://www.akdn.org/about.asp (last accessed 26 November 2015).

20 José Casanova, *Public Religions*, 4.

21 For a succinct and somewhat programmatic critique of such restrictive understanding of the subject, see Uma Kothari, 'Commentary: History, Time and Temporality in Development Discourse' in *History, Historians and Development Policy: A Necessary Dialogue*, edited by C.A. Bayly, Vijayendra Rao, Simon Szreter and Michael Woolcock, 65–70 (Hyderabad: Orient Blackswan, 2012 [2011]); cf. C.A. Bayly, 'Indigenous and Colonial Origins of Comparative Economic Development: The Case of Colonial India and Africa', ibid., 39–64 has a particular focus on 'economic development' on a comparative scale within the Empire, while Zachariah, *Developing India*, seeks to recover the complexities of the polysemic concept right from the colonial times.

22 See http://www.akdn.org/faq.asp (last accessed 26 November 2015). An overview of the AKDN's partners (national governments, government organizations as well as private institutions) is available at http://www.akdn.org/partners.asp (last accessed 26 November 2015). Together, they strive to 'improve the welfare and prospects of people in the developing world, particularly in Asia and Africa, without regard to faith, origin or gender'. See http://www.akdn.org/about.asp (last accessed 26 November 2015).

23 Sassen, *Territory, Authority, Rights*, 305.

24 See, Julia Berger, 'Religious Nongovernmental Organizations: An Exploratory Analysis', *Voluntas: International Journal of Voluntary and Nonprofit Organizations*, 14, 1 (2003): 15–39, especially at 21.

25 See http://www.akdn.org/about_akdn.asp (last accessed 26 November 2015). This rhetoric of social conscience of Islam has to be seen as part of an Ismaili worldview, one that we have seen emanating from an essentially plural understanding of Islam. In contemporary times, one thus sees in the same AKDN website the rather polemical statement emphasizing the 'inappropriateness of referring to the Shia-Sunni divide, or to interpretational differences within each branch, in the frame of an orthodoxy-heterodoxy dichotomy, or of applying the term 'sect' to any Shia or Sunni community'. See http://www.akdn.org/about_imamat. asp#evolution (last accessed 26 November 2015). And this, it has to be highlighted, is in sharp contrast to a language suffused with anti-Sunni invectives with reference to developments in early Islam that had often informed works, for instance textbooks, outlining history of the Ismailis; see, e.g., Aziz, *A Brief History of Ismailism*, 3–4. For Aziz, this provides the entry-point to his larger project of reclaiming an Ismaili cultural past for the Ismaili youth who do not have the time, courage or expertise to delve deep into what would be considered the classical canon of the community; (Ibid., 3).

26 Cf. the educational ventures of the Gülen Movement which, although drawing inspiration from Islam, do not explicitly promote Islam. Rather they invoke universal idioms of ethical conduct and morality. For a case study of Gülen-inspired schools in Tanzania underscoring this aspect, see Kristina Dohrn, 'Translocal Ethics: Hizmet Teachers and the Formation of Gülen-inspired Schools in Urban Tanzania', *Sociology of Islam*, 1, 3–4 (2013): 233–56.

27 See the section on 'Long-term commitment' at http://www.akdn.org/about_akdn.asp (last accessed 26 November 2015). The pivotal importance of the Imamate is driven home by the simple yet profound statement that it is the Imam who 'ensures the balance between the *shariah* or the exoteric aspect of the faith, and its esoteric, spiritual essence' and 'according to the needs of time and universe'. See the section on 'Principles of Shiism' at http://www.akdn.org/about_imamat.asp#evolution (last accessed 26 November 2015).

28 See http://www.akdn.org/about.asp (last accessed 26 November 2015).

29 See the section on 'Intellect and Faith' in http://www.akdn.org/about_imamat.asp (last accessed 26 November 2015).

30 For instance, the AKAM, one of the key AKDN bodies, has its own Board of Directors while His Highness the Aga Khan (IV) is its 'Chairman'. See http://www.akdn.org/agencies.asp (last accessed 26 November 2015). Indeed, recent scholars have noted crucial shift in the Ismaili apex authority: a shift from the person of the Imam to the office of the Imamate, despite the enduring nature of the practice of succession by designation. This is one of the fundamental axioms in the recent study of Aga Khan IV's Imamate and its institutional framework by Daryoush Mohammad Poor, *Authority without Territory: The Aga Khan Development Network and the Ismaili Imamate* (New York: Palgrave Macmillan, 2014).

31 Asad, *Formations of the Secular*, 1–2; Cf. the Introduction to this book

32 According to Ashis Nandy, *Bonfire of Creeds: The Essential Ashis Nandy*, 319 (New Delhi: Oxford University Press, 2004), 'development does not annihilate cultures; it merely exploits cultures to strengthen itself'. Nandy's position has to be seen as part of a postmodernist framework that sees development discourse as essentially 'an apparatus of control and surveillance'. Drawing upon the Bandung Movement of 1955, scholars have, however, shown the relevance of a certain '"third wordlist" conception of social justice' that points to the numerous 'appropriations, deflections, and challenges emerging within the overall construct of development', a process that also underscores the facileness of an argument of a single and linear power-knowledge developmental regime. See Frederick Cooper and Randall Packard, 'Introduction', to *International Development and the Social Science: Essays on the History and Politics of Knowledge*, edited by eid, 2–3 and 10 (Berkeley, Los Angeles and London: University of California Press, 1998). The ongoing discussion, hopefully, illustrates a much complex relationship between the religio-cultural *topos* and development discourse than a mere language of exploitation can connote.

33 Robert G. Gregory, *The Rise and Fall of Philanthropy in East Africa: The Asian Contribution*, 53 (New Brunswick and London: Transaction Publishers, 1992). Gregory suspects that one of the key aims of the organization had been to further the conversion of Africans into Islam, though the result was rather disappointing, (ibid.,93–4). However, even its philanthropic efforts were often received sceptically by the Africans. August H. Nimtz, *Islam and Politics in East Africa: The Sufi Order in Tanzania*, 91 (Minneapolis: University of Minnesota Press, 1980), points out that the organization was discredited since the Indian-origin Ismailis dominated it.

34 See the introductory section in the AKES website: http://www.akdn.org/akes (last accessed 26 November 2015).

35 Gregory, *The Rise and Fall of Philanthropy*, 114.

36 However, Steinberg, *Isma'ili Modern*, 73, hints at 'real tension between AKF, the nation-state, and other actors' in Pakistan and Tajikistan, where there is also a statist critique of alternative conduits of power and authority. Cf. Magnus Marsden, *Living Islam: Muslim Religious Experience in Pakistan's North-West Frontier*, especially 193–238 (Cambridge: Cambridge University Press, 2005), for interesting observations on the not-so-smooth sectarian equations in contemporary northern Pakistan where the AKDN and its ancillary bodies carry on developmental programmes at various levels and scales. It is arguable, evidently, if

there are also not different factors other than mere sectarian issues; most importantly, one would imagine, resource allocation. In this, the ruptures in northern Pakistan are somewhat different from, for example, the tensions that erupt from the pietist missionary ventures of the Tablighi Jamaat al-Dawa in parts of southern Thailand in recent times, where the locals reportedly find it uncomfortable to embrace the new values that the Tablighis bring with their inculturation. See, Alexander Horstmann, 'The Inculturation of a Transnational Islamic Missionary Movement: Tablighi Jamaat al-Dawa and Muslim Society in Southern Thailand', *Sojourn: Journal of Social Issues in Southeast Asia*, 22, 1 (2007): 107–30.

37 See Zulfikarali Mawani, 'A Brief Survey of the Development of Ismaili Education Administration from 1905-1945', in *Commemorative Issue, 1977-1978: Sixty Years of Ismaili Education in Kenya*, 19–21, at 19 (Nairobi: His Highness the Aga Khan Educational Department for Kenya, 1977–78).

38 Ibid., 20.

39 Ibid., 21.

40 Thus, *Primary Five, Book Two: People Helping People* (London: Institute of Ismaili Studies, 1997) introduces Ismaili children to a general social awareness, its rich tradition of voluntary service and, above all, the wide-ranging social activism of the AKDN. An overview of the curriculum from 'pre-school' (4–6 year-olds) to 'primary six' (11–12 year-olds) is available at the Institute of Ismaili Studies' website: http://www.iis.ac.uk/view_article. asp?ContentID=104853 (last accessed 26 November 2015). Steinberg, *Isma'ili Modern*, 93 ff. examines the role of children's texts on the formation of a global Ismaili identity. For further discussions on the educational programme, see the present chapter.

41 His Highness the Aga Khan, speaking at the Prince Claus Fund's Conference on Culture and Development, Amsterdam, 7 September, 2002; cited in the AKDN information brochure, *Aga Khan Development Network: Economic Development, Social Development, Culture*, 1 (2007), available online at: http://www.akdn.org/publications/2007_akdn.pdf (last accessed 8 December 2015).

42 A case in point is the AKF's Pamir Relief and Development Programme. Initially conceived of as an essentially-humanitarian relief programme to address the problem of food shortage, it later developed to encompass rural infrastructure, reforestation, microfinance etc. in Tajikistan. See *AKF and AKDN: A Continuum of Development, Aga Khan Foundation- An Agency of the Aga Khan Development Network*, 32 and 34 (Geneva: Aga Khan Foundation, 2011). Similarly, the FOCUS foregrounds the need 'to reduce their (people's) dependence on humanitarian aid and facilitates their transition to sustainable self-reliant, long-term development'. See http://www.akdn.org/focus (last accessed 26 November 2015).

43 Linklater, 'Cosmopolitan Citizenship', 28: 'Although Kant did not defend cosmopolitan democracy, it is arguable that the elements of a dialogic conception of global citizenship exist in his writings.'

44 See John L. Esposito, 'Islam and Civil Society' in *Modernizing Islam: Religion in the Public Sphere in Europe and the Middle East*, edited by John L. Esposito and François Burgat, 69-100, especially, 75, 76 (New Brunswick, NJ: Rutgers University Press, 2003). Furthermore, Esposito argues that since especially the 1990s in the majority of the Islamic countries, the mainstreaming of such organizations has tended to produce a professional class that has emerged as significant political force in the process, (ibid., 84).

45 Paul J. Kaiser, *Culture, Transnationalism and Civil Society: Aga Khan Social Service Institutions in Tanzania*, 82 (Westport, CT and London: Praeger Publishers, 1996). He shows, moreover, how Tanzania provided leadership in this process, (ibid., 79–97). Cf. similar developments in Burma from around the same time, whereby Ismaili schools were opened up to non-Ismaili children, and Ismailis started taking particular care to adapt to Burmese customs. See Moshe Yegar, *The Muslims of Burma: A Study of a Minority Group*, 46 (Wiesbaden: Otto Harrosowitz, 1972). Cumulatively, they marked a process of gradual rescindment of the denominational exclusiveness that frustrated ecumenical endeavours in the nineteenth century, especially in the sphere of educational reforms.

46 The figures are gleaned from the twenty-fifth anniversary official report. See http://www.akdn.org/Content/210 (last accessed 26 November 2015).

47 Malise Ruthven, 'The Aga Khan Development Network and Institutions', in *A Modern History of the Ismailis*, edited by Daftary, 189–220, at 195–96.

48 Francis Robinson, 'The Islamic World: World System to "Religious International"', in *Religious Internationals*, edited by Green and Viaene 111–35, at 112.

49 Ibid., 116.

50 Noted in A. S. Picklay, *History of the Ismailis*, 64–68 (Bombay: Published by the author, 1940).

51 J. Biddulph, *Tribes of the Hindoo Koosh*, 119–20 (Calcutta: Office of the Superintendent of Government Printing, 1880).

52 See Hafizullah Emadi, 'The End of *Taqiyya*: Reaffirming the Religious Identity of Ismailis in Shughnan, Badakhshan: Political Implications for Afghanistan', *Middle Eastern Studies*, 34, 3 (1998): 103–20, especially at 110–11.

53 Amira K. Bennison, 'Muslim Internationalism between Empire and Nation-State', in *Religious Internationals*, edited by Green and Viaene, 163–85, at 171.

54 Ibid., 164; Cf. e.g., Jalal, *Partisans of Allah*, 6 ff.

55 Bennison, 'Muslim Internationalism', 164. One should not forget, these were also issues that defined the reformist/revivalist agenda of generations of thinkers and activists since the times of Shah Wali Allah and Muhammd al-Shawkani. See, e.g., Daniel Brown, *Rethinking Tradition*, chapter 2, especially 22 ff.

56 For instance, Ayesha Jalal, 'Striking a Just Balance: Maulana Azad as a Theorist of Trans-National *Jihad*', *Modern Intellectual History*, 4, 1 (2007): 95–107 brings to the forefront a profile of Maulana Abul Kalam Azad (1888–1958) as a prominent theorist of transnational *jihad* in the tense World War I years.

57 Jalal, *Partisans of Allah*, 237.

58 See the section entitled 'Intellect and Faith' at http://www.akdn.org/about_imamat.asp (last accessed 26 November 2015). Cf. how, according to this understanding, Islam 'refers to the inner struggle of the individual'. Ibid., see the section on 'Islam: General Introduction' (last accessed 9 December 2015).

59 Ibid: See the section on 'Intellect and Faith' (last accessed 9 December 2015).

60 Ibid., (last accessed 9 December 2015).

61 Ibid., (last accessed 9 December 2015).

62 See http://www.iis.ac.uk/graduate-studies/step (last accessed 9 December 2015). Steinberg, *Isma'ili Modern*, 88 ff. explores the role of *jamaati* institutions, such as the Ismaili Tariqah and Religious Education Board (ITREB), in the making of the modern Ismaili self, and Ismaili missionary activities in especially in the Himalayan areas.

63 Barnita Bagchi, Eckhardt Fuchs and Kate Rousmaniere, 'Introduction' to *Connecting Histories of Education: Transnational and Cross-Cultural Exchanges in (Post-)Colonial Education*, edited by eid, at 2 (New York and Oxford: Berghahn Books, 2014).

64 Sabyasachi Bhattacharya, 'Towards a Global History of Education: Alternative Strategies', in *Connecting Histories of Education*, edited by Bagchi, Fuchs and Rousmaniere, 27–40, at 27.

65 Ibid., 28.

66 Ibid., 28 ff.

67 *Aga Khan Trust for Culture: The Cultural Agency of the Aga Khan Development Network*, 4 (Geneva/ Lausanne: AKTC, 2007).

68 Ibid., 7.

69 Ibid., 4.

70 Aga Khan IV's address on 26 October 2007, cited at http://www.akdn.org/Content/379 (last accessed 26 November 2015).

71 Hans-Georg Gadamer, *Truth and Method*, translated by Joel Weinsheimer and Donald G. Marshall, 159 (London and New York: Continuum, 2006 [1975]).

72 Ibid., 149, 150.

73 Stefano Bianca, 'Introduction' to *Aga Khan Historic Cities Programme: An Integrated Approach to Urban Rehabilitation*, 3 (Geneva/ Lausanne: AKTC, 2007).

74 Co-sponsors include the governments of Germany, Norway, the UK, US Department of Agriculture, the Canadian international Development Agency, the Swedish International Development Cooperation Agency, Egyptian-Swiss Development Fund, Ford Foundation, Daimler-Chrysler Fund, World Monuments Fund, the World Bank, Microsoft Inc., etc. See, ibid., 61.

75 For details of activities under the programme, see Jurjen van der Tas, 'Towards Integrated Socio-Economic Development', (ibid., 15–30).

76 Steinberg, *Isma'ili Modern*, 62.

※

Concluding Reflections

… Abraham, Moses, Jesus, and all the Prophets of Israel, are universally accepted by Islam. Muslims indeed know no limitation merely to the Prophets of Israel; they are ready to admit that there were similar Divinely-inspired messengers in other countries—Gautama Buddha, Shri Krishna, and Shri Ram in India, Socrates in Greece, the wise men of China, and many other sages and saints among peoples and civilizations of which we have now lost trace … Then what need was there for a Divine revelation to Mohammed? … In spite of its great spiritual strength, Jewish monotheism has retained two characteristics which render it essentially different from Islamic monotheism; God has remained, in spite of all, *a national and racial* God for the children of Israel, and his personality is entirely separate from its supreme manifestation, the Universe.

In far distant countries such as India and China, the purity of the Faith in the one God had been … vitiated by polytheism, by idolatry, and even by pantheism … *Christianity lost its strength and meaning for Muslims in that it saw its great and glorious founder not as a man but as God incarnate in man* … Thus there was an absolute need for the Divine Word's revelation, to Mohammed himself, *a man like the others,* of God's person and of his relations to the Universe which he had created … Islam's basic principle can only be defined as monorealism and not as monotheism.[1]

His Highness Aga Khan III, 1954; emphases mine

This book sought to explore the evolution of a Shia Ismaili identity in modern South Asia and trace the genealogies of conceptual categories and institutions that conditioned the historical process. Drawing upon a corpus of neglected primary sources, it shed light on an array of larger questions, such as, complexities of Muslim societies in colonial South Asia, the development and articulation of denominational identities, the politics of production-dissemination-reception of religio-legal knowledge, and not least both appropriations and critiques of western epistemic categories by indigenous religious elites. The quotation in the epigraph above illustrates some of the complexities that had come to exert a riveting force on religious leaders, thinkers, and intellectual elites across the world since the late nineteenth century. If the quotation encapsulates much of Aga Khan III's idea of Islam and its message, there are also clear indications of the socio-political textures of the milieu from which it emanates. One need only reiterate that the idioms of a 'national and racial God' as well as 'strength and meaning' associated with human effort rather than with a god have to be seen as part of a critical engagement with the hegemonic discursive venture of 'world religions'. While still invoking the role of 'Divine grace', the Aga Khan exemplified significant strands in Islamic thought that informed the Muslim world since the late nineteenth century, and which in the process also entailed at once a selective appropriation of Euro-centric and Christo-centric episteme as well as their deft (re)deployment against precisely those hegemonic western *topoi*. This book has illustrated that not only was the notion of the universal invoked by the proponents of aspiring as well as emerging 'world religions' in the non-West since the late nineteenth century, but it also gained an immense traction with smaller denominations, especially in their ecumenical endeavours.

This book re-assessed the tortuous legal process that, since the 1860s, recast a Shia Imami identity for the Ismailis with a line of successive living Imams, the Aga Khan(s) at the apex. It showed how this Shia Imami identity was worked out in an Anglo-Muhammadan judicial matrix by rebutting a Khoja reformist challenge, while also appropriating an array of modernist idioms that the reformists invoked. This involved an energetic defence of generally Shia, and particularly Ismaili, claims to morality and universality. Through the assertion of redoubtable qualities of the Ismailis and their charismatic leadership, E. I. Howard, the chief Defence Counsel of Aga Khan I in the 1866 law case, signalled an epistemological shift that marked a virtual redefinition of the community, and anticipated an intellectual tradition that later came to be institutionalized and labelled as Ismaili Studies. The book further illustrated how, under the long Imamate of Aga Khan III the community virtually re-invented itself first in the transregional western Indian Ocean world and gradually in the global arena. However, between the 1860s and the early twentieth century, there had also been crosscurrents in the politico-religious policies of the colonial establishment that entailed a reworking of relationship of customary and religious traditions. This question of ambiguities, largely glossed over in existing scholarship, has also been problematized in the present book.

Through a study of Aga Khan III's public career, as both the Hazir Imam of his Ismaili community as well as an important Muslim leader in late colonial South Asia with significant internationalist visions, the book further sought to illuminate his understanding of colonial modernity, the modalities of community governance, the evolution of a range of Imamate-sponsored institutions, idioms of community development, Muslim universality as well as denominational particularities. Reflecting upon these dual aspects of his public career, the book interrogated his ideas of

India, spiritual pan-Islamism, religio-cultural pluralism and ecumenism, territorial nationalism, and not least deterritorialized religious identities. These are questions of crucial contemporary relevance. The book suggested that Aga Khan III's religiously inflected ethics of social service and unease with territorial identities are among his main legacies. With some variations and adaptations, they inform the Imamate's social policy in more recent times under the present Imam, Aga Khan IV.

More recent, and burgeoning, corpus of scholarship on Islam in the age of empires tends to foreground the chequered history of the very idea of nation-state in modern Islamic thought, and indeed the ambivalent relationship that Muslim intellectuals and religious elites in large parts of the Islamicate world had come to have with the question of territoriality. The present monograph took a cue from this, and sought to suggest a way to engage meaningfully with the evolution of a Muslim denomination, with all its characteristic features and engaging critically with these questions, while at the same time marking a passage from the transregional to the global arena. The book strove to problematize the genealogy of this denominational identity within the larger rubric of postnationalism. The underlying idea was not to deny the question of 'nation' and/or 'nation-state', with their multifaceted implications, *per se*. Rather, the abiding concern was to suggest a method to engage with the complex lineages of religious communities and denominations that both draw upon some of the key props of the conceptual rubric of 'nation', at times to the point of hollowing them out, and at the same time, transcend their immediacy to render them marginal to the notion of such communities, and the imagination of those who see themselves as part of such projects. The genealogy of the Ismaili international that this book strove to trace brings us first and foremost to its historical anticipations in late colonial South Asia and the western Indian Ocean world. One sees here the evolution of a religious denomination under the charismatic leadership of its Hazir Imam not through any overt invocation of idioms of religious nationalism or territoriality, but through activation of vocabularies of the universal wedded to the denominational particularities and customs. And even when the rhetoric of religious nationalism was referred to, it happened only through substantial filtering, with significant qualifications in the specific context of a politically-inflected ecumenical endeavour in early twentieth century South Asia. The narrative that this book develops thus uses the colonial/imperial, and in physical terms transregional, space as the crucial theatre of this historical process. Aga Khan III's engagement with ideas of the nation, the state, territoriality, citizenship, community and community development, and indeed idioms of authenticity, universality, civilization and cultural diversity all took shape first and foremost in a transregional imperial space, albeit with pronounced aspirations for the global. Even as the Ismaili community spread globally, the translation of some of these ideas and projects, however, had been far from linear development towards globality. To be sure, we have pointed to the recurrent emphases by both Aga Khans III and IV on the cultural specificities, and diversities in historical pathways.[2] A centrifugal/centripetal dynamic thus holds the global Ismaili community together, a lesson valorized and systematically inculcated since the times of Aga Khan III through the community's governance apparatuses. One also sees here, not least, a community revolving around the apex religious charismatic authority of the successive Hazir Imams. Manifestations of this charismatic authority, and indeed the centrality of the Imamate in the Ismaili imagination, range from celebration of landmark dates, such as the golden and diamond jubilees of Aga Khan III's Imamate when he was weighed against gold and diamond respectively in different locations in Africa and India,[3] through more rooted and structured constitutional initiatives, and activation of the state's diverse symbols. Also, we have seen how since the times of Aga Khan III the Imamate re-invented itself in increasingly 'secular' terms. The secular, we have noted, need not be seen as the dialectical opposite to the 'religious', though.

The book has further demonstrated how the very deployment of the nomenclature of the 'Ismaili' was conditioned almost preponderantly by the experiences of the Nizari Khoja branch of the denomination in late colonial South Asia and East Africa. This need not be seen as an epistemological affront delegitimizing the Mustali branch of the Ismailis, represented in South Asia and the South Asian diasporic world on the Indian Ocean by the different sections of the Bohras. Rather, the question here is one that concerns the very nature of the historical developments whereby a certain interchangeability came to be established between the two terminologies, viz., the 'Khoja' and the 'Ismaili', even as from about the early twentieth century in particular Aga Khan III strove to stake out a Khoja/Ismaili identity through community protocols and institutionalization of scholarly projects. In more recent times though, one sees an ecumenism of a different kind, operating within and sponsored by the institutional framework of the different branches of the Ismailis and with significant cultural ramifications whereby the Mustalis and the Nizaris are juxtaposed on the same platform. Recent expressions of this Ismaili cultural ecumenism includes academic ventures, such as a sophisticated volume entitled *A Modern History of the Ismailis: Continuity and Change in a Muslim Community*, edited by the doyen of Ismaili Studies Farhad Daftary, and published under the aegis of the IIS. The volume breaks new ground by way of incorporating important contributions on both the Nizari and Tayyibi Mustali branches of the Ismailis across the globe. What requires further attention is the way each of these branches endeavour to relate to a common historical past: the Fatimid Caliphate with all its pristine glories. Indeed, the Aga Khans' efforts to relate to the Fatimid past have to be seen as part of a larger cultural project, one in which the Daudi Bohras too had had their share of investments. In her contribution to the above volume Saifiyah Qutbuddin thus points to different aspects of Fatimid cultural legacy that the Bohras see themselves as inheriting: from a more mundane use of white, the official colour of the Fatimids, in male sartorial practices, through propagation of Fatimid religious learning to especially the last *dai-al mutlaq* Mohammed Burhanuddin's restoration projects in Cairo, the heart of the Fatimid Caliphate.[4] Nor is the Daudi Bohra religious establishment, the *dawat*, based in South Asia any less sensitized to the need to engage with the ostensibly 'secular' and the 'modern'. Thus the Al Jamea Tus Saifiyah in Surat, the apex institution of the Daudi Bohra community enjoying the *dawat* blessings, stresses the importance of Fatimid educational philosophy in integrating the temporal and the spiritual aspects of human life, at once ensuring spiritual fulfilment and facilitating an ethics of social responsibility,[5] and to wed 'past wisdom' to 'contemporary knowledge'.[6]

How best do we then appreciate the distinctiveness of the Ismaili Imamate's cultural project vis-à-vis other cognate, or perhaps even contending, ventures to relate to a common Fatimid past? It can be inferred from the discussions in this book that the crux of the history of the Imami Ismailis under the Aga Khans in modern times elicits a range of interwoven questions of both scale and nature. The scalar question emanates from the community's tryst with both transregional and global contexts, while issues revolving around the question of nature relates to the diverse, and indeed cosmopolitan, responses articulated through the Imamate's institutions to conditions spurred by the question of scale. The transregional-global history of the Imami Ismailis under the Aga Khans, by the sheer scale of its multisited cultural contexts, had historically tended to stoke, and continues to do so, a wide range of complexities. Part of this also had to do with Aga Khan III shifting his base to Europe in the early part of the twentieth century itself, a development that came to condition much of the internationalism, with all its fluctuations, that we have seen him valorizing. Conceiving an Imami Ismaili subjectivity from the vantage point of the Imamate, then, was part and parcel of a project sponsored by the Imamate that endeavoured at once to relate to the universality of an Islamic cosmos as well as the distinctiveness of the denomination. This project started its life in the Anglo-Muhammadan judicial context in nineteenth century South Asia, but subsequently graduated to a much larger epistemological venture. This book has underscored the need to juxtapose each of these aspects and see them as part of a long-drawn history. It has done so by emphasizing, in particular, the epistemological bases of the Imamate's Defence in the landmark 1866 law case. The book has further illustrated how this provided a backdrop to subsequent developments that conditioned the community, viz. how community institutions were gradually restructured and customs bowdlerized to the requirements of liberal modernist ventures under Aga Khan III and creating in the process alternative conduits of communication. In more recent times, Ismaili/Jamati institutions have come to not only co-exist but collaborate with the Imamate's other non-denominational institutions to re-inscribe an Ismaili history, and customize an Ismaili subjectivity bearing in mind the ever widening nature of cultural programmes. Moreover, we have also underlined that these cultural programmes are not *just* cultural programmes, after all. They are, in effect, cogs in a larger wheel that facilitates the Imamate's endeavour to relate the present to both its perceived cultural past as well as an anticipated future. The discourse of history and heritage in the Imamate's *weltanschauung*, thus, is dovetailed to a larger developmental vision, one that is expected to connect the community along both cross-temporal and cross-spatial lines. The 'cumulative result', as has been aptly pointed out, 'is the creation of a complete sociopolitical environment' which,[7] I would like to add, holds good both literally and metaphorically. In so far as the Imamate's endeavour to posit the present with aspirations to recover a past is also dovetailed with the visions of a future – rendered meaningful through a correlation of the Fatimid past, restoration of heritage, and sustainable development – there develops a simultaneity in the Ismaili subjectivity, thus brining past, present, and future all in one temporal arc, and connecting the global ecumene through the semiotics of this exercise. More tangibly, and in more concrete terms, this means the visibility of the Imamate through its different organs,[8] if also increasingly invoking secularized idioms.

The Ismaili Imamate's endeavour to engage the Ismaili denominational specificities in a dialogic exercise with a pluralized notion of Islamic ethos and universalist messages also has interesting historical parallels beyond the Ismaili world. The depth and wide range of developmental and philanthropic activities of the contemporary Ismaili social service endeavour, viz. the AKDN and its affiliated bodies, have been thus often compared with the humanitarian activities of the Gülen Movement, named after its founder Fethullah Gülen (1941–). As has been pointed out, they indicate efforts at 'the reinterpretation of the Islamic message in light of contemporary realities and seeking to bridge the gap holistically between the Muslim world and the West'; in the process, 'the Ismaili and Gulen movements offer creative possibilities of conception, thought, and action through transnational activism embedded in Islamic principles'.[9] The four key indices of this comparative study are: the vision of Islam, the question of leadership, organizational structure and the issue of membership, and finally, the programmes they engage with. Yet although Islamic principles and ideas of service (*hizmet*) do play an instrumental role, it has been duly observed that unlike the Ismaili case, the Gülen Movement is not a sect within Islam with the living Imam at the apex.[10] Furthermore, scholars also point out how the 'neo-Nurcu' movement of Fethullah Gülen and the Nurcu movement of Said Nursi (1877–1960) have come to occupy a middle ground between secularist Kemalism and political Islam, combining elements of modernist Islam and Turkish nationalism and statism.[11] Indeed, scholars further argue that it was the backdrop of the Republic of Turkey, and particularly the reforms that it entailed, that conditioned the early development of the Gülen Movement.[12] By contrast, the distinctiveness of the Ismaili case lies in the community's religious nature under its Imamate that have always sought to dissociate itself from overt idioms of nationalism and statism while also successfully bringing the religious in dialogue with the secular.

While underscoring the distinctive aspects of Ismaili history in modern times, especially under Aga Khan III, the book has also tried not to fall a prey to any straightjacketed discourse of exclusivism. In other words, it has been a very conscious effort to relate the course of Ismaili history since the late nineteenth century to the larger issues that defined the history of Islam and Muslim societies in modern South Asia. Thus issues stemming from critical understandings of colonial modernity, religious authority, variations of the idea of community, and cosmopolitan and postnational imagination have all been crucially important in this study. It is against this larger backdrop that the book strove to situate the denominational history of the Ismailis in the broader maze of universality/particularities, and indeed the politics of ecumenism. Moreover, a further important aspect of the present endeavour has been to problematize the very definition of an 'Ismaili'. To be sure, we have seen how, with the Bombay Khojas in the vanguard, this definition marked momentous methodological shifts, and carved out an epistemological space in the course of the 1866 Aga Khan Case. Latent in this epistemological venture was also an essentially protean element, which in the course of time became a crucial component in the Imamate's projects of developing an Ismaili interconnectedness out of compositeness. This protean element was the conceptual counterpoise steadfastly invoked by the Imamate in its efforts to balance the heightened institutional efforts at standardization. The very idea of a global Ismaili ecumene in contemporary times, clinically deterritorialized and depoliticized, is premised on a canonized set of religious normativity, and is reinforced by a cultural and ethnic cosmopolitanism. This complex balance, we have seen, somewhat critically engages with standard Kantian understanding, while signalling decisive efforts to conceive of a cluster of ethical aspirations beyond the statist confines. The present book, then, is also an effort to better understand the genealogies of this complex ideational constellation from a historical perspective.

Endnotes

1 Aga Khan III, *The Memoirs of the Aga Khan*, 174–75.

2 After all, there are significant scepticisms in scholarship about the very idea of a 'global intellectual history'. A key area of contention has been the very idea of the global, and its often overt associations with the modern. There is, therefore, a particular emphasis on both 'plurality of universalisms' and 'time depth of connections'. See Frederick Cooper, 'How Global Do We Want Our Intellectual History To Be?' in *Global Intellectual History*, edited by Moyn and Sarori, 283–94, at 291.

3 Hollister, *The Sh'ia of India*, 373–74 thus points to the meticulous preparations for the

diamond jubilee chaperoned by the Aga Khan Legion which, by 1943, boasted of about 40,000 members on its rolls.

4 Saifiyah Qutbuddin, 'History of the Da'udi Bohra Tayyibis in Modern Times: the Da'is, the Da'wat, and the Community' in *A Modern History of the Ismailis*, edited by Daftary, 297–330.

5 See the Al Jamea tus Saifiyah website: http://jameasaifiyah.edu/fatemi-philosophy-of-education-2/ (last accessed 28 November 2015). This institution was the outcome of an intellectual revival that developed the earlier Dars-e Saifee (established in 1818, Surat) into the present form under the spiritual leadership of the fifty-first *dai* Taher Saifuddin. Under the fifty-second *dai* Mohammed Burhanuddin the dimensions of learning in the institution are said to have widened considerably. The institution now boasts of four campuses, viz. in Surat, Karachi, Nairobi, and Mumbai (the latter two are currently under construction), all of which model themselves on Fatimid architectural patterns. Indeed, the very emblem of the institution adapts the arch of the Jame Azhar mosque of Cairo of the Fatimid era.

6 See http://jameasaifiyah.edu/realisation-of-aljamea-tus-saifiyah/ (last accessed 28 November 2015).

7 Steinberg, *Isma'ili Modern*, 64.

8 Steinberg's ethnographic account of the Himalayan Nizaris in contemporary times thus suggests that the semiotics of the AKDN institutions virtually 'conjure the image of the imam to the local Isma'ilis' (Ibid., 74).

9 Sara Shroff, *Muslim Movements Nurturing a Cosmopolitan Muslim Identity: The Ismaili and Gulen Movement*, ii (Master of Arts Thesis, School of Continuing Studies and The Graduate School of Arts and Sciences, Georgetown University, Washington DC, 2009). However, it should be added that the topology of the Gülen Movement becomes meaningful with reference to the Turkish socio-cultural specificities, viz., certain 'Turkish Islam' as some scholars argue, drawing upon a Said Nursi's (1877–1960) *Nurcu* or *Nur* (light) movement. For a brief overview, see Bulent Aras and Omer Caha, 'Fethullah Gulen and His Liberal "Turkish Islam" Movement', *Middle East Review of International Affairs*, 4, 4 (2000): 30–42.

10 Shroff, *Muslim Movements*, 63.

11 M. Kakan Yavuz, 'Towards an Islamic Liberalism?: The Nurcu Movement and Fethullah Gülen', *Middle East Journal*, 53, 4 (1999): 584–605.

12 See for instance Helen Rose Ebaugh, *The Gülen Movement: A Sociological Analysis of a Civic Movement Rooted in Moderate Islam* (Heidelberg, London and New York: Springer, 2010), the chapters entitled 'Islam and the State Throughout Turkish History' and 'Fethullah Gülen: His Life, Beliefs and the Movement That He Inspires'.

※

Select Bibliography[1]

Primary Sources

A. Manuscripts and Archival Documents

The British Library

India Office Records and Private Papers:
Political and Secret Department Records, 1916, 1918, 1924.
Public and Judicial Department Records, 1884, 1885, 1886.
Public Office Records, 1923.
Sir Fazli Hussain Collection.

The Asia Pacific and Africa (formerly Oriental and India Office) Collections:
Goolamali, Karim. 1986 [1932]. *An Appeal (Containing 'A Voice from India', 'Northcote Memorial' etc.) to Mr. Ali Solomon Khan, son of H.H. the Aga Khan.* Karachi: Khoja Reformers' Society. Cf. 'Published Primary Sources' section for specific references to compilations.
The Khoja Shia Imami Ismaili Council. 1913. *The Khoja Shia Imami Ismaili Council, Poona: Rules and Regulations.* Poona: The Khoja Shia Imami Ismaili Council.

The Cambridge University Library

Crewe Papers
The Centre of South Asian Studies, University of Cambridge
Gilbert Wiles Papers.
Malcolm Darling Papers.

Archives of the League of Nations, The United Nations Archives, Geneva

Records of the Fifteenth Ordinary Session of the Assembly Meetings, Twelfth Plenary Meeting, 1934.
Records of the Sixteenth Ordinary Session of the Assembly Meetings, Sixth Plenary Meeting, 1935.
Verbatim Record of the Seventeenth Ordinary Session of the Assembly of the League of Nations, 1936.

---

[1] For references to websites accessed see notes in the chapters.

Verbatim Record of the Thirteenth Ordinary Session of the Assembly of the League of Nations, 1932.

Maharashtra State Archives

Educational Department, Building Grants, 1902, 1906

Home Department, (Special), 1921

National Archives of India

Badruddin Tyabji Papers.

Home Department, Judicial Branch, 1880.

Home Department, Public Branch, 1879.

The Norwegian Nobel Institute

Papers related to the nomination of Aga Khan III for Nobel Peace Prize, 1924, 1925.

The Parliamentary Archives of the United Kingdom

Lloyd George Papers.

Politisches Archiv des Auswärtigen Amts (The Political Archives of the Federal Foreign Ministry, Germany)

Politisches Archiv des Auswärtigen Amts, Abteilung A, Englische Besitzungen in Asien, No. 2, Britische Indien, Bd. 49, vom 1 März 1912 bis 15 April 1913.

B. Published Primary Sources (official publications, memoirs, speeches, publications of individuals and organizations etc.)

H. H. The Aga Khan. 1918. *India in Transition: A Study in Political Evolution*. London: Philip Lee Warner.

_____. 1954. *The Memoirs of the Aga Khan: World Enough and Time*. London: Cassell & Co. Ltd.

Aga Khan, Prince and Zaki Ali. 1954 [1944]. *Glimpses of Islam*. Lahore: Sh. Muhammad Ashraf.

2007. *Aga Khan Trust for Culture: The Cultural Agency of the Aga Khan Development Network*. Geneva/Lausanne: AKTC.

Aitken, E. H. 1907. *Gazetteer of the Province of Sind, Volume 'A'*. Karachi: Mercantile Steam Press.

2011. *AKF and AKDN: A Continuum of Development, Aga Khan Foundation – An Agency of the Aga Khan Development Network*. Geneva: Aga Khan Foundation.

Al-Husayni, Shihabu'd-Din Shah. 1947 [1933]. *Risala dar Haqiqat-i Din*, translated by Wladimir Ivanow as *True Meaning of Religion*. Mumbai: Thacker & Co.

Ali, Syed Ameer. 1902. *The Spirit of Islâm Or, The Life and Teachings of Mohammed*. Kolkata: S.K. Lahiri & Co.

_____. 1946 [1891]. *The Spirit of Islâm: A History of the Evolution and Ideals of Islâm. With a Life of the Prophet*. London: Christophers.

Anonymous. 1986 [1932]. 'A Voice from India. Being an Appeal to the British Legislature, by Khojahs of Bombay, against the usurped and oppressive domination of Hussain Hussanee, commonly called and known as Aga Khan, by a Native of Bombay, 1864', in *An Appeal to Mr. Ali Solomon Khan, Son of H.H. the Aga Khan*, edited by Karim Goolamali, 1–51. Karachi: Khoja Reformers' Society.

_____. 1986 [1932]. 'An Open Letter to H.H. the Aga Khan', in *An Appeal to Mr. Ali Solomon Khan, Son of H.H. the Aga Khan*, edited by Karim Goolamali, 82–102. Karachi: Khoja Reformers' Society.

_____. 1986 [1932]. 'The Northcote Memorial', in *An Appeal to Mr. Ali Solomon Khan, Son of H.H. the Aga Khan*, edited by Karim Goolamali, 52–81. Karachi: Khoja Reformers' Society.

Aziz, Abualy A. 1974. *A Brief History of Ismailism*. Dar es Salam.

Aziz, K. K. (ed.). 1997. *Aga Khan III: Selected Speeches and Writings of Sir Sultan Muhammad Shah, Volume II, 1928–1955*. London and New York: Kegan Paul International.

_____. (ed.). 1998. *Aga Khan III: Selected Speeches and Writings of Sir Sultan Muhammad Shah, Volume I, 1902–1927*. London and New York: Kegan Paul International.

Baines, J. A. 1882. *The Imperial Census of 1881: Operations & Results in the Presidency of Bombay, Including Sind, Vol. I*. Bombay: Government Central Press.

Bianca, Stefano. 2007. 'Introduction', in *Aga Khan Historic Cities Programme: An Integrated Approach to Urban Rehabilitation*, 2–5. Geneva/ Lausanne: AKTC.

Biddulph, J. 1880. *Tribes of the Hindoo Koosh*. Kolkata: Office of the Superintendent of Government Printing.

Burton, Richard F. 1973 [1851]. *Sindh and the Races that Inhabit the Valley of the Indus, with Notices on the Topography and History of the Province*. Karachi: Oxford University Press.

Campbell, James A. (ed.). 1899. *Gazetteer of the Bombay Presidency, Volume IX, Part 2, 1899*. Bombay: Government Central Press.

Census of India. 1875. *Census of the Bombay Presidency: General Reports and Tables of the Population, Houses, & c., 1872, Part II*. Bombay: Government Central Press.

Digby, William. 1901. *'Prosperous' British India. A Revelation from Official Records*. London: Unwin.

Enthoven, R. E. 1902. *Census of India, 1901, Vol. IX, Bombay, Part I*. Bombay: Government Central Press.

Frere, Bartle. 1876. 'The Khojas: The Disciples of the Old Man of the Mountain, II', *Macmillans Magazine* XXXIV: 430–38.

Goolamali, Karim. 1986 [1932]. 'An Appeal', in *An Appeal to Mr. Ali Solomon Khan, Son of H.H. the Aga Khan*, edited by Karim Goolamali, i–vii. Karachi: Khoja Reformers' Society.

H. R. H. Prince Aga Khan Ismailia Federal Council for Pakistan. 1962. *The Constitution of the Councils and Jamats of Shia Imami Ismaili Muslims of Pakistan*. Karachi: H. R. H. Prince Aga Khan Ismailia Federal Council for Pakistan.

Hasan, Mushirul (ed.). 1979. *Muslims and the Congress: Select Correspondence of Dr. M. A. Ansari 1912–1935*. New Delhi: Manohar.

His Highness the Aga Khan Supreme Shia Imami Ismailia Council for Africa. 1962. *The Constitution of the Khoja Imami Ismailis in Africa*. Nairobi: His Highness the Aga Khan Supreme Shia Imami Ismailia Council for Africa.

Howard, E. I. 1866. *The Shia School of Islam and its Branches, Especially that of the Imamee–Ismailies*. Being a Speech delivered by Edward Irving Howard, Esq., Barrister-at-Law, in the Bombay High Court in 1866. Bombay: Oriental Press.

Hunter, W. W. 2004 [1871]. *The Indian Musalmans*. New Delhi: Rupa & Co.

Iqbal, Mohammad. 1960 [1930]. *The Reconstruction of Religious Thought in Islam*. Lahore: Shaikh Muhammad Ashraf.

Ivanow, Wladimir. 1948. 'Note by the Editor', in *Collectanea (The Ismaili Society's Non-periodical Collection of Articles)*, *Vol. I, 1948*, edited by Wladimir Ivanow. Leiden: Brill.

Khoja Sunnat Jamat. 1969. *The Sunni Khojas: An Account of the Khoja Sunnat Jamat Bombay*. Mumbai: Khoja Sunnat Jamat.

Mawani, Zulfikarali. 1977–78. 'A Brief Survey of the Development of Ismaili Education Administration from 1905–1945', in *Commemorative Issue, 1977–1978: Sixty Years of Ismaili Education in Kenya*. Nairobi: His Highness the Aga Khan Educational Department for Kenya.

Muir, William. 1861. *The Life of Mahomet: With Introductory Chapters on the Original Sources for the Biography of Mahomet, and on the Pre-Islamite History of Arabia, Vol. I*. London: Smith, Elder & Co.

_____. 1882. 'Sura V, v. 9 (The Coran)', *The Hebrew Student*, 1 and 2 (May): 14.

Nag, Kalidas. 1926. *Greater India (Greater India Society Bulletin No. 1)*. Kolkata: Greater India Society.

Nehru, J. L. 1974. 'His Highness the Aga Khan', in *Selected Works of Jawaharlal Nehru, Vol. VI*, 470–74. New Delhi: Orient Longman.

Picklay, A. S. 1940. *History of the Ismailis*. Mumbai: Published by the author.

Pirzada, Syed Sharifuddin (ed.). 1969. *The Foundations of Pakistan, All-India Muslim League Documents: 1906–1947, Vol. I, 1906–1924*. Karachi and Dhaka: National Publishing House.

_____. 1984. *The Collected Works of Quaid-e-Azam Mohammad Ali Jinnah, Vol. I, 1906–1921*. Karachi: East and West Publishing Company.

1997. *Primary Five, Book Two: People Helping People*. London: Institute of Ismaili Studies, 1997.

Rose, H. A. 1990 [1833]. *A Glossary of the Tribes and Castes of the Punjab and North-West Frontier Province*. Chandigarh: The Language Department of the Punjab.

Roy, M. N. 1971 [1922]. *India in Transition*. Mumbai: Nachiketa Publications Limited.

Sprenger, Alois. 1856. 'On the Origin and Progress of Writing down Historical Facts among the Musalmans', *Journal of the Asiatic Society* XXV (IV): 303–29.

_____. 1856. 'On the Origin and Progress of Writing Down Historical Facts among the Musalmans', *Journal of the Asiatic Society* XXV (V): 375–81.

van der Tas, Jurjen. 2007. 'Towards Integrated Socio-Economic Development', in *Aga Khan Historic Cities Programme: An Integrated Approach to Urban Rehabilitation*, 15–30. Geneva/ Lausanne: AKTC.

Visvesvaraya, Mokshagundam. 1920. *Reconstructing India*. London: P.S. King & Son Ltd.

von Hammer-Purgstall, Joseph. 1835. *The History of the Assassins, Derived from Oriental Sources*, translated by O. Charles Wood. London: Smith and Elder.

Zaidi, Z. H. (ed.). 1993. *Quaid-i-Aẓam Mohammad Ali Jinnah Papers: Prelude to Pakistan 20 February-2 June 1947, First Series, Vol. I, Part 1*. Islamabad and Lahore: National Archives of Pakistan/Ferozons Pvt. Ltd.

1997. *Primary Five, Book Two: People Helping People*. London: Institute of Ismaili Studies.

C. Law Cases and Judgements

1875. *Hirbae* v. *Gorbae*, (1875), 12 Bombay High Court Reporter, 294 ff.

1909. *Haji Bibi* v. *H.H. Sir Sultan Mahomed Shah, the Aga Khan*, (1909), 11 Bombay Law Reporter, 409 ff.

1912. *Hirbae* v. *Sonbae*, or the *Khojas and Memons' Case*, (1847), Cases Illustrative of Oriental Life and the Application of English Law to India, Decided in H. M. Supreme Court at Bombay by Sir Erskine Perry, 110; reprinted in *The Indian Decisions, (Old Series), Vol. IV*, 707 ff. Mumbai and Chennai: T.A.Venkaswamy Row and T.S. Krishnaswamy Row.

1965. *Advocate General* v. *Muhammad Husen Huseni*, (1866), 12 Bombay High Court Reporter, 323 ff. Reported in A.A.A. Fyzee, *Cases in the Muhammadan Law of India and Pakistan*, 504–49. Oxford: Clarendon Press.

Printed Secondary Works, Dissertations and Theses

Agamben, Giorgio. 2005. *The Time That Remains: A Commentary on the Letter to the Romans*. Stanford: Stanford University Press.

Akhtar, Iqbal. 2014. 'Negotiating the Racial Boundaries of Khōjā Caste Membership in Late Nineteenth-Century Colonial Zanzibar (1878–1899)', *Journal of African Religions* 2 (3): 297–316.

Alam, Muzaffar. 2014 [2004]. *The Languages of Political Islam in India, c. 1200–1800*. New Delhi/Ranikhet: Permanent Black.

Alavi, Seema. 2015. *Muslim Cosmopolitanism in the Age of Empire*. Cambridge, MA: Harvard University Press.

Althusser, Louis. 1984. *Essays on Ideology*. London: Verso.

Amiji, Hatim M. 1971. 'Some Notes on Religious Dissent in Nineteenth-Century East Africa', *African Historical Studies* 4 (3): 603–16.

Amrith, Sunil S. 2010. 'Indians Overseas? Governing Tamil Migration to Malaya, 1870–1941', *Past and Present* 208 (1): 231–61.

_____. 2011. *Migration and Diaspora in Modern Asia*. Cambridge and New York: Cambridge University Press.

Anderson, Benedict. 1983. *Imagined Communities: Reflections on the Origin and Spread of Nationalism*. London and New York: Verso.

Anderson, Michael R. 1993. 'Islamic Law and the Colonial Encounter in British India', in *Institutions and Ideologies: A SOAS Reader*, edited by David Arnold and Peter Robb, 165–85. Richmond: Curzon Press.

Appiah, Kwame Anthony. 1996. 'Cosmopolitan Patriots', in *For Love of Country: Debating the Limits of Patriotism. Martha C. Nussbaum with Respondents* edited by Joshua Cohen, 21–29. Boston: Beacon Press.

_____. 2006. *Cosmopolitanism: Ethics in a World of Strangers*. New York: W.W. Norton.

Aras, Bulent and Omer Caha. 2000. 'Fethullah Gulen and His Liberal "Turkish Islam" Movement', *Middle East Review of International Affairs* 4 (4): 30–42.

Arnold, David and Stuart Blackburn. 2004. 'Introduction: Life Histories in India', in *Telling Lives in India: Biography, Autobiography, and Life History*, edited by David Arnold and Stuart Blackburn, 1–28. Bloomington and Indianapolis: Indiana University Press.

Arvidsson, Stefan. 2006. *Aryan Idols: Indo-European Mythology as Ideology and Science*, translated by Sonia Wichmann. Chicago and London: University of Chicago Press.

Asad, Talal. 1993. *Genealogies of Religion: Discipline and Reasons of Power in Christianity and Islam*. Baltimore and London: The Johns Hopkins University Press.

_____. 2003. *Formations of the Secular: Christianity, Islam, Modernity*. Stanford: Stanford University Press.

Aydin, Cemil. 2007. *The Politics of Anti-Westernism in Asia: Visions of World Order in Pan-Islamic and Pan-Asian Thought*. New York: Columbia University Press.

_____. 2013. 'Globalizing the Intellectual History of the Idea of the "Muslim World"', in *Global Intellectual History*, edited by Samuel Moyn and Andrew Sartori, 159–86. New York: Columbia University Press.

Bagchi, Barnita, Eckhardt Fuchs and Kate Rousmaniere (eds.). 2014. *Connecting Histories of Education: Transnational and Cross-Cultural Exchanges in (Post-)Colonial Education*. New York and Oxford: Berghahn Books.

Ballhatchet, Kenneth. 1957. *Social Policy and Social Change in Western India, 1817–1830*. London: Oxford University Press.

Baughan, Emily. 2012. 'The Imperial War Relief Fund and the All British Appeal:

Commonwealth, Conflict and Conservatism within the British Humanitarian Movement, 1920–1925', *Journal of Imperial and Commonwealth History* 40 (5): 845–61.

Bayly, Christopher A. 2012 [2011]. 'Indigenous and Colonial Origins of Comparative Economic Development: The Case of Colonial India and Africa', in *History, Historians and Development Policy: A Necessary Dialogue*, edited by C. A. Bayly, Vijayendra Rao, Simon Szreter and Michael Woolcock, 39–64. Hyderabad: Orient Blackswan.

_____. 2012. *Recovering Liberties: Indian Thought in the Age of Liberalism and Empire*. Cambridge and New Delhi: Cambridge University Press.

Bayly, Christopher A. and Leila Fawaz. 2002. 'Introduction: The Connected World of Empires', in *Modernity and Culture: From the Mediterranean to the Indian Ocean*, edited by L. Fawaz and C. A. Bayly, 1–27. New York: Columbia University Press.

Bayly, Susan. 1995. 'Caste and "Race" in the Colonial Ethnography of India', in *The Concept of Race in South Asia*, edited by Peter Robb, 165–218. New Delhi: Oxford University Press.

_____. 2004. 'Imaging "Greater India": French and Indian Visions of Colonialism in the Indic Mode', *Modern Asian Studies* 38 (3): 703–44.

Beckerlegge, Gwilym. 2000. *Swami Vivekananda's Legacy of Service: A Study of the Ramakrishna Math and Mission*. New Delhi: Oxford University Press.

_____. 2006. *The Ramakrishna Mission: The Making of a Modern Hindu Movement*. New Delhi: Oxford University Press.

Bennison, Amira K. 2012. 'Muslim Internationalism between Empire and Nation-State', in *Religious Internationals in the Modern World: Globalization and Faith Communities Since 1750*, edited by Abigail Green and Vincent Viaene, 163–85. Basingstoke and New York: Palgrave Macmillan.

Benton, Lauren. 1999. 'Colonial Law and Cultural Difference: Jurisdictional Politics and the Formation of the Colonial State', *Comparative Studies in Society and History* 41 (3): 563–88.

Berger, Julia. 2003. 'Religious Nongovernmental Organizations: An Exploratory Analysis', *Voluntas: International Journal of Voluntary and Nonprofit Organizations* 14 (1): 15–39.

Bhabha, Homi K. 2004 [1994]. *The Location of Culture*. New York: Routledge.

Bharucha, Rustom. 2014 [2006]. *Another Asia: Rabindranath Tagore and Okakura Tenshin*. New Delhi: Oxford University Press.

Bhatia, Mohita. 2013. 'Secularism and Secularisation: A Bibliographical Essay', *Economic and Political Weekly* XLVIII (50) (December): 103–10.

Bhattacharya, Neeladri. 2003. 'Predicaments of Mobility: Peddlers and Itinerants in Nineteenth Century Northwestern India', in *Society and Circulation: Mobile People and Itinerant Cultures in South Asia*, edited by Claude Markovits, Jacques Pouchepadass and Sanjay Subrahmanyam, 163–214. Ranikhet/New Delhi: Permanent Black.

_____. 2005. 'Notes Towards a Conception of the Colonial Public', in *Civil society, Public Sphere and Citizenship: Dialogues and Perceptions*, edited by Rajeev Bhargava and Helmut Reifeld, 130–56. New Delhi: Sage.

Bhattacharya, Sabyasachi. 2014. 'Towards a Global History of Education: Alternative Strategies', in *Connecting Histories of Education: Transnational and Cross-Cultural Exchanges in (Post-)Colonial Education*, edited by Barnita Bagchi, Eckhardt Fuchs and Kate Rousmaniere, 27–40. New York and Oxford: Berghahn Books.

Bilgrami, Akeel. 2012. 'Secularism: Its Content and Context, 2012', *Economic and Political Weekly* XLVII (4): 89–100.

Blyth, Robert J. 2003. *The Empire of the Raj: India, Eastern Africa and the Middle East, 1858-1947*. Basingstoke and New York: Palgrave Macmillan.

Boivin, Michel. 1994. 'The Reform of Islam in Ismaili Shī'ism from 1885 to 1957', in *Confluence of Cultures: French Contributions to indo-Persian Studies*, edited by Françoise Delvoye. Delhi: Manohar, translated by Rashmi Patni.

Bose, Sugata. 2006. *A Hundred Horizons: The Indian Ocean in the Age of Global Empire*. Cambridge MA and London: Harvard University Press.

_____. 2010. 'Different Universalisms, Colorful Cosmopolitanisms: The Global Imagination of the Colonized', in *Cosmopolitan Thought Zones: South Asia and the Global Circulation of Ideas*, edited by Sugata Bose and Kris Manjapra, 97–111. Basingstoke and New York: Palgrave Macmillan.

Bourdieu, Pierre, 1990. *The Logic of Practice*, translated by Richard Nice. Stanford: Stanford University Press.

Brass, Paul. 1974. *Language, Religion and Politics in North India*. Cambridge: Cambridge University Press.

_____. 1979. 'Elite Groups, Symbol Manipulation and Ethnic Identity among the Muslims of South Asia', in *Political Identity in South Asia*, edited by David Taylor and Malcolm Yapp, 35–77. London and Dublin: Curzon Press.

_____. 1991. *Ethnicity and Nationalism: Theory and Comparison*. New Delhi: Sage.

Brown, Daniel. 1999 [1996]. *Rethinking Tradition in Modern Islamic Thought*. Cambridge: Cambridge University Press.

Casanova, José. 1994. *Public Religions in the Modern World*. Chicago and London: University of Chicago Press.

_____. 2008. 'Public Religions Revisited', in *Religion: Beyond the Concept*, edited by Hent de Vries, 101–19. New York: Fordham University Press.

Chaghatai, M. Ikram. 1998. *Hammer-Purgstall and the Muslim India*. Lahore: Iqbal Academy Pakistan.

Chatterjee, Partha. 1993. *The Nation and its Fragments: Colonial and Postcolonial Histories*. Princeton, New Jersey: Princeton University Press.

Chaudhuri, K. N. 1985. *Trade and Civilisation in the Indian Ocean: An Economic History from the Rise of Islam to 1750*. Cambridge: Cambridge University Press.

_____. 1990. *Asia before Europe: Economy and Civilisation of the Indian Ocean from the Rise of Islam to 1750*. Cambridge: Cambridge University Press.

Cohn, Bernard S. 2006 [1987]. *An Anthropologist among Historians and Other Essays*, 224–54. New Delhi: Oxford University Press.

Comaroff, J. and J. Comaroff. 1992. *Ethnography and the Historical Imagination*. Boulder: Westview Press.

Cooper, Frederick and Randall Packard (eds.). 1998. *International Development and the Social Science: Essays on the History and Politics of Knowledge*. Berkeley, Los Angeles and London: University of California Press.

Cooper, Frederick. 2001. 'What is the Concept of Globalization Good for? An African Historian's Perspective', *African Affairs* 100 (399): 189–213.

_____. 2013. 'How Global Do We Want Our Intellectual History To Be?', in *Global Intellectual History*, edited by Samuel Moyn and Andrew Sartori, 283–94. New York: Columbia University Press.

Daftary, Farhad. 1972. 'W. Ivanow: A Biographical Notice', *Middle Eastern Studies* 8 (2): 241–44.

_____. 1990. *The Ismāʿīlīs: Their History and Doctrines*. Cambridge: Cambridge University Press.

_____ (ed). 1996. *Medieval Ismaʿili History and Thought*. Cambridge: Cambridge University Press.

_____ (ed). 2011 [2010]. *A Modern History of the Ismailis: Continuity and Change in a Muslim Community*. London and New York: I.B. Tauris.

Davies, Merryl Wyn. 1988. *Knowing One Another: Shaping an Islamic Anthropology*. London and New York: Mansell.

Delanty, Gerard. 2006. 'The Cosmopolitan Imagination: Critical Cosmopolitanism and Social Theory', *The British Journal of Sociology* 57 (1): 25–47.

Devji, Faisal. 2007. 'The Minority as Political Form', in *From the Colonial to the Postcolonial: India and Pakistan in Transition*, edited by Dipesh Chakrabarty, Rochona Majumdar and Andrew Sartori, 85–95. New Delhi: Oxford University Press.

_____. 2009. 'Preface to Marc van Grondelle', in *The Ismailis in the Colonial Era: Modernity, Empire and Islam*, ix–xvi. New York: Columbia University Press.

_____. 2010. 'The Language of Muslim Universality', *Diogenes* 57 (2): 36–49.

_____. 2013. *Muslim Zion: Pakistan as a Political Idea*. Cambridge, MA: Harvard University Press.

Dharampal. 1972. *The Madras Panchayat System, Vol II: A General Assessment*. Delhi: Impex India.

Dobbin, Christine. 1972. *Urban Leadership in Western India: Politics and Communities in Bombay City, 1840–1885*. London: Oxford University Press.

Dohrn, Kristina. 2013. 'Translocal Ethics: Hizmet Teachers and the Formation of Gülen-inspired Schools in Urban Tanzania', *Sociology of Islam* 1 (3–4): 233–56.

Dreyer, Jaco S. 2004. 'Theological Normativity: Ideology or Utopia?: Reflections on the Possible Contribution of Empirical Research', in *Normativity and Empirical Research in Theology*, edited by Johannes A. van der Ven and Michael Sherer-Rath, 3–16. Leiden: Brill.

Duara, Prasenjit. 2001. 'The Discourse of Civilization and Pan-Asianism', *Journal of World History* 12 (1): 99–130.

_____. 2010. 'Asia Redux: Conceptualizing a Region for Our Times', *The Journal of Asian Studies*, 69 (4): 963–83.

Ebaugh, Helen Rose. 2010. *The Gülen Movement: A Sociological Analysis of a Civic Movement Rooted in Moderate Islam*. Heidelberg, London, New York: Springer.

Emadi, Hafizullah. 1998. 'The End of *Taqiyya*: Reaffirming the Religious Identity of Ismailis in Shughnan, Badakhshan: Political Implications for Afghanistan', *Middle Eastern Studies* 34 (3): 103–20.

Esenbel, Selçuk. 2004. 'Japan's Global Claim to Asia and the World of Islam: Transnational Nationalism and World Power, 1900–1945', *The American Historical Review* 109 (4): 1140–70.

Esposito, John L. 2003. 'Islam and Civil Society', in *Modernizing Islam: Religion in the Public Sphere in Europe and the Middle East*, edited by John L. Esposito and François Burgat, 69–100. New Brunswick, NJ: Rutgers University Press.

Forward, Martin. 1995. 'Syed Ameer Ali: A Bridge-builder?', *Islam and Christian-Muslim Relations* 6 (1): 45–62.

Gadamer, Hans-Georg. 2006 [1975]. *Truth and Method*, translated by Joel Weinsheimer and Donald G. Marshall. London and New York: Continuum.

Geertz, Clifford. 1973. *The Interpretation of Cultures*. New York: Basic Books.

Goodson, Ivor. 1995. 'The Story So Far', *Life History and Narrative*, edited by J. A. Hatch and R. Wiesniewski, 89–98. Washington DC: Falmer Press.

Goswami, Chhaya. 2011. *The Call of the Sea: Kachchhi Traders in Muscat and Zanzibar, c. 1800–1880*. Hyderabad and New Delhi: Orient BlackSwan.

Gottschalk, Peter. 2013. *Religion, Science, and Empire: Classifying Hinduism and Islam in British India*. New York: Oxford University Press.

Green, Abigail and Vincent Viaene. 2012. 'Introduction: Rethinking Religion and Globalization', in *Religious Internationals in the Modern World: Globalization and Faith Communities Since 1750*, edited by Abigail Green and Vincent Viaene, 1–19. Basingstoke and New York: Palgrave Macmillan.

Green, Nile. 2008. 'Islam for the Indentured Indian: A Muslim Missionary in Colonial South Africa', *Bulletin of School of Oriental and African Studies* 71 (3): 529–53.

_____. 2011. *Bombay Islam: The Religious Economy of the West Indian Ocean, 1840–1915*. New York: Cambridge University Press.

_____. 2012. 'Africa in Indian Ink: Urdu Articulations of Indian settlement in East Africa', *Journal of African History* 53 (2): 131–50.

Greenblatt, Stephen. 1980. *Renaissance Self-Fashioning: From More to Shakespeare.* Chicago: University of Chicago Press.

Gregory, Robert G. 1992. *The Rise and Fall of Philanthropy in East Africa: The Asian Contribution.* New Brunswick and London: Transaction Publishers.

Guha, Ranajit. 2003. 'Discipline and Mobilize', in *Subaltern Studies, Volume VII: Writings on South Asian History and Society,* edited by Partha Chatterjee and Gyanendra Pandey, 69–120. New Delhi: Oxford University Press.

Hajjar, Sami G. and Steven J. Brzeznski. 1977. 'The Nizārī Ismā' īli Imam and Plato's Philosopher King', *Islamic Studies* 16 (1): 303–16.

Hall, Stuart. 1996. 'Politics of Identity', in *Culture, Identity and Politics: Ethnic Minorities in Britain,* edited by Terence Ranger, Yunas Samad and Ossie Stuart, 129–35. Aldershot: Avebury.

Harder, Hans. 2011. *Sufism and Saint Veneration in Contemporary Bangladesh: The Maijbhandaris of Chittagong.* London and New York: Routledge.

Hardy, Peter. 1998 [1972]. *The Muslims of British India.* Cambridge and New Delhi: Cambridge University Press.

Hasan, Mushirul. 2012 [1997]. *Legacy of a Divided Nation: India's Muslims since Independence.* New Delhi: Oxford University Press.

Hashim, Abdulkadir. 2012. 'Shaping of the Sharia Courts: British Policies of Transforming the Kadhi Courts in Colonial Zanzibar', *Social Dynamics: A Journal of African Studies* 38 (3): 381–97.

Haynes, Douglas E. 1991. *Rhetoric and Ritual in Colonial India: The Shaping of a Public Culture in Surat City, 1852–1928.* Berkeley: University of California Press.

Hazareesingh, Sandip. 2007. *The Colonial City and the Challenge of Modernity: Urban Hegemonies and Civic Consciousness in Bombay, 1900–1925.* Hyderabad: Orient Longman.

Heng, Geraldine. 2012. 'Sex, Lies, and Paradise: The Assassins, Prester John, and the Fabulation of Civilizational Identities', *differences: A Journal of Feminist Cultural Studies,* 23 (1): 1–31.

Hinnells, John R. 2008. 'Changing Perceptions of Authority among Parsis in British India', in *Parsis in India and the Diaspora,* edited by John R. Hinnells and Alan Williams, 100–18. London and New York: Routledge.

Hirji, Zulfikar. 2011. 'The Socio-Legal Formation of the Nizari Ismailis of East Africa, 1800–1950', in *A Modern History of the Ismailis: Continuity and Change in a Muslim Community,* edited by Farhad Daftary, 129–59. London: IB Tauris.

Hollister, J. N. 1953. *The Sh'ia of India.* London: Luzac & Co. Ltd.

Horstmann, Alexander. 2007. 'The Inculturation of a Transnational Islamic Missionary Movement: Tablighi Jamaat al-Dawa and Muslim Society in Southern Thailand', *Sojourn: Journal of Social Issues in Southeast Asia* 22 (1): 107–30.

Iriye, Akira. 2002. *Global Community: The Role of International Organizations in the Making of the Contemporary World*. Berkeley and Los Angeles: University of California Press.

Jaffrelot, Christophe. 1993. 'Hindu Nationalism: Strategic Syncretism in Ideology Building', *Economic and Political Weekly* XXVIII (12–13) (March): 517–24.

_____. 1996. *The Hindu Nationalist Movement and Indian Politics, 1925 to the 1990s: Strategies of Identity Building, Implantation and Mobilisation (with special reference to Central India)*. London: Hurst & Company.

Jalal, Ayesha. 1998. 'Exploding Communalism: The Politics of Muslim Identity in South Asia', in *Nationalism, Democracy and Development: State and Politics in India*, edited by Sugata Bose and Ayesha Jalal, 76–103. Delhi: Oxford University Press.

_____. 2000. *Self and Sovereignty: Individual and Community in South Asian Islam since 1850*. London and New York: Routledge.

_____. 2007. 'Striking a Just Balance: Maulana Azad as a Theorist of Trans-National Jihad', *Modern Intellectual History* 4 (1): 95–107.

_____. 2008. *Partisans of Allah: Jihad in South Asia*. Cambridge, MA. and London: Harvard University Press.

Jerolmack, Colin and Douglas Porpora. 2004. 'Religion, Rationality, and Experience: A Response to the New Rational Choice Theory of Religion', *Sociological Theory* 22 (1): 140–60.

Jones, Justin. 2009. 'The Local Experience of Reformist Islam in a "Muslim" Town in Colonial India: The Case of Amroha', *Modern Asian Studies* 43 (4): 871–908.

_____. 2012. *Sh'ia Islam in Colonial India: Religion, Community and Sectarianism*. Cambridge and New York: Cambridge University Press.

Jones, Kenneth. 1981. 'Religious Identity and the Indian Census', in *The Census in British India: New Perspectives*, edited by N. Gerald Barrier, 73–101. Delhi: Manohar.

_____. 1989. *Socio-Religious Reform Movements in British India*. Cambridge and New Delhi: Cambridge University Press/Orient Longman.

Kadende-Kaiser, Rose M. and Paul J. Kaiser. 1998. 'Identity, Citizenship, and Transnationalism: Ismailis in Tanzania and Burundians in the Diaspora', *Africa Today* 45 (3–4): 461–80.

Kaiser, Paul J. 1996. *Culture, Transnationalism and Civil Society: Aga Khan Social Service Institutions in Tanzania*. Westport, CT and London: Praeger Publishers.

Kassam, Zayn R. 2011 [2010] 'Gender Policies of Aga Khan III and Aga Khan IV', in *A Modern History of the Ismailis: Continuity and Change in a Muslim Community*, edited by Farhad Daftary, 247–64. London and New York: I.B. Tauris.

Kaviraj, Sudipta. 2012 [2010]. 'On the Structure of Nationalist Discourse', in *The Imaginary Institution of India*, edited by Sudipta Kaviraj, 85–126. New Delhi/Ranikhet: Permanent Black.

Khan, Dominique-Sila and Zawahir Moir. 1999. 'Coexistence and Communalism: The Shrine of Pirana in Gujarat', *South Asia: Journal of South Asian Studies* XXII (Special Issue): 133–54.

Khan, Dominique-Sila. 2004. *Crossing the Threshold: Understanding Religious Identities in South Asia*. London: I.B. Tauris.

Kidambi, Prashant. 2012 [2011]. 'From "Social Reform" to "Social Service": Indian Civic Activism and the Civilizing Mission in Colonial Bombay c. 1900–1920', in *Civilizing Missions in Colonial and Postcolonial South Asia: From Improvement to Development*, edited by Carey A. Watt and Michael Mann, 217–39. London, New York and Delhi: Anthem.

Koselleck, Reinhart. 2004. *Futures Past: On the Semantics of Historical Time*, translated and introduced by Keith Tribe. New York: Columbia University Press.

Kothari, Uma. 2012 [2011]. 'Commentary: History, Time and Temporality in Development Discourse', in *History, Historians and Development Policy: A Necessary Dialogue*, edited by C. A. Bayly, Vijayendra Rao, Simon Szreter and Michael Woolcock, 65–70. Hyderabad: Orient Blackswan.

Kurzman, Charles (ed.). 1998. *Liberal Islam: A Sourcebook*. Oxford and New York: Oxford University Press.

_____. 1999. 'Liberal Islam: Prospects and Challenges', *Middle East Review of International Affairs* 3 (3): 11–19.

Legg, Stephen. 2014. 'An International Anomaly? Sovereignty, the League of Nations and India's Princely Geographies', *Journal of Historical Geography* 43: 96–110.

Lelyveld, David. 1996 [1978]. *Aligarh's First Generation: Muslim Solidarity in British India*. Delhi: Oxford University Press.

Levitan, Kathrin. 2011. *A Cultural History of the British Census: Envisioning the Multitude in the Nineteenth Century*. Basingstoke and New York: Palgrave Macmillan.

Lewis, Bernard. 2003 [1967]. *The Assassins: A Radical Sect in Islam*. New York: Basic Books.

Lewis, Thomas A. 2011. 'On the Role of Normativity in Religious Studies', in *The Cambridge Companion to Religious Studies*, edited by Robert A. Orsi, 168–85. Cambridge: Cambridge University Press.

Linklater, Andrew. 1998. 'Cosmopolitan Citizenship', *Citizenship Studies* 2 (1): 23–41.

Loimeier, Roman. 2009. *Between Social Skills and Marketable Skills: The Politics of Islamic Education in 20th Century Zanzibar*. Leiden and Boston: Brill.

Madan, T. N. 2015 [2004]. 'Introduction-India's Religions: Plurality and Pluralism', in *India's Religions: Perspectives from Sociology and History*, edited by T. N. Madan, 1–35. New Delhi: Oxford University Press.

Mahmood, Saba. 2005. *Politics of Piety: The Islamic Revival and the Feminist Subject*. Princeton, NJ: Princeton University Press.

Majeed, Javed. 2007. *Autobiography, Travel and Postnational Identity: Gandhi, Nehru and Iqbal*. Basingstoke and New York: Palgrave Macmillan.

_____. 2009. *Muhammad Iqbal: Islam, Aesthetics and Postcolonialism*. London and New Delhi: Routledge.

Makarem, Sami. 1967. 'The Philosophical Significance of the Imām in Ismāʻīlism', *Studia Islamica* 27: 41–53.

Manela, Erez. 2007. *The Wilsonian Moment: Self-Determination and the International Origins of Anticolonial Nationalism*. Oxford and New York: Oxford University Press.

Manjapra, Kris. 2006. 'The Illusions of Encounter: Muslim "Minds" and Hindu Revolutionaries in First World War Germany and After', *Journal of Global History* 1 (3): 363–82.

_____. 2014. *The Age of Entanglement: German and Indian Intellectuals across Empire*. Cambridge, MA. and London: Harvard University Press.

Marchand, Suzanne L. 2013 [2009]. *German Orientalism in the Age of Empire: Religion, Race, and Scholarship*. Cambridge and New York: Cambridge University Press.

Marsden, Magnus. 2005. *Living Islam: Muslim Religious Experience in Pakistan's North-West Frontier*. Cambridge: Cambridge University Press.

_____. 2008. 'Muslim Cosmopolitans? Transnational Life in Northern Pakistan', *The Journal of Asian Studies* 67 (1):213–47.

Masselos, J. 1973. 'The Khojas of Bombay: The Defining of Formal Membership Criteria During the Nineteenth Century', in *Caste and Social Stratification among the Muslims*, edited by Imtiaz Ahmad, 1–19. New Delhi: Manohar.

Masuzawa, Tomoko. 2005. *The Invention of World Religions, Or, How European Universalism Was Preserved in the Language of Pluralism*. Chicago and London: University of Chicago Press.

McPherson, Kenneth. 1993. *The Indian Ocean: A History of the People and the Sea*. Delhi: Oxford University Press.

Menon, Nivedita. 2009. 'Thinking through the Postnation', *Economic and Political Weekly* XLIV (10, Special issue 'The Postnational Condition'): 70–77.

Metcalf, Thomas A. 2007. *Imperial Connections: India in the Indian Ocean Arena, 1860–1920*. New Delhi/ Ranikhet: Permanent Black.

Minault, Gail and David Lelyveld. 1974. 'The Campaign for a Muslim University, 1898–1920', *Modern Asian Studies* 8 (2): 145–89.

Minault, Gail. 1982. *The Khilafat Movement: Religious Symbolism and Political Mobilization in India*. New York: Columbia University Press.

_____. 1998. *Secluded Scholars: Women's Education and Muslim Social Reform in. Colonial India*. New Delhi: Oxford University Press.

_____. 2011. 'Aloys Sprenger: German Orientalism's "Gift" to Delhi College', *South Asia Research* 31 (7): 7–23.

Morris, H. S. 1958. 'The Divine Kingship of the Aga Khan: A Study of Theocracy in East Africa', *Southwestern Journal of Anthropology* 14 (4): 454–72.

_____. 1968. *Indians in Uganda*. London: Weidenfeld and Nicolson.

Mufti, Aamir. 2007. *Enlightenment in the Colony: The Jewish Question and the Crisis of Postcolonial Culture*. Princeton: Princeton University Press.

Mukherjee, Soumen. 2011. 'Being "Ismaili" and "Muslim": Some Observations on the Politico-Religious Career of Aga Khan III', *South Asia: Journal of South Asian Studies* 34 (2): 188–207.

_____. 2014. 'Universalising Aspirations: Community and Social Service in the Isma'ili Imagination in Twentieth Century South Asia and East Africa', *Journal of the Royal Asiatic Society*, Series 3, 24 (3): 435–53.

Nandy, Ashis. 1998. 'The Politics of Secularism and the Recovery of Religious Tolerance', in *Secularism and its Critics*, edited by Rajeev Bhargava, 321–44. Delhi: Oxford University Press.

_____. 2004. *Bonfire of Creeds: The Essential Ashis Nandy*. New Delhi: Oxford University Press.

Nanji, Azim. 2008. '*Millet*' in Idem, *The Penguin Dictionary of Islam*. London: Penguin.

Nimtz, August H. 1980. *Islam and Politics in East Africa: The Sufi Order in Tanzania*. Minneapolis: University of Minnesota Press.

Nizami, K. A. 1995. *History of the Aligarh Muslim University, Vol. 1, 1920–1945*. Delhi: Idara-i Adabiyat-i Delli.

Nussbaum, Martha. 1996. 'Patriotism and Cosmopolitanism', in *For Love of Country: Debating the Limits of Patriotism. Martha C. Nussbaum with Respondents*, edited by Joshua Cohen, 2–17. Boston: Beacon Press.

Oberoi, Harjot. 1994. *The Construction of Religious Boundaries: Culture, Identity and Diversity in the Sikh Tradition*. New Delhi: Oxford University Press.

Palsetia, Jesse S. 2001 'Mad Dogs and Parsis: The Bombay Dog Riots of 1832', *Journal of the Royal Asiatic Society*, Series 3, 11 (1): 13–30.

Pandey, Gyanendra. 1990. *The Construction of Communalism in Colonial North India*. Delhi: Oxford University Press.

Pollock, Sheldon, Homi K. Bhabha, Carol A. Breckenridge and Dipesh Chakrabarty. 2000. 'Introduction: Cosmopolitanisms', *Public Culture* 12 (3): 577–89.

Poor, Daryoush Mohammad. 2014. *Authority without Territory: The Aga Khan Development Network and the Ismaili Imamate*. New York: Palgrave Macmillan.

Purohit, Teena. 2011. 'Identity Politics Revisited: Secular and "Dissonant" Islam in Colonial South Asia', *Modern Asian Studies* 45 (3): 709–33.

_____. 2012. *The Aga Khan Case: Religion and Identity in Colonial India*. Cambridge, MA. and London: Harvard University Press.

Putnam, Hilary. 1996. 'Must We Choose Between Patriotism and Universal Reason?', in *For Love of Country: Debating the Limits of Patriotism. Martha C. Nussbaum with Respondents*, edited by Joshua Cohen, 91–97. Boston: Beacon Press.

Qutbuddin, Saifiyah. 2011 [2010]. 'History of the Da' udi Bohra Tayyibis in Modern Times: the Da' is, the Da' wat, and the Community', in *A Modern History of the Ismailis: Continuity and Change in a Muslim Community*, edited by Farhad Daftary, 297–330. London and New York: I.B. Tauris.

Raheja, Gloria Goodwin. 1996. 'Caste, Colonialism, and the Speech of the Colonized: Entextualization and Disciplinary Control in India', *American Ethnologist* 23 (3): 494–513.

Rahman, Matiur. 1970. *From Consultation to Confrontation: A Study of the Muslim League in British Indian Politics, 1906-1912*. London: Luzac & Company Ltd.

Raza, Ali, Franziska Roy and Benjamin Zachariah (eds.). 2015. *The Internationalist Moment: South Asia, Worlds, and World Views, 1917-39*. New Delhi: Sage.

Reinwald, Brigitte and Jan-Georg Deutsch (eds.). 2002. *Space on the Move: Transformations of the Indian Ocean Seascape in the Nineteenth and Twentieth Century*. Berlin: Klaus Schwarz.

Robinson, Francis. 1979. 'Islam and Muslim Separatism', in *Political Identity in South Asia*, edited by David Taylor and Malcolm Yapp, 78–112. London and Dublin: Curzon Press.

_____. 2004. 'Other-Worldly and This-Worldly Islam and Islamic Revival: A Memorial Lecture for Wilfred Cantwell Smith', *Journal of the Royal Asiatic Society*, Series 3, 14 (1): 47–58.

_____. 2012 [2000]. 'Nation Formation: The Brass Thesis and Muslim Separatism', in Idem, *Islam and Muslim History in South Asia*, 156–76. New Delhi: Oxford University Press.

_____. 2012 [2000]. 'Religious Change and the Self in Muslim South Asia since 1800', in Idem, *Islam and Muslim History in South Asia*, 105–21. New Delhi: Oxford University Press.

_____. 2012 [2001]. *The Ulama of Farangi Mahall and Islamic Culture in South Asia*. New Delhi: Permanent Black.

_____. 2012. 'The Islamic World: World System to "Religious International"', in *Religious Internationals in the Modern World: Globalization and Faith Communities Since 1750*, edited by Abigail Green and Vincent Viaene, 111–35. Basingstoke and New York: Palgrave Macmillan.

_____. 2013. 'Strategies of Authority in Muslim South Asia in the 19th and 20th Centuries', in *Muslim Voices: Community and the Self in South Asia*, edited by Usha Sanyal, David Gilmartin and Sandria B. Freitag, 16–36. New Delhi: Yoda Press.

Rorty, Richard. 2003 [1982]. *Consequences of Pragmatism*. Minneapolis: University of Minnesota Press.

Rothermund, Dietmar. 1970. 'Emancipation or Re-integration', in Idem, *The Phases of Indian Nationalism and Other Essays*, 26-56. Bombay: Nachiketa Publications Limited.

Ruthven, Malise. 2011 [2010]. 'The Aga Khan Development Network and Institutions', in *A Modern History of the Ismailis: Continuity and Change in a Muslim Community*, edited by Farhad Daftary, 189–220. London and New York: I.B. Tauris.

Sassen, Saskia. 2006. *Territory, Authority, Rights: From Medieval to Global Assemblages.* Princeton: Princeton University Press.

Saunier, Pierre-Yves. 2009. 'Transnational', in *The Palgrave Dictionary of Transnational History*, edited by Akira Iriye and Pierre-Yves Saunier, 1047–55. Basingstoke and New York: Palgrave Macmillan.

Sevea, Iqbal Singh. 2013 [2012]. *The Political Philosophy of Muhammad Iqbal: Islam and Nationalism in Late Colonial India.* Cambridge and New Delhi: Cambridge University Press.

Shaikh, Farzana. 1989. *Community and Consensus in Islam: Muslim Representation in Colonial India, 1860–1947.* Cambridge: Cambridge University Press.

Sheriff, Abdul. 2001. 'The Records of the "Wakf Commission" as a Source of Social and Religious History of Zanzibar', in *Islam in East Africa: New Sources*, edited by Biancamaria Scarcia Amoretti, 27–45. Rome: Herder.

Shodhan, Amrita. 2001. *A Question of Community: Religious Groups and Colonial Law.* Kolkata: Samya

Shroff, Sara. 2009. *Muslim Movements Nurturing a Cosmopolitan Muslim Identity: The Ismaili and Gulen Movement.* Master of Arts Thesis, School of Continuing Studies and The Graduate School of Arts and Sciences, Georgetown University, Washington DC.

Skinner, Quentin. 1974. 'Some Problems in the Analysis of Political Thought and Action', *Political Theory* 2 (3): 277–303.

Smith, Wilfred Cantwell. 1981. 'The Historical Development in Islam of the Concept of Islam as an Historical Development', in Idem, *On Understanding Islam: Selected Studies*, 41–77. The Hague: Mouton Publishers.

Stark, R. and R. Finke. 2000. *Acts of Faith: Explaining the Human Side of Religion.* Berkeley: University of California Press.

Steinberg, Jonah. 2011. *Isma'ili Modern: Globalization and Identity in a Muslim Community.* Chapel Hill: University of North Carolina Press.

Stolte, Carolien and Harald Fischer-Tiné. 2012. 'Imagining Asia in India: Nationalism and Internationalism (ca. 1905–1940)', *Comparative Studies in Society and History* 54 (1): 65–92.

Taylor, Charles. 2007. *A Secular Age.* Cambridge, MA: Harvard University Press.

Tejani, Shabnum. 2014 [2007]. *Indian Secularism: A Social and Intellectual History.* New Delhi/Ranikhet: Permanent Black.

Titus, M. T. 1959. *Islam in India and Pakistan: A Religious History of Islam in India and Pakistan.* Kolkata: YMCA Press.

Tönnies, Ferdinand. 1955. *Community and Association*, translated by Charles P. Loomis. London: Routledge & Kegan Paul.

van der Veer, Peter. 1994. *Religious Nationalism: Hindus and Muslims in India.* Berkeley: University of California Press.

Viswanathan, Gauri. 2008. 'Secularism in the Framework of Heterodoxy', *Publications of the Modern Language Association* 123 (2): 466–76.

Watt, Carey A. 2005. *Serving the Nation: Cultures of Service, Association, and Citizenship.* New Delhi: Oxford University Press.

_____. 2012 [2011]. 'Philanthropy and Civilizing Missions in India c. 1820-1960: States, NGOs and Development', in *Civilizing Missions in Colonial and Postcolonial South Asia: From Improvement to Development*, edited by Carey A. Watt and Michael Mann, 271–316. London, New York and Delhi: Anthem.

Wells, Ian Bryant. 2005. *Ambassador of Hindu Muslim Unity: Jinnah's Early Politics.* New Delhi: Permanent Black.

Willis, John M. 2010. 'Debating the Caliphate: Islam and the Nation in the Work of Rashid Rida and Abul Kalam Azad', *The International History Review* 32 (4): 711–32.

_____. 2014. 'Azad's Mecca: On the Limits of Indian Ocean Cosmopolitanism', *Comparative Studies of South Asia, Africa and the Middle East* 34 (3): 574–81.

Wright Jr., Theodore P. 1976. 'Muslim Kinship and Modernization: The Tyabji Clan of Bombay', in *Family, Kinship and Marriage among Muslims in India*, edited by Imtiaz Ahmad, 217–38. Delhi: Manohar.

Yavuz, M. Kakan. 1999. 'Towards an Islamic Liberalism?: The Nurcu Movement and Fethullah Gülen', *Middle East Journal* 53 (4): 584–605.

Yegar, Moshe. 1972. *The Muslims of Burma: A Study of a Minority Group.* Wiesbaden: Otto Harrosowitz.

Zachariah, Benjamin. 2012 [2005]. *Developing India: An Intellectual and Social History, c. 1930–50.* New Delhi: Oxford University Press.

Index